COMMUNISM AND ANTI-COMMUNISM IN THE UNITED STATES

GARLAND REFERENCE LIBRARY
OF SOCIAL SCIENCE
(VOL. 379)

COMMUNISM AND ANTI-COMMUNISM
IN THE UNITED STATES
An Annotated Guide to Historical Writings

John Earl Haynes

GARLAND PUBLISHING, INC. • NEW YORK & LONDON
1987

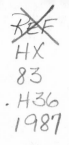

Library of Congress Cataloging-in-Publication Data

Haynes, John Earl.
Communism and Anti-Communism in the United States.

(Garland Reference Library of Social Science ;
v. 379)
Includes index.
1. Communism—United States—History—Bibliography.
2. Anti-communist movements—United States—History—
Bibliography. I. Title. II. Series.
Z7164.S67H4   1987   [HX83]   016.33543′0973   86-25821
ISBN 0-8240-8520-5 (alk. paper)

Printed on acid-free, 250-year-life paper
Manufactured in the United States of America

CONTENTS

PREFACE...xi

INTRODUCTION: HISTORIANS AND AMERICAN COMMUNISM......xiii

1. GENERAL HISTORIES OF THE COMMUNIST PARTY OF THE UNITED
   STATES OF AMERICA: ORIGINS TO THE 1950s............3

2. THE ORIGINS OF AMERICAN COMMUNISM....................5
   BIOGRAPHICAL MATERIAL..............................7

3. THE COMMUNIST PARTY IN THE 1920s....................9
   BIOGRAPHICAL MATERIAL.............................10

4. THE COMMUNIST PARTY: 1930-1945.....................11
   THE COMMUNIST PARTY AND WAR ISSUES................14

5. THE COMMUNIST PARTY: 1945 AND AFTER................15

6. COMMUNISTS, RADICALS, AND AMERICAN POLITICS........17
   GENERAL...17
   COMMUNISM AND THE La FOLLETTE PROGRESSIVE PARTY OF
      1924...17
   THE NEW DEAL, THE POPULAR FRONT, AND WORLD WAR
      II...18
   COMMUNISM, HENRY WALLACE, AND THE 1948 PROGRESSIVE
      PARTY..20
   COMMUNISM AND POLITICS IN NEW YORK: THE 1930s AND
      1940s..23
      Vito Marcantonio..............................24
   COMMUNISM AND POLITICS IN MINNESOTA...............26
   COMMUNISM AND POLITICS IN WISCONSIN...............28
   COMMUNISM AND POLITICS IN CALIFORNIA..............28
   COMMUNISM AND POLITICS IN WASHINGTON STATE........29
   COMMUNISM AND POLITICS IN OREGON..................29

7. THE NATURE AND STRUCTURE OF THE COMMUNIST PARTY.....31

8. SCHISMATIC COMMUNIST MOVEMENTS.....................37
   GENERAL...37
   TROTSKYISM, THE SHACHTMANITES.....................37

9. COMMUNISM AND THE AMERICAN LABOR MOVEMENT..........41
   GENERAL...41
   COMMUNIST LABOR POLICY DURING WORLD WAR II........46

GOVERNMENT, UNION POLITICS, AND THE COMMUNIST
    PARTY....................................47
LABOR, ANTI-COMMUNISM, AND FOREIGN POLICY.........50
ROMAN CATHOLICS AND ANTI-COMMUNISM IN THE LABOR
    MOVEMENT.................................54
COMMUNISM AND THE CIO: GENERAL....................56
COMMUNISM AND LABOR: BY UNION, INDUSTRY, AND
    REGION...................................58
    Auto Industry and the United Auto Workers
        (UAW)................................58
    Needle Trades..............................63
    Social Service Employees...................64
    Packinghouse Workers.......................64
    Furniture Workers..........................65
    Longshore and Maritime.....................65
    Electrical and Machine.....................67
    Mine, Mill and Smelter Workers.............69
    Teachers's Unions..........................69
    United Steel Workers.......................70
    Transport Workers' Union...................71
    Lumber and Wood............................72
    Trucking: the Teamsters....................73
    Coal: United Mine Workers..................74
    Textiles...................................75
    Culinary Unions............................76
    Newspaper Guild............................76
    Shipbuilding...............................76
    Labor in California........................77
    Labor in Minnesota.........................77
    Labor in the Pacific Northwest.............77
    Labor in Missouri..........................78
    Labor in Wisconsin.........................78
COMMUNISM AND THE UNEMPLOYED......................78
BIOGRAPHICAL MATERIAL.............................79

10. COMMUNISM, ETHNICITY, AND NATIONALITY..............83
    GENERAL..83
    CROATS...83
    FINNS..83
    ITALIANS.......................................87
    JEWS...87
    MEXICANS.......................................89
    SWEDES...90

11. COMMUNISM AND BLACK AMERICANS......................91
    GENERAL..91
    COMMUNISM AND BLACKS IN NEW YORK CITY AND HARLEM..93
    THE NATIONAL NEGRO CONGRESS....................95
    SOVIET AND COMINTERN POLICY TOWARD BLACK
        AMERICANS..................................95
    BLACKS AND COMMUNIST-LED UNIONS................96

SCOTTSBORO, INTERNATIONAL LABOR DEFENSE AND THE
    CIVIL RIGHTS CONGRESS........................98
BIOGRAPHICAL MATERIAL............................99

12. THE COMINTERN AND INTERNATIONAL AFFAIRS...........107
    GENERAL..107
    THE KUZBAS PROJECT.............................108
    THE SPANISH CIVIL WAR..........................108

13. COMMUNISM, FARMERS, AND FARM WORKERS..............111
    GENERAL..111
    NATIONAL FARMERS UNION.........................112
    COMMUNISM AND SOUTHERN AGRICULTURE..............112
    COMMUNISM AND WEST COAST AGRICULTURE............114
    COMMUNISM AND MIDWESTERN AGRICULTURE............115

14. COMMUNISM AND WOMEN...............................117

15. COMMUNISM AND THE CHURCHES........................119
    GENERAL..119
    ANTI-COMMUNISM, THE SPANISH CIVIL WAR, AND
        CATHOLICISM................................121
    BIOGRAPHICAL MATERIAL..........................122

16. FRIENDS OF COMMUNISM AND THE SOVIET UNION.........125
    GENERAL..125
    ORGANIZATIONS ASSOCIATED WITH COMMUNISM.........126
    AMERICAN VISITORS TO COMMUNIST SOCIETIES........127
    THE MOSCOW TRIALS..............................128
    JOURNALS OF OPINION AND THE PRESS...............128
        Monthly Review............................129
        National Guardian.........................129
        The Nation................................129
        The New Republic..........................130
    BIOGRAPHICAL MATERIAL..........................130

17. COMMUNISM, EDUCATION, AND YOUTH...................133
    GENERAL..133
    TEACHING ABOUT COMMUNISM IN SECONDARY SCHOOLS....134
    COMMUNISM, ANTI-COMMUNISM, AND HIGHER
        EDUCATION..................................135
    YOUTH AND STUDENTS.............................139

18. COMMUNISM, INTELLECTUALS, AND CULTURE.............143

19. COMMUNISM, WRITERS AND LITERATURE.................147
    GENERAL..147
    ORGANIZED WRITERS..............................149
    PROLETARIAN LITERATURE.........................150
        Mike Gold..................................151
    BIOGRAPHICAL MATERIAL..........................152

20. COMMUNISM AND POETS.................................157

21. COMMUNISM AND ART...................................159

22. COMMUNISM, RADICALISM, AND DRAMA...................161
    BIOGRAPHICAL MATERIAL.............................163

23. COMMUNISM, FILM, RADIO, AND TELEVISION............165
    RADICAL PHOTOGRAPHY AND DOCUMENTARY FILM.........165
    COMMUNISM AND HOLLYWOOD..........................166
    BLACKLISTING OF COMMUNISTS AND COMMUNIST
        SYMPATHIZERS.................................168
    THE COLD WAR AND ANTI-COMMUNISM IN FILMS.........169
    BIOGRAPHICAL MATERIAL 170

24. COMMUNISM AND MUSIC................................173

25. ESPIONAGE..177
    GENERAL..177
    ESPIONAGE CASES..................................178
        Elizabeth Bentley...........................178
        Noel Field..................................179
        The Hiss-Chambers Case......................179
        Walter Krivitsky............................186
        J. Robert Oppenheimer 186
        The Rosenbergs..............................187
        Michael Straight............................189
        Harry Dexter White..........................190

26. SUBSIDIARY TREATMENTS OF COMMUNIST HISTORY........191

27. BIOGRAPHICAL MATERIAL..............................195

28. PUBLIC PERCEPTION OF COMMUNISM AND THE SOVIET
    UNION..207

29. THE COLD WAR AND THE DOMESTIC COMMUNIST ISSUE.....211
    GENERAL..211
    POLAND...212
    CHINA..213
        Anna Louise Strong..........................215
        Agnes Smedley...............................216

30. ANTI-COMMUNIST LIBERALS AND RADICALS..............217
    GENERAL..217
    THE AMERICANS FOR DEMOCRATIC ACTION..............221
    THE SOCIALIST PARTY..............................222
    PARTISAN REVIEW..................................222
    V.F. CALVERTON AND THE MODERN QUARTERLY 224
    BIOGRAPHICAL MATERIAL............................225

31. ANTI-COMMUNIST LAWS AND DEMOCRATIC LIBERTIES......231

32. THE "RED SCARE" OF 1919-1920....................237
        GENERAL.....................................237
            THE "RED SCARE" IN NEW YORK.............239
            THE "RED SCARE" IN NEW HAMPSHIRE........240
            THE "RED SCARE" IN DENVER...............240
            THE SEATTLE GENERAL STRIKE..............240

33. THE FEDERAL LOYALTY-SECURITY PROGRAM.............241

34. CONGRESSIONAL INVESTIGATIONS OF COMMUNISM........245

35. THE FEDERAL BUREAU OF INVESTIGATION AND
        COMMUNISM...................................249

36. RIGHT-WING ANTI-COMMUNISM AND McCARTHYISM........255
        GENERAL.....................................255
        McCARTHYISM AND CATHOLICS...................259
        SENATOR JOSEPH McCARTHY.....................260
            McCarthy in Wisconsin...................263
        RIGHT-WING ANTI-COMMUNIST ORGANIZATIONS.....264
        THE NATURE OF McCARTHYISM AND FAR RIGHT ANTI-
            COMMUNISM...............................265
        ANTI-COMMUNISM AND McCARTHYISM IN THE STATES.....268
            Anti-Communism in the Midwest...........269
            Anti-Communism in the South.............269
            Anti-Communism in Arkansas..............270
            Anti-Communism In California............270
            Anti-Communism in Hawaii................271
            Anti-Communism in Indiana...............271
            Anti-Communism In Illinois..............272
            Anti-Communism in Maryland..............272
            Anti-Communism in Michigan..............272
            Anti-Communism in Minnesota.............272
            Anti-Communism in Missouri..............272
            Anti-Communism in New York..............272
            Anti-Communism in South Dakota..........272
            Anti-Communism In Texas.................273
            Anti-Communism In Washington............273
        BIOGRAPHICAL MATERIAL.......................274

37. HISTORIOGRAPHIC AND BIBLIOGRAPHIC WORKS..........281

ADDENDA...287

AUTHOR INDEX..291

PREFACE

In the late 1970s publication on topics related to the history of American Communism increased from a few items a year to an astonishing level of several hundred. A new organization, the Historians of American Communism, formed in 1982 to link scholars whose research touched upon Communist history. The author has edited the Historians of American Communism's **Newsletter** since it originated. One of the initial projects of the **Newsletter** was the publication of an annual bibliography of books and essays dealing with aspects of American Communist history. From that endeavor this present book developed.

This bibliography lists published books, essays, and articles, unpublished dissertations and theses, and a few unpublished essays dealing with the history of American Communism and anti-Communism. Scholarly and historical studies, not primary materials or journalistic accounts, are the chief subjects of this bibliography, although some autobiographies and journalistic works are also included.

The emphasis is on material dealing with the history of the mainstream Communist movement: the Communist Party, United States of America. Some material on the major splinter groups from the Communist Party (Trotskyism, the Lovestonites, and others) is also included. Generally, studies of theoretical Marxism and Leninism are not included unless such works deal directly with the American Communist movement. Chronologically, the material listed covers American Communism from its founding shortly after the Bolshevik Revolution up through the near disintegration of the American Communist Party in the mid-1950s. Some material also deals with those pre-Bolshevik radical movements out of which American Communism developed, and some items discuss the American Communism in the 1960s and 1970s.

The history of domestic American anti-Communism is intimately related to the history of Communism and the chronological coverage is similar. The emphasis in anti-Communist material listed is on the history of opposition to the domestic Communist movement, not on opposition to Soviet or other foreign Communist movements operating in a foreign arena. Works dealing with foreign policy

issues are cited when they are connected with domestic
concern about Communism.

Although a good deal of the material cited has
Communism (or anti-Communism) as a major topic, a
significant amount of coverage occurs in works mainly
concerned with other matters but in which American
Communists play a role. For example, many of the authors
who wrote material cited in the section on the labor
movement were not principally writing "about" Communists
in the union movement. Instead, they were writing about
a particular union or a particular incident and found
that Communists played a role at some point in their
story.

The annotation provided attempts to aid the reader
in deciding if a cited work is relevant to the reader's
interests. When a title is sufficiently clear as to what
may be expected, often annotation is not provided. A
number of items not examined by the author are also not
annotated. Items are grouped by subject area. The
Contents lists the chronological and thematic
categories and subcategories. Within a category or
subcategory, items are listed alphabetically by author.
Further, there is an author index.

Cross references are provided when an item listed in
one subject matter category has significant relevance for
another as well, and where one item has as its subject
another item. Cross references and the author index are
to item number, not to page number.

INTRODUCTION:
HISTORIANS AND AMERICAN COMMUNISM

With the publication in 1920 of **Revolutionary Radicalism** [item 17] by an investigative committee of the New York Legislature, the writing of the history of American Communism began almost with the movement itself. However, even though **Revolutionary Radicalism** is useful to historians because it reprints a number of otherwise unavailable documents, few would confuse the committee's political expose with scholarship. The thirty years that followed produced a significant amount of polemical material and journalistic coverage of American Communism (some of very high quality), but very little scholarly history. Only a few academically trained scholars looked at American Communism as a subject of research. Even had more done so, the barriers to scholarship were formidable because primary material was generally not open to research and the events were too recent for perspective.

Starting in the early 1950s, however, scholarly writing on the history of American Communism began in earnest and grew, very slowly, until the late 1970s. At that point, a tremendous increase in the volume of research occurred and continues until the present time (1986). The body of historical research on American Communism is now so broad and varied that generalizations about it are subject to numerous exceptions, and some of the viewpoints represented are unique and defy categorization. These caveats noted, one can discern three broad waves of historical scholarship on American Communism. The first, the pioneering scholarship of the 1950s and early 1960s, took place within an anti-Communist framework. The second, the "revisionist" scholarship of the late 1960s and early 1970s, concentrated its attention, usually unsympathetic, on anti-Communism in American life. The third wave, starting in the late 1970s and continuing, is far heavier in volume than the preceding waves and more varied in its interpretive framework. The majority of the writers in this third wave, however, are noticeably hostile to anti-Communism and see Communists as having made significant and largely beneficial contributions to American life.

The one characteristic shared by all three waves of scholarship is the extent to which political attitudes

set the context for historical interpretations.
Historians examining Communism and anti-Communism are not
so distant from the contest that they can easily maintain
the perspective with which one can, for example, view the
political struggle between the Guelphs and the
Ghibellines of medieval Italy. The events under question
are recent, and the issues involved are still under
dispute. This century has been one of violent
conflicting ideologies; and the contest between
Communism, capitalism, democracy, nationalism,
Christianity, and socialism in all their forms and
combinations is not at an end. That scholars should have
convictions on these matters should be no surprise.

Political commitment need not, however, prevent a
conscientious historian from carrying out one's
scholastic responsibilities. Successful scholarship in
this area requires self-discipline, a willingness to
"give the devil his due," and sensitivity to one's own
assumptions. It also requires on the part both of the
writer and the reader a recognition that ethical
assumptions will influence how a historical issue is
framed. Some historians have produced and will continue
to produce partisan histories. But among those who have
written about American Communism and anti-Communism there
are many able scholars with divergent political outlooks.
Many of these, despite their political preferences, have
published studies in which evidence has been
conscientiously evaluated and fairly presented and from
which scholars of varying views can draw an understanding
of the past.

The first wave: The 1950s produced the first
substantial volume of academically-based studies of
American Communism. The best known of these are the ten
books of the "Communism in American Life" series
commissioned by the Fund for the Republic [items 11, 33,
76, 207, 225, 849, 933, 1030, 1814, and 2047].

Virtually all of the books of the first wave broke
new ground because very little preceded them.
Pioneering, however, is a difficult enterprise. Due to
the lack of a body of prior research, these scholars had
little opportunity to evaluate and measure their findings
against those of others. Because they were the first,
there was little opportunity for these researchers to
take part in a scholarly dialogue. Others that followed
would benefit from examining the strengths and weaknesses
of their research, but these pioneers had few
opportunities to benefit from the work of other scholars.

The lack of an adequate base of specialized
monographs often reduced the depth of the scholarship of
1950s and early 1960s. For example, many of the volumes
of the "Communism in American Life" series were broad in
scope, such as Robert W. Iversen's **The Communists and the
Schools** [item 933]. Iversen was handicapped by the lack
of detailed studies of particular incidents and
controversies, biographies of relevant personalities, and
histories of particular institutions. Iversen had to
write a synthesis when there was, as yet, no body of
scholarship to synthesize.

Two of the books of the "Communism in American Life"
series, however, deserve special note. Theodore Draper's
The Roots of American Communism [item 11] and **American
Communism and Soviet Russia** [item 33] are internal
political and organizational histories which tell the
story of the Party's founding and its formative years up
to 1929. Both are superb works of history and remain
essential reading for anyone seriously interested in the
history of American Communism. Draper was amazingly
successful in collecting primary material. The period of
Draper's research was also prior to the Party's spread
into a variety of complex arenas, and he was less
handicapped by the lack of complementary research than
others in the "Communism in American Life" series who
concentrated on the 1930s and 1940s. Two other books
from the first wave of scholarship also remain highly
useful. Earl Latham's **The Communist Controversy in
Washington** [item 1814] provides a reliable narrative
history for anyone needing an introduction to the House
Un-American Activities Committee, the Smith Act, the
controversy over loyalty programs, the Hiss-Chambers
Case, the Amerasia affair, and the saga of Senator Joseph
McCarthy. Irving Howe and Lewis Coser's **The American
Communist Party, A Critical History** [item 4] is excellent
critical scholarship and remains the best one-volume
history of American Communism available. (The Howe-Coser
book was not part of the "Communism in American Life"
series.)

The political attitude of these pioneering scholars
varied; most were liberals, radicals or socialists and a
very few were conservatives. But no one reading them can
fail to note that, whatever their particular orientation,
these writers disliked Communism. To them, Communism was
an antidemocratic political movement that sought to
replace America's pluralistic social order and system of
democratic liberties with a totalitarian regime. Most of
these writers also regarded American Communism as
irrevocably linked and subordinate to Soviet Communism.
This latter point was of key importance because many of

these writers regarded Soviet Communism as a totalitarian
horror second only to Nazi Germany in its barbarism and
its threat to Western civilization.

In the late 1940s an ideological civil war among
liberals set anti-Communist liberals against a Popular
Front alliance of liberals who sought accommodation with
the Soviet Union abroad and cooperation with American
Communists at home. Both anti-Communist and Popular
Front liberals claimed to be the legitimate successors to
Roosevelt's New Deal. Their internecine struggle to
control the direction and nature of liberalism was hard-
fought, intensely emotional, and regarded as deadly
serious by those involved. Henry Wallace's crushing
defeat and the election of Harry Truman in 1948, along
with the expulsion of Communists from the labor movement,
marked the triumph of anti-Communist liberalism in this
fight.

Victorious anti-Communist liberals regarded
Communists as illegitimate participants in liberal and
labor institutions. Consequently, they often saw such
participation as a matter of infiltration and conspiracy.
When they looked back at the history of such
participation in the 1930s and 1940s, they tended to
understate the extent to which some New Deal politicians
and institutions welcomed such participation because such
recognition tended to support the claim of Popular Front
liberals that they were also heirs of the New Deal. Some
of the interpretations of the pioneering historians of
American Communism reflect the outlook of the victorious
anti-Communist liberals. David Shannon in **The Decline of
American Communism** [item 76] and Max Kampelman in **The
Communist Party versus the CIO** [item 387] clearly saw
American Communists as illegitimate participants in
liberal politics and the labor movement and as having
significant conspiratorial characteristics. Morris L.
Ernst and David Loth's **Report on the American Communist**
[item 204] and Gabriel Almond's **The Appeals of Communism**
[item 188] linked attraction to Communism to
psychological disorders.

In the 1950s, Senator Joseph McCarthy and other
right-wing anti-Communists attacked liberals as little
better than Communists or as the front men for a
Communist conspiracy. Perhaps in response, some of the
scholars of the first wave appeared to pursue a defensive
agenda as much concerned with protecting liberal
reputations as with delineating Communist history. Ralph
Roy's **Communism and the Churches** [item 849], for example,
defended various religious bodies and clergy from right-
wing attack and, in the process, understated the extent

to which various religious figures found common grounds
with the Communist Party in the 1930s and 1940s.

The Second Wave: The scholars of the second wave
were interested in American anti-Communism, not American
Communism. They regarded McCarthyism and the popular
anti-Communism of the 1950s as a horrible and despicable
phenomenon which had inflicted grave damage on American
society and culture, subverted democratic liberties, and
ruined the lives of many people. These writers set
themselves the task of explaining the origins of
McCarthyism.

What gave these scholars their cohesiveness was the
extent to which they placed the blame for McCarthyism on
anti-Communist liberals, or the "Cold War liberals" as
they often called them. In the mainstream histories
written in the 1950s and early 1960s, anti-Communist
liberals usually had received positive and often glowing
treatment. The often self-consciously "revisionist"
historians of the late 1960s and early 1970s, however,
had a negative evaluation of anti-Communist liberalism.
Although these writers differed among themselves on some
matters, their common approach can be seen in **The
Specter: Original Essays on the Cold War and the Origins
of McCarthyism** [item 1807]. Here, Robert Griffith and
Athan Theoharis, two of the leading revisionist
historians, brought together most of the major
revisionist scholars in a collection of essays which
battered anti-Communist liberalism from every quarter.

To these revisionists, anti-Communist liberals had
legitimated anti-Communism and thereby set the stage for
the eruption of McCarthyism and the evils that flowed
from it. In their eyes, anti-Communism was inextricably
infected with the malignancy of McCarthyism. Often, the
revisionists went further and tied America's involvement
in Vietnam to anti-Communism and to McCarthyism. Thus,
the anti-Communist liberals of the late 1940s and 1950s
were assigned partial responsibility for the Vietnam War.
And because the revisionists were, virtually without
exception, hostile to America's involvement in Vietnam,
that partial responsibility was more evidence of the
inherent immorality of anti-Communism.

One of the curious features of revisionist writing
is the extent to which anti-Communism was treated in a
vacuum. The revisionists were historians of anti-
Communism and they had almost nothing to say about
American Communism. If one were to read the
revisionists' books and essays and nothing else one would
gain the impression that the American Communist Party was

largely a figment of the imagination of anti-Communists.
At times, anti-Communists, including anti-Communist
liberals, are treated as paranoid or deluded individuals
embarked on a witch hunt for nonexistent witches. At
other times, anti-Communists are treated as coldblooded
opportunists who consciously created a mythical Communist
conspiracy in order to serve their political needs and
justify their oppressive actions.

The American Communist Party, to the extent it shows
up in revisionist histories at all, is regarded as an
organization of little importance. Communists activities
were seen as far too insignificant to have justified a
rational or genuine counter action. In revisionist
histories, those who the anti-Communist liberals fought
were often vaguely defined as progressives, or social
liberals, or some other undifferentiated coalition in
which it might be acknowledged that Communists played
some unspecified role. Often, the only Communists one
finds in the revisionist histories are those whom the
revisionists skeptically refer to as "alleged"
Communists.

In revisionist writing the Soviet Union appeared as
a nation without unusual characteristics; it was often
absolved of responsibility for the Cold War. The
attitude toward Soviet society and government varied from
an indifferent agnosticism to an indifferent
acknowledgement that the Soviet regime was not an
admirable one. One is struck at the contrast in
revisionist writing between the indignation and highly
emotional abhorrence they had toward McCarthyism and the
cool indifference toward the Soviet Union. Because the
revisionists were indifferent toward the nature of Soviet
Communism, they either dismissed or found
incomprehensible the hostility toward Soviet Communism
shown by anti-Communist liberals.

The Third Wave: The third wave of historical
writing began in the late 1970s with the appearance of a
very large number of essays, articles, theses, and
dissertations on a broad array of Communist activities.
These latest researchers are able to work with extensive
collections of archival material that were lacking in the
1950s and 1960s. Partially as a consequence of the rich
archival resources, this third wave has supplied what the
pioneers of Communist history lacked, an extensive base
of monographic studies.

In addition to the expected large volume of studies
of Communist activities in the labor movement, in this
huge outpouring of essays and books one can find detailed

examinations of an astounding array of topics: of
Communist influence on folk music, on drama, on poetry,
or on specific major and minor literary figures; of
Communist activity among Jews, Finns, Blacks, and
Mexicans; of Communist work among Alabama and Arkansas
sharecroppers, among grain farmers in Iowa, South Dakota,
and Minnesota, and dairy farmers in New York; of
Communist influence on social gospel Protestants,
professional social workers, and socially conscious
lawyers, and even on the Communist influence in sports.
This body of research demonstrates the existence of a
significant Communist role in certain areas of American
life. Yet most of the standard histories of the 1930s,
1940s, and 1950s ignore or minimize the role of American
Communism. A major task facing historians of recent
American history is the need to integrate this new body
of scholarship into mainstream history.

Several books in this body of scholarship deserve
special mention for their contribution to the field.
Three fill out the chronological history of the Party
begun by Draper: Harvey Klehr's **The Heyday of American
Communism: The Depression Decade** [item 59], Maurice
Isserman's **Which Side Were Your On? The American
Communist Party During the Second World War** [item 56],
and Joseph Starobin's **American Communism in Crisis, 1943-
1957** [item 80]. In addition to an internal
organizational and political history, Klehr provides
extensive coverage of Communist activity in the labor
movement, among students and blacks, its influence among
intellectuals, and its involvement, through its Popular
Front relationship, with elements in the New Deal
coalition. Klehr's book, with its combination of broad
coverage and meticulous scholarship, is essential reading
on Communism in the 1930s. Several noteworthy books of
more specialized interest are Allen Weinstein's **Perjury:
The Hiss-Chambers Case** [item 1311], Ronald Radosh and
Joyce Milton's **The Rosenberg File: A Search for the Truth**
[item 1342], Mark Naison's **Communists in Harlem During
the Depression** [item 661], Lowell Dyson's **Red Harvest,
The Communist Party and American Farmers** [item 783],
William L. O'Neill **A Better World, The Great Schism:
Stalinism and the American Intellectuals** [item 1560], and
Bert Cochran's **Labor and Communism: The Conflict that
Shaped American Unions** [se item 381].

The interpretive approaches used by historians in
the third wave are more diverse than in earlier periods.
Today one can find interpretations ranging from criticism
of the American Communist Party for insufficient
revolutionary vigor, to open partisanship for Communism,
to positive but critical evaluations, to negative

judgements. The major poles of interpretation, however,
are two: one with a largely positive evaluation of
American Communism although critical of various aspects
of Party history, and one largely critical.

Recent scholars who take a critical view of
Communism in American history are often compared to the
pioneering authors of the "Communism in American Life"
series. Most of the critical scholars share the
judgement of the pioneers that the Communist Party was a
antidemocratic, totalitarian political movement
irrevocably linked to Soviet Communism. But their views
differ from their forebears in several other ways. They
are less partisan and their writing lacks the polemical
tone of many of the pioneering scholars. They also see a
large and significant Communist role in American history
in the 1930s and 1940s, a role that was larger than that
described by the pioneering generation of historians.
Although none sees Communists as predominate or
controlling actors, they write of a powerful Communist
role in the CIO, in liberal politics in New York,
Minnesota, Wisconsin, Washington, Oregon, and California,
and in a variety of cultural and intellectual arenas.
They also see that role as less conspiratorial than did
the pioneering anti-Communist writers and explore the
circumstances that led non-Communists to find common
ground with Communists in the 1930s and 1940s.

The predominant tendency in recent scholarship,
however, is far more positive in its evaluation of
American Communism. Where these scholars differ from
recent critical scholars is in a more favorable
evaluation of American Communism and in their emphatic
negative interpretation of the anti-Communist reaction to
Communist activity. Whereas they see Communists as
having contributed positively to the labor movement, they
judge anti-Communist union activists as having robbed the
labor movement of its dynamism and social activism.
Whereas they see Communism as having enriched literary
and intellectual life, they see anti-Communism as having
stifled intellectual life and prostituted culture to the
service of America's imperial ambitions.

In a bibliographic essay, Maurice Isserman calls
those who take a positive view of Communist history (of
whom he is a leading figure) the "new historians." He
describes them as largely veterans of the student New
Left of the late 1960s and early 1970s whose interest in
Communist history derived from a desire to answer through
historical study the questions and dilemmas presented in
their own radical political experience. He commented
that:

the new history of Communism has examined particular
communities, particular unions, particular working
class and ethnic cultures, particular generations,
and other sub-groupings within the Party. Though
critical of the CP's authoritarian internal
structure, and its overall subservience to the
Soviet Union, the new historians have been alert to
the ways in which the American CP was shaped by the
environment in which it operated and by the people
who enlisted under its banners. . . . [T]he new
historians of Communism are willing to see American
Communists as real human beings who held and
discarded illusions, learned some lessons from their
mistakes and failed to learn others, interpreted
events as either substantiation or refutation of
passionately held belief--in short, as a group of
people involved in, shaping, and shaped by an
historical process. [Item 2018, p. 539-40.]

The "social history" approach to American Communism
described by Isserman is strongly rejected by historians
taking a critical view of Communist history. Almost
without exception, critical scholars regard Communism as
a political movement and approach it through political
history. They see Communism as a movement which
interpreted the world through an all-encompassing
political ideology and which infused all aspects of life
with political content. Consequently, they regard a
social history approach to American Communism as beside
the point, trivial, or, at best, an interesting
supplement to a political history.

In 1985, Theodore Draper, who had turned to other
subjects after publication of **American Communism and
Soviet Russia** in 1960, returned to the history of
American Communism. In two lengthy essays reviewing
recent scholarship in the field, he lauded Klehr's work
and harshly criticized Isserman and those taking a social
history approach to Communist history. Draper later
included these essays in new editions of **The Roots of
American Communism** and **American Communism and Soviet
Russia** along with some comment regarding his own one-time
membership in the Communist Party. Draper's essays and
the heated exchanges that followed suggest that many
scholars who, like Draper and Klehr, take a political
(and largely critical) approach regard the social history
approach championed by Isserman and others as not only
inappropriate but deliberately evasive of the key issues
confronting historians of American Communism [items 2009,
20010, and 2011].

Critical scholars find it difficult to credit the depreciation (deprecation, in some cases) of a political history approach to American Communism by scholars whose commitment to radical politics is obvious. Just as almost no one reading the books of the "Communism in American Life" series could miss the anti-Communist commitment of its authors, few reading the "new historians" can miss their radical political orientation. A number of these historians are also associated with or publish in those journals (**Radical America, Radical History Review, Science and Society, Socialist Review,** and **Marxist Perspectives**) which seek to fuse scholarship with a radical political perspective. (As noted above, Isserman allows that the interest of the "new historians" in Communist history had its origins in their radical political commitment. He maintains, however, that their perspective later shifted away from the partisan search for a "usable past.")

The "new historians" display a wide variety of left-wing positions, but most share a hostility to capitalism, a hostility to anti-Communism, and a hostility to American society and culture as it has been and is now constituted. These convictions are strongly felt and constitute a driving force in the relatively sympathetic treatment of Communism provided by these scholars. They see American Communists, whatever their faults, as kindred spirits and as colleagues in the fight against capitalism and established American institutions. Many of these "new historians" acknowledge and are critical of a variety of Communist shortcomings. But, they do not regard those shortcomings as of decisive importance when compared to Communism's contribution to the fight to destroy capitalism and reconstruct American culture along Marxist lines.

Radicalism by itself is not the determining factor; many of the pioneering anti-Communist historians (and some of the recent critical ones as well) were also hostile to capitalism and adhered to some variety of left-wing ideology. What is key is the extent to which radicalism is combined with a commitment to political democracy and pluralism. Those radicals who place a high value on democracy and pluralism regard Communists as opponents rather than as colleagues. One should also note that despite their contribution to the rehabilitation of the Communist Party in American history, some of the work of the "new historians" is not appreciated by the Communist Party itself. Isserman's writings, for example, have been denounced in Communist publications as revisionist because of his relatively favorable treatment of "Browderism" [item 2083].

When discussing the viewpoint of the "new historians," Isserman has commented that:

> to a certain extent, the new historians of American Communism, and the traditionalists like Klehr, are speaking at cross-purposes. The new historians have conceded what Klehr called the 'essential clue' to the nature of the American CP: that its political line changed in accord with the prevailing winds from Moscow. They have then gone on to ask new questions. [Item 2018, p. 544.]

Isserman, however, misunderstands what most "traditionalists" mean when they look at the link between American Communism and Soviet Communism. Isserman appears to understand that relationship as the inappropriate projection on to the American scene of political themes current in the Soviet Union. Although such projection is of interest, it is a surface phenomenon which by itself speaks more to the political acumen of American Communist leaders than it does to the nature of American Communism. What "traditionalists" see in American Communism's link to Soviet Communism is much more than that; what they see is an indication of the inner-nature and ultimate purposes of the American Communist Party. To the "traditionalists," the relationship of American Communism to Soviet Communism is a manifestation of its essential totalitarian character and an indication that the American Communist Party, had it been successful, would have reconstructed the United States on the model of the Soviet Union. This point is not conceded or even much discussed by most "new historians."

One of the striking features about most "new historians" is their parochial attitude toward American Communism. Many of these historians know American Communism, and they have a familiarity with theoretical Marxism. Only a few, however, display any evidence that they have read widely in the history of Communism in the Soviet Union, Eastern Europe, or China. Most, it is safe to assert, have never heard of the White Sea Canal and would be mystified by the argument that the history of the canal's construction says something about the nature of Communism. Scholars of American Communism, however, ought to be familiar with the history of Communism in those places where it has been a living and breathing reality for generations. Further, the American Communist Party was inspired by Communism in the Soviet Union and has regarded Soviet Communism as the model for the new America it hopes to build. Consequently, to interpret

the nature of American Communism without familiarity with
the history of Soviet Communism is a grave mistake.

This error has equal force regarding the historical
evaluation of anti-Communism in American life. The
strength and fervor of American anti-Communism was not
inspired by philosophical rejection of Marxism-Leninism
or by fear of the popular support commanded by Earl
Browder, William Z. Foster, or other American Communist
leaders. Rather, anti-Communists loathed and feared what
they saw in the Soviet Union. They hated and loathed the
American Communist Party not for itself but for the
Soviet Communism which they believed American Communists
wished to bring to America. And yet, many of the "new
historians" seek to explain anti-Communism as if the
history and character of Communism in the Soviet Union,
Eastern Europe, and China were irrelevant.

If questions of historical interpretation were
decided by counting the books and essays taking one view
or another then there would be little doubt as to what is
the "winning" interpretation in the history of American
Communism. The "new historians" would be easy winners.
And, indeed, their positive evaluation of American
Communism and scathing indictment of anti-Communism may
become the reigning interpretation. This acceptance may
be aided by the politization of a significant segment of
history faculties in the last fifteen years and the
acceptance of politically committed radical history by
the major professional organizations of historians.

The "new historians" have produced a tremendous
amount of valuable historical research and include a
number of able scholars. But their interpretation of the
role of Communism and anti-Communism in American life
will lack intellectual credibility until they are able to
reconcile their interpretation of American Communism with
the history of Communism wherever it has come to power.

COMMUNISM AND ANTI-COMMUNISM

IN THE UNITED STATES

GENERAL HISTORIES OF THE COMMUNIST PARTY OF
THE UNITED STATES OF AMERICA: ORIGINS TO THE 1950s

1. Bart, Philip, ed. **Highlights of A Fighting History:
    60 Years of the Communist Party USA.** New York:
    International Publishers, 1979. Documentary
    history sponsored by the Communist Party.

2. Bittelman, Alexander. **Milestones in the History of
    the Communist Party.** New York: Workers Library,
    1937. Review of episodes in Party history by a
    prominent Communist official.

3. Foster, William Z. **History of the Communist Party of
    the United States.** New York: International
    Publishers, 1952. Party history written by one of
    the Party's principal figures. A major theme of
    the book is the discrediting of Earl Browder and
    "Browderism."

4. Howe, Irving, and Lewis Coser. **The American
    Communist Party, A Critical History, 1919-1957.**
    Boston: Beacon Press, 1957. Surveys the political
    history of the Communist Party; emphasizes its
    obedience to Moscow and its hostility to democracy;
    best one volume history of the Party available.
    Howe and Coser were leading Left anti-Communist
    intellectuals of the 1950s and 1960s. See item
    2010.

5. Mason, Daniel. "Aspects of the Struggle to Create a
    Leninist Party." **Political Affairs** 53 (Sept. 1974).
    Celebrates episodes in Communist Party history.

6. Oneal, James, and G.A. Werner. **American Communism.**
    New York: Dutton, 1947. Oneal, a Socialist Party
    leader, participated in the expulsion of the
    Socialist Party left-wing in 1919; an expansion and
    updating of Oneal's earlier book cited below as
    item 19.

2

THE ORIGINS OF AMERICAN COMMUNISM

7. American Institute for Marxist Studies. "How
   Lenin's Letter Was Delivered." New York: American
   Institute for Marxist Studies, n.d. Recounts how
   Lenin's letter to American workers regarding the
   nature of Bolshevism was delivered to John Reed
   for American distribution.

8. Anderson, Paul H. **The Attitude of American Leftist
   Leaders Toward the Russian Revolution 1917-1923.**
   Notre Dame: University of Notre Dame Press, 1942.

9. Bell, Daniel. "The Origins of American Communism."
   New Leader 35 (May 26, 1952).

10. Buhle, Paul. "Anarchism and American Labor."
    International Labor and Working Class History 23
    (1983). Discusses co-option of anarchism into
    Communism in the course of reviewing historical
    treatment of anarchist movements.

11. Draper, Theodore. **The Roots of American Communism.**
    New York: Viking Press, 1957. Well written and
    indispensable scholarly study of the origins of
    the American Communist Party; emphasizes the power
    of Soviet Bolshevism in inspiring and shaping
    American Communism and the rapid subordination of
    American Communism to Soviet leadership.

12. Dubofsky, Melvyn. **We Shall Be All: A History of the
    Industrial Workers of the World.** Chicago:
    Quandrangle, 1969. Discusses the IWW reaction to
    the development of Communism.

13. Falk, Julius. "The Origins of the Communist
    Movement in the United States." **The New
    International** (Fall 1955). Discusses the
    Socialist Propaganda League and other predecessors
    to the Communist Party.

14. Held, Abraham. "The Launching of the Communist
    Party of the United States." Master's thesis.
    University of Chicago, 1939. Discusses the split
    in the Socialist Party and the organization of the
    Communist Party to 1921.

15. Ilkka, Richard Jacob. "The Rhetorical Vision of the
    American Communist Movement: Origin and Debut,
    1918-1920." Ph.D. dissertation. University of
    Minnesota, 1974. Finds that early Communist
    rhetorical fantasies cast the Socialist Party
    moderates in the role of Russian counter-
    revolutionaries, the Socialist Party Left in the
    role of the Bolsheviks, and presented the new
    Soviet state as the prototype of a new society.
    In the simplified drama of Communist rhetoric,
    self-righteousness was the most common theme,
    occurring more often than hatred of capitalism and
    hatred of moderate socialists. Much of the
    rhetoric symbolically acted out visions of self
    esteem and mastery: the Communist as vigilant
    guardian of the movement, preacher-militant
    educating the masses, and revolutionary martyr.

16. Johnson, Oakley C. "1919, Crucial Year on the Left:
    a Study of the Proletarian Party." **Political
    Affairs** 53 (Dec. 1974).

17. Joint Legislative Committee Investigating Seditious
    Activities. **Revolutionary Radicalism, Its
    History, Purpose and Tactics, with an Exposition
    and Discussion of the Steps Being Taken and
    Required to Curb It, Part I, Revolutionary and
    Subversive Movements Abroad and at Home.** Albany:
    J.B. Lyon, 1920. Prepared by an investigative
    committee (Lusk Committee) of the New York
    Legislature. The earliest history of American
    Communism; includes many documents.

18. Klehr, Harvey. "The Bridgeman Delegates." **Survey** 22
    (Spring 1976).

19. Oneal, James. **American Communism, A Critical
    Analysis of its Origins, Development and Programs.**
    New York: Rand Book Store, 1927. Oneal, a
    Socialist Party leader, saw the Communist Party as
    sectarian, utopian, out of touch with American
    traditions, and excessively influenced by events
    in Europe and the Soviet Union.

20. Weinstein, James. **The Decline of Socialism in
    America, 1912-1925.** New York: Monthly Review

Press, 1967. Discusses the split over Bolshevism
in the Socialist Party.

21. Whitney, Richard M. **Reds in America**. New York: The
    Beckwith Press, 1924. A radical-hunting expose
    reproducing many early Communist Party documents.

BIOGRAPHICAL MATERIAL

John Reed

22. Balabanoff, Angelica. "John Reed's Last Days."
    Modern Monthly (Jan. 1937). Memoir by a
    colleague. Reed, one of the founders of American
    Communism, died of disease in the Soviet Union in
    the 1920s.

23. Eastman, Max. **Heroes I Have Known**. New York: Simon
    & Schuster, 1952.

24. Hicks, Granville. **John Reed: The Making of a
    Revolutionary**. New York: Macmillan, 1936.

25. Rosenstone, Robert. **Romantic Revolutionary: A
    Biography of John Reed**. New York: Knopf, 1975.

    See items 7, 757, 872, 1148, 1274, 1395, and 1448.

William Haywood

26. Carlson, Peter. **Roughneck: The Life & Times of Big
    Bill Haywood**. New York: Norton, 1983. Biography
    of the IWW leader who fled to the Soviet Union to
    escape prosecution in the U.S.

27. Conlin, Joseph R. **Big Bill Haywood and the Radical
    Union Movement**. Syracuse: Syracuse University
    Press, 1969.

28. Dubofsky, Melvyn. "The Radicalism of the
    Dispossessed: William Haywood and the IWW."
    **Dissent: Explorations in the History of American
    Radicalism**. Alfred F. Young, ed. DeKalb: Northern
    Illinois University Press, 1968.

29. Haywood, William D. **Bill Haywood's Book: The
    Autobiography of William D. Haywood**. New York:
    International Publishers, 1929. This
    autobiography may have been ghostwritten by the
    Communist Party.

30. Hein, Carl. "William Haywood and the Syndicalist
     Faith." **American Radicals.** Harvey Goldberg, ed.
     New York: Monthly Review Press, 1969.

31. Palmer, Bryan D. "'Big Bill' Haywood's Defection To
     Russia and the IWW: Two Letters." **Labor History**
     17,2 (Spring 1976). Discusses the anger of the
     IWW with Haywood and the Communist Party when
     Haywood's defection left the IWW with the costs of
     paying Haywood forfeited bond.

3

THE COMMUNIST PARTY IN THE 1920s

32. Cannon, James P. **The First Ten Years of American Communism.** New York: Pathfinder Press, 1962. Memoir by a Communist and later Trotskyist leader.

33. Draper, Theodore. **American Communism and Soviet Russia, The Formative Period.** New York: Viking Press, 1960. Well written and thorough scholarly study of the Communist Party in the 1920s; this key history of American Communism finds that Soviet-Comintern policy decisively shaped the American Communist Party.

34. Eisman, Louis. "The First Decade of the Communist Party." Master's thesis. University of California, 1935.

35. Raymond, Orin Ralph, 2d. "The American Communist Party and United States 'Imperialism', 1920-1928: Application of Doctrine." Ph.D. dissertation. Harvard University, 1971.

36. Shaffer, Ralph E. "Formation of the California Communist Labor Party." **Pacific Historical Quarterly** 36 (Feb. 1967).

37. Shaffer, Ralph E. "Communism in California, 1919-1924: 'Orders From Moscow' or Independent Western Radicalism." **Science and Society** 34,4 (Winter 1970). Argues that California Communists were indigenous radicals.

38. Shapiro, Stanley. "Hand and Brain: The Farmer-Labor Party of 1920." Unpublished paper, 1981 Organization of American Historians annual meeting.

39. Wolfe, Bertram D. "The Sixth Congress and the American Communist Party." **Survey [Great Britain]** 24,1 (1979). Personal recollection by Wolfe, an

American Communist Party delegate, of the 1928
Comintern Congress.

BIOGRAPHICAL MATERIAL

John Pepper

40. Jaszi, Oscar. **Revolution and Counter-Revolution in
    Hungary.** London: P.S. King & Son, 1924. Notes the
    role of John Pepper, later a powerful Comintern
    Representative to the American Communist Party, in
    the short-lived Hungarian Soviet Republic.

41. Kaas, Baron Albert, and Fedor de Lazarovics.
    Bolshevism in Hungary. London: Grant Richards,
    1931. Discusses the Hungarian background of John
    Pepper.

42. Malusz, Elemer. **The Fugitive Bolsheviks.** London:
    Grant Richards, 1931. Discusses the Hungarian
    background of John Pepper.

43. Deleted.

See items 1402-1407 and 1451-1453.

4

THE COMMUNIST PARTY: 1930-1945

44. Alperin, Robert Jay. "Organization in the Communist Party, USA 1931-1938." Ph.D. dissertation. Northwestern University, 1959. Finds that Communist Party organization was weak in the early 1930s but improved as schools and classes were organized to reduce membership turnover; argues that Marxism remained a driving organizational principle.

45. Browder, Earl. "How Stalin Ruined the American Communist Party." **Harper's Magazine** 220 (March 1960). Browder looks back at the Duclos article.

46. Browder, Earl. "The American Communist Party in the Thirties." **As We Saw the Thirties.** Rita J. Simon, ed. Urbana: University of Illinois Press, 1967.

47. Buhle, Paul. "And Finally." **Cultural Correspondence** (Spring 1977). Discusses the nature of the Popular Front.

48. Burgchardt, Carl R. "Two Faces of American Communism: Pamphlet Rhetoric of the Third Period and the Popular Front." **Quarterly Journal of Speech** 66,4 (1980). Compares Communist Party pamphlets before July 1935 with those printed after that time. The former called for the destruction of capitalism in dogmatic and lurid language. The latter tried to convey a positive and less threatening image of Communism.

49. Clark, Joseph. "Why Did They Stay?" **Dissent** 30,2 (1983). Review essay discussing Isserman's **Which Side Were You On?**

50. Daniels, Roger. **The Bonus March.** Westport: Greenwood, 1971. Discusses Communist involvement in the veterans bonus march on Washington in 1932.

51. Draper, Hal. **New York Review of Books** (May 10,
    1984). Essay-review of Klehr's **Heyday of American
    Communism.** Exchanges with Elmer Benson and Robert
    Claiborne, December 6, 1984.

52. Gerstle, Gary L. "Mission From Moscow: American
    Communism in the 1930s." **Reviews in American
    History** 12,4 (Dec. 1984). Review-essay critical
    of Klehr's **Heyday of American Communism.**

53. Gordon, Max. "The Communist Party of the Nineteen-
    Thirties and the New Left." **Socialist Revolution** 6
    (Jan.-March 1976). This defense of the Popular
    Front as a proper socialist strategy by a former
    Communist Party activist includes an exchange with
    James Weinstein.

54. Gordon, Max. "The Communist Party: An Exchange."
    New York Review of Books (April 14, 1983). An
    exchange with Harvey Klehr over the nature of
    Communist policy in the 1930s and 1940s.

55. Isserman, Maurice. "Peat Bog Soldiers: The American
    Communist Party during the Second World War, 1939-
    1945." Ph.D. dissertation. University of
    Rochester, 1979.

56. Isserman, Maurice. **Which Side Were You On? The
    American Communist Party During the Second World
    War.** Middletown: Wesleyan University Press, 1982.
    Well researched and scholarly political history of
    the Communist Party from the late 1940s to the end
    of World War II. Concentrates on the Communist
    Party's internal political life. Maintains that
    the generation of Communists who joined the Party
    in the 1930s were oriented toward a democratized
    and Americanized Communist movement but were
    frustrated by the structure of the Communist
    Party. See items 49, 2009-2011, 2024, and 2031.

*   Jacobson, Phyllis. "The 'Americanization' of the
    Communist Party." **New Politics** (1986). Cited as
    item 2045.

57. Jaffe, Philip J. "The Rise and Fall of Earl
    Browder." **Survey** 18 (Spring 1972).

58. Jaffe, Philip J. **The Rise and Fall of American
    Communism.** New York: Horizon Press, 1975. Partly
    a biography of Earl Browder, partly a history of
    the Communist Party from 1939 to 1945, and partly
    a compilation of Communist Party documents.

59. Klehr, Harvey. **The Heyday of American Communism:**
     The Depression Decade. New York: Basic Books,
     1984. Extremely well researched history and
     analysis of the Communist Party; the indispensable
     book on Communism in the 1930s. Finds that
     Communist strategy and tactics were shaped by a
     perception of what served and pleased the Soviet
     Union. Although emphasizing the Party's internal
     life and political activity, the book also
     contains ample material on Communist work in the
     labor movement and among farmers, ethnic groups,
     blacks, intellectuals, the unemployed, and youth.
     See items 51, 52, 54, and 2009-2011.

60. Kling, Joseph M. "Making the Revolution -- Maybe:
     Deradicalization and Stalinism in the American
     Communist Party, 1928-1938." Ph.D. dissertation.
     City University of New York, 1983. Concludes that
     the Communist Party became deradicalized after
     1936. The deradicalization was not due directly
     to the decision to support the New Deal. Rather,
     the Party became deradicalized because it
     supported the New Deal without placing that
     support in a class struggle context and because it
     withdrew from the ideological struggle against
     capitalism.

61. Lynd, Staughton. "The United Front in America: A
     Note." **Radical America** 8 (July-August 1974).

62. Lyons, Eugene. **The Red Decade: The Stalinist**
     Penetration of America. Indianapolis: Bobbs
     Merrill, 1941. Journalistic expose of Communist
     Party involvement in the political and cultural
     life of the 1930s. See item 901.

63. Moore, John Hammond. "Communists and Fascists in a
     Southern City: Atlanta, 1930." **South Atlantic**
     Quarterly 67 (1968).

64. Naison, Mark. "Lefties and Righties: The Communist
     Party and Sports During the Great Depression."
     Radical America 13,4 (July-Aug. 1979). Recounts
     the active effort of the Communist Party to
     promote independent sports organizations in the
     1920s, '30s, and '40s, the high quality of
     reporting on sports in Party publications, and the
     role of Communists in promoting racial integration
     of major league sports.

65. Ottanelli, Michele Fraser. "Origins of the Popular
     Front Policy in the United States; 1933-1935."

Unpublished paper, 1983 American Historical
Association graduate history forum of central New
York State, State University of New York,
Cortland. Sees the Popular Front as more of a
product of domestic concerns than a response to
Moscow's direction.

66. Ottanelli, Michele Fraser. "Communists and the New
Deal: An American Popular Front." Unpublished
paper, 1985 Organization of American Historians
convention.

67. Stanley, William Oliver, III. "The Communist Party
and Education, 1928-1939: The Union of Theory and
Practice." Ph.D. dissertation. University of
Illinois at Urbana-Champaign, 1974. Examines the
Communist Party's internal educational philosophy
and its critique of public schools.

See items 1388-1394.

THE COMMUNIST PARTY AND WAR ISSUES

68. Bilderback, William Winch. "The American Communist
Party and World War II." Ph.D. dissertation.
University of Washington, 1974. Surveys the
Communist Party's stance toward the war and war
related issues.

69. Boller, Paul F., Jr. "Hiroshima and the American
Left: August 1945." **International Social Science
Review** 57,1 (Winter 1982). Finds that in 1945 the
Communist Party and those associated with it were
the strongest defenders of the use of nuclear
weapons against Japan. In contrast, the strongest
critics of the attack were anti-Communist liberals
and radicals such as Reinhold Niebuhr, Norman
Thomas, and most Trotskyists.

70. Chatfield, Charles. **For Peace and Justice, Pacifism
in America, 1914-1941.** Knoxville: University of
Tennessee Press, 1971. Notes Communist attempts
to enter the Keep America Out of War Congress
after the Hitler-Stalin Pact.

71. Doenecke, Justus D. "Non-Interventionism on the
Left: The Keep America Out of the War Congress,
1938-1941." **Journal of Contemporary History** 12
(April 1977). Discusses the relationship of the
Communist Party to the pacifist movement.

5

THE COMMUNIST PARTY: 1945 AND AFTER

72. Dennis, Peggy. "A Half-View of History is not Good Enough." Privately circulated essay, 1982. Critical of Isserman's "Half-Swept House" as too heavily influenced by the perspective of those associated with John Gates.

73. Isserman, Maurice. "The 1956 Generation: An Alternative Approach to the History of American Communism." **Radical America** 14,2 (March-April 1980). Argues that the near disintegration of the Communist Party in 1956 demonstrates that it contained a complex and diverse internal membership and that many members were oriented toward a democratized and independent socialist movement.

74. Isserman, Maurice. "Half-Swept House: American Communism in 1956." **Socialist Review** (Feb. 1982). Examines the shifting factional lines and attempts at internal reform of the Communist Party in 1956. See item 72.

75. Lee, Mark Wilcox. "An Analysis of Selected Speeches of William Z. Foster During the Reconstitution Period of the Communist Party, 1945-1950." Ph.D. dissertation. University of Washington, 1966. Finds that Foster's rhetoric had a simple two valued system (capitalism is evil, the Soviet Union is good), that he frequently spoke in an "Aesopian" style understood by insiders and confusing to outsiders, and that he made frequent use of invectives and slogans.

76. Shannon, David. **The Decline of American Communism: A History of the Communist Party of the United States Since 1945.** New York: Harcourt, Brace and Co., 1959. A critical history which treats the Communist Party as subservient to Moscow and an illegitimate participant in liberal politics.

77. Starobin, Joseph R. "1956, A Memoir." **Problems of Communism** 15 (Nov.-Dec. 1966). Memoir of the Communist Party's 1956 crisis.

78. Starobin, Joseph R. "The American Left and the Dilemmas of the Cold War, 1945-1952." Unpublished paper, 1969 American Historical Association meeting.

79. Starobin, Joseph R. "American Communism and the Cold War: an Obscure Chapter in the Pre-history of the Sino-Soviet Schism." Ph.D. dissertation. Columbia University, 1970.

80. Starobin, Joseph R. **American Communism in Crisis, 1943-1957.** Cambridge: Harvard University Press, 1972. Well researched, poignant scholarly study by the former foreign editor of the **Daily Worker.** Argues that Browder was leading the Communist Party in the direction of a positive participation in American politics when he was expelled. Maintains that the American Communists were caught-up in a "mental Comintern" that caused them to slavishly follow what they thought, occasionally erroneously, were Moscow's wishes. Suggests that Moscow made little effort to understand the condition of the American Communist Party and regarded it with minimal interest.

81. Wiener, Jon. "The Communist Party Today and Yesterday: An Interview with Dorothy Healy." **Radical America** 11,3 (May-June 1977). Healy, a longtime leader of the Communist Party in California, discusses Gus Hall, the Communist Party's recruitment of minorities, and compares the West Coast branch of the party with the what she sees as a more rigid Eastern element.

82. Wigren, James C. "Eugene Dennis and the 'Americanization' of the Communist Party, U.S.A., 1956-1960." Master's thesis. George Washington University, 1985.

6

COMMUNISTS, RADICALS, AND AMERICAN POLITICS

GENERAL

83. Brody, David. "On the Failure of US Radical Politics: a Farmer-Labor Analysis." **Industrial Relations** 22 (Spring 1983).

84. Haynes, John Earl. "The New History of the Communist Party in State Politics: the Implications for Mainstream Political History." Unpublished paper, 1985 Organization of American Historians convention. Argues that studies of state and local politics in New York, California, Minnesota, Wisconsin, and Washington State show significant Communist participation in mainstream politics in the late 1930s and 1940s. Suggests the need to revise the treatment of Communism in mainstream political histories and to reinterpret the origins of anti-Communist liberalism.

86. Perlman, Selig, and Philip Taft. **History of Labor in the United States, 1896–1932.** New York: Macmillan, 1935. Discusses Communist involvement in the Farmer-Labor movement of 1919-24.

87. Saposs, David. **Communism in American Politics.** Washington: Public Affairs Press, 1960. Unsympathetic survey of the Communist Party in politics; suggests significant Communist participation in politics in scattered areas of the nation; treats Communism as an illegitimate participant in democratic politics.

COMMUNISM AND THE La FOLLETTE PROGRESSIVE PARTY OF 1924

88. MacKay, Kenneth Campbell. **The Progressive Movement of 1924.** New York: Columbia University Press, 1947. Notes Communist Party involvement in the movement and La Follette's repudiation of Communist support.

89. Shideler, James H. "La Follette Campaign."
     Wisconsin Magazine of History 33 (1950).

90. Simson, Arthur. "Communism and the La Follette
     Campaign." **Political Affairs** 53 (Nov. 1974).
     Communist Party version of its role in the
     La Follette campaign.

THE NEW DEAL, THE POPULAR FRONT, AND WORLD WAR II

91. Bellush, Bernard and Jewel Bellush. "A Radical
     Response to the Roosevelt Presidency: The
     Communist Party (1933-1945)." **Presidential Studies
     Quarterly** 10,4 (1980). Surveys shifts in
     Communist Party attitudes toward FDR; notes that
     shifts followed changes in Soviet foreign policy.

92. Blum, John Morton. **V Was for Victory: Politics and
     American Culture During World War II.** New York:
     Harcourt Brace Javanovich, 1976. Discusses the
     domestic political and cultural atmosphere of the
     war years.

93. Garraty, John A. "Radicalism in the Great
     Depression." **Essays on Radicalism in Contemporary
     America.** Jerome L. Rodnitzky, Frank Ross Peterson,
     Kenneth R. Philip, and John A. Garraty, eds.
     Austin: University of Texas Press, 1972.
     Commentary on the lack of radical change in
     American and Europe in the 1930s.

94. Hincheyst, Mary. "The Frustration of the New Deal
     Revival, 1944-1946." Ph.D. dissertation.
     University of Missouri, 1965.

95. Klehr, Harvey. "The Strange Case of Roosevelt's
     'Secret Agent': Frauds, Fools, & Fantasies."
     Encounter [Great Britain] 59,6 (1982). Discusses
     Josephine Truslow Adams, a mentally unstable woman
     known casually by Eleanor Roosevelt. She
     convinced Earl Browder that she had close ties
     with Franklin D. Roosevelt; Browder subsequently
     attempted to use her as a liaison with the White
     House.

96. Lipset, Seymour Martin. "Roosevelt and the Protest
     of the 1930s." **University of Minnesota Law Review**
     (Fall 1983).

97. Lovin, Hugh T. "The Fall of the Farmer-Labor
     Parties, 1936-38." **Pacific Northwest Quarterly** 62

(Jan. 1971). Surveys the decline of the farmer-labor third party movement.

98. Lovin, Hugh T. "The 'Farmer-Labor' Movement in Idaho, 1933-1938." **Journal of the West** 28 (1979).

99. McCoy, Donald. **Angry Voices: Left-of-Center Politics in the New Deal Era.** Lawrence: University of Kansas Press, 1958. Sees only a limited and restricted Communist role in New Deal Politics.

100. McElvaine, Robert S. "Thunder Without Lightning; Working Class Discontent in the U.S., 1929-1937." Ph.D. dissertation. State University of New York, Binghamton, 1974. Concludes that workers were ready for radical action in the 1930s but this did not come about because of the strength of the two party system, weaknesses of the Socialist Party and the Communist Party, Roosevelt's clever rhetoric, and the deaths of Floyd Olson and Huey Long; sees the politics of Wisconsin, Minnesota, and California as demonstrating the radical potential of the 1930s.

101. McFarland, C.K. "Coalition of Convenience: Lewis and Roosevelt, 1933-1940." **Labor History** 13 (Summer 1972). Notes the changing Communist Party attitude toward Roosevelt and John L. Lewis.

102. Miller, Donald L. **The New American Radicalism: Alfred M. Bingham and Non-Marxian Insurgency in the New Deal Era.** Port Washington: Kennikat, 1979. Notes Bingham's opposition to Communist participation in the American Commonwealth Political Federation and other left-of-center political movements.

103. Notaro, Carmen Anthony. "Franklin D. Roosevelt and the American Communist, Peacetime Relations, 1932-1941." Ph.D. dissertation. State University of New York, Buffalo, 1969. Surveys the shifting attitude of the Communist Party toward the Roosevelt administration.

104. Salmond, John A. **A Southern Rebel: The Life and Times of Aubrey Willis Williams, 1890-1965.** Chapel Hill: University of North Carolina Press, 1983. Biography of a important New Deal official who on occasion acted as a link with Popular Front figures and who was eventually driven from office for his advanced New Deal views.

* Stephenson, Anders. "The CPUSA Conception of the Rooseveltian State." Thesis. New College, Oxford University, 1977. Cited as item 2064. See item 105.

105. Stephenson, Anders. "The CPUSA Conception of The Rooseveltian State, 1933-1939." **Radical History Review** 24 (1980). Commentary on the Communist Party's analysis of the structure of government, politics, and power under the New Deal.

COMMUNISM, HENRY WALLACE, AND THE 1948 PROGRESSIVE PARTY

106. Barto, Harold. "Clark Clifford and the Presidential Election of 1948." Ph.D. dissertation. Rutgers University, 1970. Discusses Clifford's role in devising a Truman administration strategy against Henry Wallace and the Communist-influenced Progressive Party.

107. Bintner, Stuart John. "Clark Clifford and the 1948 Presidential Campaign." Master's thesis. University of Missouri-Kansas City, 1969.

108. Brandt, Harvey V. "The Ideological Function of the Progressive Party of 1948." Master's thesis. Columbia University, 1949.

109. Brown, John Cotton. "The 1948 Progressive Campaign: A Scientific Approach." Ph.D. dissertation. University of Chicago, 1949. Brown, a graduate student of Rexford Tugwell, attended a number of important private Progressive Party convention meetings as Tugwell's assistant.

110. Divine, Robert. "The Cold War and the Election of 1948." **Journal of American History** 59 (June 1972).

111. Hamby, Alonzo. "Henry Wallace, the Liberals, and Soviet-American Relations." **Review of Politics** 30,4 (1968).

112. Hamby, Alonzo. "Sixty Million Jobs and the People's Revolution: The Liberals, the New Deal and World War II." **Historian** 30 (August 1968).

113. Hamilton, Mary A. "A Progressive Publisher and the Cold War: J.W. Gitt and **The Gazette and Daily,**

York, Pennsylvania, 1946-1956." Ph.D.
dissertation. Michigan State University, 1980.
Surveys the journalism and political activity of
Gitt, whose newspaper was one of the very few
commercial dailies to support Henry Wallace.
Discusses Gitt's concern about the Communist role
in the Progressive Party and his resignation from
the Party leadership in 1950 over its stance on
the Korean war.

114. Hasting, Anne Celeste. "Intraparty Struggle: Harry
S. Truman, 1945-1946." Ph.D. dissertation. Saint
Louis University, 1972. Treats the attacks on
Henry Wallace for cooperating with the Communist
Party as a ploy by Truman supporters.

115. Jaffe, Philip J. "The Varga Controversy and the
American Communist Party." **Survey [Great Britain]**
18,3 (1972). Examines the relationship of the
Communist Party's decision to support a third
party in 1948 with Zhdanov's speech and the
attacks on Varga's unorthodox views on
capitalism. See item 761.

116. MacDougall, Curtis D. **Gideon's Army.** New York:
Marzani & Munsell, 1965. MacDougall, a prominent
participant in the Wallace campaign, reviews in
detail the history of Henry Wallace's Progressive
Party; finds no significant Communist influence.

117. Markowitz, Norman D. "The Rise and Fall of the
People's Century: Henry A. Wallace and American
Liberalism, 1941-1948." Ph.D. dissertation.
University of Michigan, 1970.

118. Markowitz, Norman D. **The Rise and Fall of the
People's Century: Henry A. Wallace and American
Liberalism, 1941-1948.** New York: Free Press,
1973. A political history of Wallace's variety
of liberalism; notes a Communist role in the
Progressive Party. Argues that the "Cold War
liberals" who defeated Wallace were opportunists
who suffered from a failure of nerve when they
did not support Wallace's "social liberal" vision
in the postwar world.

119. Markowitz, Norman D. "A View from the Left: From
the Popular Front to Cold War Liberalism." **The
Specter.** Robert Griffith and Athan Theoharis,
eds. New York: 1974. Critical evaluation of
anti-Communist liberalism.

120. Peterson, Frank Ross. "Fighting the Drive Toward
      War: Glen H. Taylor, the 1948 Progressives, and
      the Draft." **Pacific Northwest Quarterly** 61 (Jan.
      1970).

121. Peterson, Frank Ross. "Harry S. Truman and His
      Critics: The 1948 Progressives and the Origins of
      the Cold War." **Essays on Radicalism in
      Contemporary America.** Jerome L. Rodnitzky, Frank
      Ross Peterson, Kenneth R. Philip, and John A.
      Garraty, eds. Austin: University of Texas Press,
      1972. Sympathetic analysis of the attack on
      Truman's anti-Communist liberalism by Henry
      Wallace and Glen Taylor.

122. Peterson, Frank Ross. **Prophet Without Honor: Glen
      H. Taylor and the Fight for American Liberalism.**
      Lexington: University Press of Kentucky, 1974.
      Admiring political biography of Glen Taylor, the
      one-term U.S. Senator and vice-presidential
      nominee of Henry Wallace's Progressive Party in
      1948. Treats claims of a Communist Party role in
      the Progressive Party as contrived by Democrats.

123. Rosen, Jerold A. "Henry A. Wallace and American
      Liberal Politics, 1945-1948." **Annals of Iowa** 44
      (Fall 1978).

124. Schapsmeier, Edward L., and Frederick Schapsmeier.
      Henry A. Wallace and the War Years, 1940-1965.
      Ames: Iowa State University Press, 1970. This
      detailed scholarly biography discusses Wallace's
      dealings with the Communist Party and its allies
      in the late 1940s.

125. Schmidt, Karl M. "The Wallace Progressive Party."
      Ph.D. dissertation. Johns Hopkins University,
      1951.

126. Schmidt, Karl M. **Henry A. Wallace: Quixotic
      Crusade 1948.** Syracuse: Syracuse University
      Press, 1960.

127. Walton, Richard J. **Henry Wallace, Harry Truman,
      and the Cold War.** New York: The Viking Press,
      1976. Argues that Wallace and his Progressive
      Party were right and that Truman and the anti-
      Communist liberals were wrong.

128. Yarnell, Allen. "The Impact of the Progressive
      Party on the Democratic Party in the 1948
      Presidential Election." Ph.D. dissertation.
      University of Washington, 1969.

129. Yarnell, Allen. The Democratic Party's Response to
      the Progressive Party in 1948." **Research Studies**
      39 (March 1971).

130. Yarnell, Allen. **Democrats and Progressives: The
      1948 Presidential Election as a Test of Postwar
      Liberalism.** Berkeley: University of California
      Press, 1974. Discusses the use of anti-Communism
      as a Truman campaign theme against Henry Wallace;
      denies that the Wallace campaign moved Truman to
      the Left.

      See items 1569-1574.

COMMUNISM AND POLITICS IN NEW YORK: THE 1930s AND 1940s

131. Bakunin, Jack. "The Role of the Socialists in the
      Formation of the American Labor Party." Master's
      thesis. City College of New York, 1965.
      Discusses Socialist attitudes toward Communist
      participation in the ALP.

132. Bone, Hugh A. "Political Parties in New York
      City." **American Political Science Review** 40
      (April 1946).

133. Carter, Robert Frederick. "Pressure From the Left:
      The American Labor Party, 1936-1954." Ph.D.
      dissertation. Syracuse University, 1965. Surveys
      the political history of the ALP.

134. Flournoy, Houston Irvine. "The Liberal Party in
      New York State." Ph.D. dissertation. Princeton
      University, 1956. A history of the withdrawal of
      the International Ladies Garment Workers Union
      and other anti-Communists from the American Labor
      Party to form the rival Liberal Party.

135. Gerson, Simon W. **Pete, The Story of Peter V.
      Cacchione, New York's First Communist Councilman.**
      New York: International Publishers, 1976.

136. Gordon, Max. "The Party and the Polling Place: A
      Response." **Radical History Review** 23 (1980). In
      a commentary on Waltzer's "The Party and the
      Polling Place," Gordon, a former Communist
      official, defends the Popular Front strategy.

137. Licht, Walter. "An Analysis of a Political
      Experiment: The American Labor Party (1936-
      1940)." Senior honors thesis. Harvard University,
      1967.

138. Sarasohn, Stephen Beisman. "The Struggle for
     Control of the American Labor Party 1936-1948."
     Master's thesis. Columbia University, 1948.

139. Steinbock, Julius. "The Emergence of the Liberal
     Party in New York State: A Study in Minor
     Parties." Master's thesis. Ohio State University,
     1947.

140. Steward, William James. "A Political History of
     the American Labor Party 1936-1944." Master's
     thesis. American University, 1959.

141. Waldman, Louis. Labor Lawyer. New York: Dutton,
     1941. Memoir by an anti-Communist figure in the
     American Labor Party.

142. Waltzer, Kenneth. "The American Labor Party: Third
     Party Politics in New Deal-Cold War New York,
     1936-1954." Ph.D. dissertation. Harvard
     University, 1977. Well researched and well
     written history of the American Labor Party;
     discusses the powerful role of the Communist
     Party in the ALP and the nature of the Popular
     Front alliance.

143. Waltzer, Kenneth. "The Party and the Polling
     Place: American Communism and an American Labor
     Party in the 1930's." Radical History Review 23
     (Dec. 1980). Well researched history of the role
     of the Communist Party in New York's American
     Labor Party. Discusses the nature of the Popular
     Front stance. See item 136.

144. Wolfe, Allan. "The Withering Away of the American
     Labor Party." Rutgers University Library Journal
     31 (1968).

145. Zeller, Belle and Hugh A. Bone. "The Repeal of
     P.R. in New York City." American Political
     Science Review 42 (1948). Notes the desire to
     minimize Communist Party electoral success as a
     cause of the repeal of proportional
     representation in New York City.

Vito Marcantonio

146. Bingham, Arthur Walker. "The Congressional
     Elections of Vito Marcantonio." Senior honors
     thesis. Harvard University, 1950.

147. Blum, Jacob, and John Wilhelm. "Vito Marcantonio:
      The Politics of Dissent." Honors thesis. Yale
      University, 1967.

148. Jackson, Peter. "Vito Marcantonio and Ethnic
      Politics in New York." **Ethnic and Racial Studies**
      [Great Britain] 6,1 (1983).

149. Kaner, Norman J. "Toward a Minority of One: Vito
      Marcantonio and American Foreign Policy." Ph.D.
      dissertation. Rutgers University, 1968.

150. La Gumina, Salvatore. "Vito Marcantonio, Labor and
      the New Deal 1935-1940." Ph.D. dissertation. St.
      Johns University, 1966.

151. La Gumina, Salvatore. **Vito Marcantonio: The**
      People's Politician. Dubuque: Kendall-Hunt, 1969.

152. La Gumina, Salvatore. "The New Deal, the
      Immigrants and Congressman Vito Marcantonio."
      International Migration Review 4,2 (1970).
      Discusses the conflict between Representative
      Marcantonio, a close ally of the Communist Party,
      with the Roosevelt administration over
      immigration policies.

153. La Gumina, Salvatore. "Vito Marcantonio: A Study
      in the Functional and Ideological Dynamics of a
      Labor Politician." **Labor History** 13,3 (Summer
      1972).

154. Lieberman, Donna. "Vito Marcantonio: A
      Biographical Study." Senior honors thesis.
      Brandeis University, 1969.

155. Meyer, Gerald. "Vito Marcantonio, A Successful New
      York City Radical Politician." Ph.D.
      dissertation. City University of New York, 1984.
      Concludes that Marcantonio's political strength
      was based on a personal political machine, ethnic
      appeals to Italians and Puerto Ricans, and money
      and manpower supplied by the Communist Party.

156. Rubenstein, Annette T., ed. **I Vote My Conscience:**
      Debates, Speeches, Writings of Vito Marcantonio,
      1933-1950. New York: 1956.

157. Sasuly, Richard. "Vito Marcantonio: The People's
      Politician." **American Radicals.** Harvey Goldberg,
      ed. New York: Monthly Review Press, 1957.

158.   Schaffer, Alan. **Vito Marcantonio: Radical in
        Congress.** Syracuse: Syracuse University Press,
        1966.

159.   Waltzer, Kenneth. "The FBI, Congressman Vito
        Marcantonio, and the American Labor Party."
        Beyond the Hiss Case. Athan Theoharis, ed.
        Philadelphia: Temple University Press, 1982.

COMMUNISM AND POLITICS IN MINNESOTA

160.   Berman, Hyman. "Political Antisemitism in
        Minnesota During the Great Depression." **Jewish
        Social Studies** 38,3-4 (Summer-Fall 1976). Notes
        the use of anti-Communist as well as anti-Semitic
        themes in political attacks on Governor Elmer
        Benson of Minnesota; notes the role of Communists
        in the Benson administration.

161.   Gieske, Millard. **Minnesota Farmer-Laborism: The
        Third-Party Alternative.** Minneapolis: University
        of Minnesota Press, 1979. Notes the Communist
        Party's entrance into the powerful Minnesota
        Farmer-Labor movement in the mid-1930s.

162.   Haynes, John Earl. "Liberals, Communists, and the
        Popular Front in Minnesota: The Struggle to
        Control the Political Direction of the Labor
        Movement and Organized Liberalism, 1936-1950."
        Ph.D. dissertation. University of Minnesota,
        1978. Similar to Haynes' **Dubious Alliance** except
        for greater emphasis on internal labor movement
        activity. See item 163.

163.   Haynes, John Earl. **Dubious Alliance: The Making of
        Minnesota's DFL Party.** Minneapolis: University of
        Minnesota Press, 1984. Detailed narrative
        history of the conflict within Minnesota liberal
        institutions between a Popular Front faction,
        which included a leading Communist Party element,
        and anti-Communist liberals. The struggle began
        in 1936 when Communists entered the powerful
        Minnesota Farmer-Labor Party and ended in 1948
        when Hubert Humphrey's anti-Communist liberals
        established their control over the Democratic-
        Farmer-Labor Party.

164.   Humola, Hulda F. "The Farmer-Labor Party in
        Minnesota, 1930-38." Master's thesis. University
        of Chicago, 1944. Notes growing influence of
        Communists in Farmer-Labor affairs under Governor
        Benson.

165. Krause, Fayette F. "A Study of Left Wing Politics
     in the Roosevelt Era." Master's thesis.
     University of Minnesota, 1966. Sees little
     Communist Party influence in the Minnesota
     Farmer-Labor movement.

166. Mitau, G. Theodore. "The Democratic-Farmer-Labor
     Party Schism of 1948." **Minnesota History** 34
     (Spring 1955).

*   Montgomery, David. "The Farmer-Labor Party."
     **Working for Democracy: American Workers from the
     Revolution to the Present.** Paul Buhle and Alan
     Dawley, eds. Urbana: University of Illinois
     Press, 1985. Cited as item 2061. Didactic;
     summary of Farmer-Labor history from a
     ideological, hard Left perspective.

167. Naftalin, Arthur A. "A History of the Farmer-Labor
     Party of Minnesota." Ph.D. dissertation.
     University of Minnesota, 1948. Sees significant
     Communist infiltration into the Minnesota Farmer-
     Labor Party in the 1930s.

168. O'Connell, Thomas Gerald. "Toward the Cooperative
     Commonwealth: An Introductory History of the
     Farmer-Labor Movement in Minnesota (1917-1948)."
     Ph.D. dissertation. Union Graduate School, 1979.

169. Shields, James M. **Mr. Progressive: A Biography of
     Elmer Austin Benson.** Minneapolis: T.S. Dennison &
     Co., 1971. Laudatory biography of a Minnesota
     governor and U.S. Senator who was a prominent
     Popular Front liberal.

170. Stuhler, Barbara. "The One Man Who voted 'Nay',
     The Story of John T. Bernard's Quarrel With
     American Foreign Policy 1937-1939." **Minnesota
     History** 43 (Fall 1972). Recounts, without noting
     his Communist Party links, Congressman Barnard's
     support for an anti-Fascist foreign policy.

*   Valelly, Richard M. "State-Level Radicalism and
     the Nationalization of American Politics: The
     Case of the Minnesota Farmer-Labor Party." Ph.D.
     dissertation, Harvard University, 1984. Cited as
     item 2050. Discusses the factors transforming
     the Minnesota Farmer-Labor Party from a unique
     state-level radical movement into a more typical
     participant in national liberal politics.

COMMUNISM AND POLITICS IN WISCONSIN

171.   Haney, Richard Carlton. "A History of the
       Democratic Party of Wisconsin since World War
       Two." Ph.D. dissertation. University of
       Wisconsin, 1970. Notes that many of those who
       led the revival of the Democratic Party after
       World War II had been active in the anti-
       Communist faction of the American Veterans
       Committee.

172.   Kunkel, Joseph A., III. "The Ideological Party in
       American Politics: The Case of the Milwaukee
       Social Democrats." Ph.D. dissertation. University
       of Minnesota, 1980.

173.   Lorence, James J. "Socialism in Northern
       Wisconsin, 1910-1920: An Ethno-Cultural
       Analysis." **Mid-America** 64,3 (1982). Notes that
       the association of the Social Democrats with
       Communism contributed to the decline of rural
       Socialist voting strength after the Bolshevik
       revolution.

174.   McCoy, Donald. "The Development and Dissolution of
       the Wisconsin Progressive Party of 1934-46."
       Master's thesis. University of Chicago, 1949.

175.   Olson, Frederick. "The Milwaukee Socialist, 1897-
       1941." Ph.D. dissertation. Harvard Univ., 1952.

176.   Schmidt, Lester F. "The Farmer-Labor Progressive
       Federation: The Story of a 'United Front'
       Movement among Wisconsin Liberals, 1934-1941."
       Ph.D. dissertation. University of Wisconsin,
       1954. Notes extensive conflict between anti-
       Communist and Popular Front factions within the
       Wisconsin Progressive Party.

177.   Stachowski, Floyd. "The Political Career of Daniel
       Webster Hoan." Ph.D. dissertation. Northwestern
       University, 1966. Mayor of Milwaukee in the
       1930s, Hoan was a leading Wisconsin Socialist and
       anti-Communist.

COMMUNISM AND POLITICS IN CALIFORNIA

178.   Blake, Fay M., and H. Morton Newman. "Upton
       Sinclair's EPIC Campaign." **California History**
       63,4 (Fall 1984). Notes Communist hostility to
       EPIC.

179. Burke, Robert. **Olson's New Deal for California.**
      Berkeley: University of California Press, 1953.
      Notes Governor Olson's association with some
      Communist-led organizations.

180. Frost, Richard. **The Mooney Case.** Stanford:
      Stanford University Press, 1968. Discusses
      Communist Party involvement in the campaign to
      free Tom Mooney.

181. Furmanovsky, Michael. "'Cocktail Picket Party':
      The Hollywood **Citizen-News** Strike, the Newspaper
      Guild, and the Popularization of the 'Democratic
      Front' in Los Angeles." **UCLA Historical Journal** 5
      (1984). Discusses the success of Popular Front
      tactics in winning support for a newspaper
      strike.

182. Moremen, Merrill Raymond. "The Independent
      Progressive Party of California, 1948." Master's
      thesis. Stanford University, 1950.

183. Murdock, Steve. "California Communists - Their
      Years of Power." **Science and Society** 34,4 (1970).
      Maintains that the Communist Party had
      significant influence in California in the 1930s,
      '40s, and '50s.

COMMUNISM AND POLITICS IN WASHINGTON STATE

184. Acena, Albert A. **The Washington Commonwealth
      Federation: Reform Politics and the Popular
      Front.** Ph.D. dissertation. University of
      Washington, 1975. Detailed scholarly study of the
      WCF and its role in Washington State liberal
      politics. Notes that the WCF was controlled by a
      Popular Front faction dominated by the Communist
      Party.

185. Krause, Fayette F. "Democratic Party Politics in
      the State of Washington during the New Deal,
      1932-1940." Ph.D. dissertation. University of
      Washington, 1971. Describes a powerful Popular
      Front faction with a significant Communist
      presence in the Washington Democratic Party.

COMMUNISM AND POLITICS IN OREGON

186. Herzig, Jill H. "The Oregon Commonwealth
      Federation: The Rise and Decline of a Reform

Organization." Master's thesis. University of
Oregon, 1963. Notes a struggle between anti-
Communists and a Communist-led Popular Front
faction in the OCF in the late 1930s.

187. Lovin, Hugh T. "Toward a Farmer-Labor Party in
Oregon, 1933-1938." **Oregon Historical Quarterly**
76 (1975).

7

THE NATURE AND STRUCTURE OF THE COMMUNIST PARTY

188. Almond, Gabriel A. **The Appeals of Communism.**
     Princeton: Princeton University Press, 1954.
     Critical commentary on the appeal of Communism
     based on interviews with American and foreign
     Communists and on Communist literature.

189. Bell, Daniel. "The Background and Development of
     Marxian Socialism in the United States."
     Socialism and American Life. Donald Drew Egbert
     and Stow Persons, eds. Princeton: Princeton
     University Press, 1952. Critical commentary on
     the intellectual and cultural outlook of the
     early Socialist Party and Communist Party.

190. Bell, Daniel. **Marxian Socialism in the United
     States.** Princeton: Princeton University Press,
     1967.

191. Bell, Daniel. "The Failure of American Socialism:
     The Tension of Ethics and Politics." **The End of
     Ideology.** New York: The Free Press, 1961. Judges
     that the main appeal of the Communist Party in
     the 1930s and 1940s was to the dispossessed
     intelligentsia of the Depression generation and
     to "engineers of the future" who were attracted
     by its elitist character.

192. Bell, Daniel. "First Love and Early Sorrows."
     Partisan Review 48,4 (1981). Sees chiliastic and
     gnostic sources contributing to the willingness
     of Communists and other Leftists to use violence
     and terror to redeem the world.

193. Briendel, Eric M. "The Communists & the
     Committees." **Commentary** (Jan. 1981). Critical
     commentary on books and films depicting American
     Communists as romantic idealists.

194. Briendel, Eric M. "The Stalinist Follies."
     Commentary 74,4 (1982). Critical commentary on
     the writings of former Communists who, despite a

personal break with the Communist Party, continue
to minimize Stalin's crimes, defend the Hitler-
Stalin Pact, the Hungarian invasion, or the Czech
invasion.

195. Budenz, Louis. **Men Without Faces: The Communist
Conspiracy in the USA.** New York: Harper &
Brothers, 1948. Budenz, once editor of the **Daily
Worker,** became a fervid anti-Communist and
frequently testified about the conspiratorial
nature of Communism in the late 1940s and 1950s.

196. Budenz, Louis. **The Techniques of Communism.**
Chicago: Regnery, 1954. Emphasizes the
conspiratorial nature of the Communist Party.

197. Burnham, James. **The Struggle for the World.** New
York: John Day, 1947. Burnham, a leading
Marxist-Leninist theoretician in the 1930s,
became a prominent right-wing intellectual.

198. **Chronicles of Culture.** "Gornick's Machinations."
Chronicles of Culture 2 (March-April 1978).
Critical review-essay of Gornick's **The Romance of
American Communism.**

199. Cohn, Werner. "'A Clear Provocation,' Esoteric
Elements in Communist Language." **Encounter [Great
Britain]** 64,5 (May 1985). Discusses the origins
of Communist jargon which defines revelation of
an embarrassing truth as provocation.

200. Dies, Martin. **Trojan Horse in America.** New York:
Dodd, Mead, 1940. Dies chaired and brought to
prominence what became the House Un-American
Activities Committee.

201. Dirscherl, Dennis. "The Many Faces of Treason."
Ukrainian Quarterly 37,4 (1981).

202. Dixler, Elsa Jane. "The American Communist Party
and the Revolution." **American Behavioral
Scientist** 20,4 (March-April 1977). Discusses the
meaning of revolution in the American context.

203. Draper, Theodore. "The Ghost of Social Fascism."
Commentary (Feb. 1969). Discusses the
development of the Communist Party's concept of
"social fascism."

204. Ernst, Morris L., and David Loth. **Report on the
American Communist.** New York: Henry Holt and Co.,

1952. Examines the Communist Party's membership;
sees Communists as compensating for personal
deficiencies in extremist politics.

205. Evans, William Barrett. "'Revolutionist Thought'
in the **Daily Worker**, 1919-1939." Ph.D.
dissertation. University of Washington, 1965.
Finds no consistent theoretical perspective on
revolution; instead, there was a consistent
reflection of Soviet and Comintern
pronouncements.

206. Fry, William Welz. "Communist United Front
Strategy and Tactics: Origins and some recent
Applications." Ph.D. dissertation. Georgetown
University, 1962.

207. Glazer, Nathan. **The Social Basis of American
Communism.** New York: Harcourt, Brace & World,
1961. Examines the socioeconomic background of
American Communists.

208. Glazer, Nathan. "The Social Basis of American
Communism." Ph.D. dissertation. Columbia
University, 1962.

209. Gornick, Vivian. **The Romance of American
Communism.** New York: Basic Books, 1977. Based
upon interviews with forty-seven former Communist
Party members. Gornick sees Communists as
idealistic, finds party life to have been largely
fulfilling, and generally presents an appealing
"human face" to American Communism. See items
198, 218, 2010, 2012, and 2014.

210. Hook, Sidney. **Heresy, Yes--Conspiracy, No!** New
York: John Day, 1953. Argues that the Communist
Party is more of a conspiracy than a dissenting
political movement.

211. Hook, Sidney. "The Communist Peace Offensive."
Partisan Review 51,4 & 52,1 (1984 & 1985).
Memoir of the 1949 "Waldorf Conference" peace
campaign.

212. Kintner, William R. "Communist Organization and
the Unlimited Quest for Power." Ph.D. dissertation. Georgetown University, 1949.

213. Klehr, Harvey. "Marxist Theory in Search of
America." **Journal of Politics** 35,2 (1973).
Discusses the difficulty of Marxist analysis of

American history and the failure of the Communist
Party to develop an adequate theory of "American
exceptionalism."

214. Klehr, Harvey. "Leninism and Lovestoneism."
     Studies in Comparative Communism 7 (Spring-Summer
     1974). Discusses the argument between Foster and
     Lovestone over the nature of American capitalism.
     Finds that both continued the Leninist
     misunderstanding of American history.

215. Klehr, Harvey. "Leninist Theory in Search of
     America." **Polity** 9,1 (1976). Notes the variety
     of images of the US offered by Lenin.

216. Klehr, Harvey. "Leninism, Lewis Corey, and the
     Failure of American Socialism." **Labor History**
     18,2 (Spring 1977).

217. Klehr, Harvey. **Communist Cadre: The Social
     Background of the American Communist Party Elite.**
     Stanford: Hoover Institution Press, 1978.
     Analyzes biographical information on 212
     Communist Party Central Committee members (1920-
     1961). Finds that native-born Communists rose
     faster than the foreign-born, blacks were more
     likely to remain loyal to the Communist Party
     than whites, non-Jews rose quicker in the
     hierarchy that Jews, and that women rose in the
     cadre, but slowly.

218. Kramer, Hilton. "Beautiful Reds." **New York Times
     Book Review** (April 2, 1978). Critical review of
     Vivian Gornick's **The Romance of American
     Communism.**

219. Krugman, Herbert. "The Interplay of Social and
     Psychological Factors in Political Deviance: An
     Inquiry into Some Factors Underlying the
     Motivation of Intellectuals Who Became
     Communists." Thesis. Columbia University, 1952.

220. Lasswell, Harold D., and Dorothy Blumenstock.
     World Revolutionary Propaganda. New York: Knopf,
     1939.

221. Le Blanc, Paul. "The Tragedy of American
     Communism." **Michigan Quarterly Review** (Summer
     1982).

222. Lyons, Paul. "The Communist as Organizer: the
     Philadelphia Experience, 1936-1956." Ph.D.
     dissertation. Bryn Mawr College, 1980.

223. Lyons, Paul. **Philadelphia Communists, 1936-1956.**
Philadelphia: Temple University Press, 1982.
Sympathetic examination of Communist Party
activists based on interviews with thirty-six
current or former members.

224. McCrackin, Bobbie. "The Etiology of Radicalization
among American and British Communist
Autobiographers." Ph.D. dissertation. Emory
University, 1980. Examines the autobiographies
of seventy-eight U.S. and British Communists to
discover the sources of their radicalism. The
factors which appear important are an upbringing
in a radical family or subculture, the impact of
a crisis such as the Depression, or frustrated
ambitions finding an outlet. Examines the
relevance of several psychological theories.

225. Meyer, Frank S. **The Moulding of Communists; The
Training of the Communist Cadre.** New York:
Harcourt, Brace and Co., 1961. Psychological
analysis finding Communists to be largely
neurotic.

226. Monnerot, Jules. **The Sociology and Psychology of
Communism.** Boston: Beacon, 1953.

227. Moore, Barrington. "The Communist Party of the
USA; An Analysis of a Social Movement." **American
Political Science Review** 39 (Feb. 1945).

228. Palmer, Edward E., ed. **The Communist Problem in
America.** New York: Thomas Y. Crowell, 1951.

*   Rossiter, Clinton. **Marxism: The View from America.**
New York: Harcourt, Brace and Co., 1960. Cited
as item 2047.

229. Selznick, Philip. **The Organizational Weapon: A
Study of Bolshevik Strategy and Tactics.** New
York: McGraw-Hill, 1952. Sees the organizational
structure of the Communist Party as that of a
weapon aimed at the destruction of American
society.

230. Shils, Edward. "The Burden of 1917." **Survey**
(Summer-Autumn 1976). Discusses the influence of
the Bolshevik model on thinking about
contemporary socialism and revolution.

231. Stripling, Robert (Robert Consideine, ed.). **The
Red Plot Against America.** Drexel Hill: Bell,

1949. Journalistic expose by the longtime staff
director of House Un-American Activities
Committee.

232. Wheeler, Robert Hullings Lappe. "American
Communists: Their Ideology and Their
Interpretation of American Life, 1917-1939."
Ph.D. dissertation. Yale University, 1953.

233. Wriggins, William H. "The Image of the Ideal
Communist Militant as Depicted in Communist Party
Publications." Ph.D. dissertation. Yale
University, 1953.

8

SCHISMATIC COMMUNIST MOVEMENTS

GENERAL

234. Alexander, Robert J. **The Right Opposition: The Lovestoneites and the International Communist Opposition of the 1930's.** Westport: Greenwood Press, 1981. Surveys the fate of the Right Opposition in America and in other nations after its expulsion from the Communist Party.

235. Eastland, Terry. "The Communists and the Klan." **Commentary** 69,5 (1980). Discusses the violent confrontation between the Ku Klux Klan and the Communist Workers' Party (Workers' Viewpoint Organization) in November 1979 in Greensboro, North Carolina.

236. O'Brien, Jim. "American Leninism in the 1970s." **Radical America,** 11,6 & 12,1 (1977-78), Surveys the wide variety of Leninist organizations; concludes that the Communist Party is likely to remain the dominant body.

237. Deleted

See items 1355 and 1356.

TROTSKYISM, THE SHACHTMANITES

238. Belton, John. "The Commission of Inquiry into Charges Made Against Leon Trotsky in the Great Purge Trials in Moscow." Master's thesis. Emory University, 1977. History of the Commission (Dewey Commission) of American intellectuals who investigated Soviet charges against Trotsky.

239. Buhle, Paul, ed. **The Legacy of the Workers Party, 1940-1949: Recollections and Reflections.** New York: Tamiment Institute, 1985. Edited transcript of oral recollections of former Workers Party (Shachtmanites) activists.

240. Cannon, James P. **The History of American Trotskyism.** New York: Pathfinder Press, 1944, 1972. Written by an American Trotskyism dominant figure.

241. Carlson, Oliver. "Recollections of American Trotskyist Leaders." **Studies in Comparative Communism** 10,1-2 (1977). Memoir by a Trotskyist mentioning conversations with William Foster, Karl Radek, James Cannon, Max Shachtman and others in the 1920s and 1930s.

242. Fields, A.B. "Trotskyism and Maoism: A Comparative Analysis of Theory and Practice in France and the United States." **Studies in Comparative Communism** 16 (Spring-Summer 1983).

243. Glotzer, Albert. "Max Shachtman -- A Political-Biographical Essay." **Bulletin of the Tamiment Institute, Ben Josephson Library** 50 (April 1983). The issue also contains a guide to the extensive Shachtman collection of the Tamiment Institute.

244. Myers, Constance Ashton. "American Trotskyists, 1928-1941." Ph.D. dissertation. University of South Carolina, 1974.

245. Myers, Constance Ashton. **The Prophet's Army: Trotskyists in America, 1928-1941.** Westport: Greenwood, 1977. History of the internal politics of Trotskyism in America from the time of the expulsion from the Communist Party to the expulsion of the Shachtmanites from the Socialist Workers Party.

246. Myers, Constance Ashton. "'We Were a Little Hipped on the Subject of Trotsky,' Literary Trotskyists in the 1930s." **Cultural Politics.** Jerold Starr, ed. New York: Praeger, 1985.

247. Pahl, Thomas L. "The G-String Conspiracy, Political Reprisal or Armed Revolt?: The Minneapolis Trotskyite Trial." **Labor History** 8,1 (Winter 1967). Discusses government prosecution of the Socialist Workers Party in the early 1940s.

248. Shachtman, Max. "Radicalism in the Thirties: The Trotskyist View." **As We Saw the Thirties.** Rita J. Simon, ed. Urbana: University of Illinois Press, 1967.

249. Wald, Alan M. "Memorials of the John Dewey
     Commission: Forty Years Later." **Antioch Review** 38
     (1977).

250. Wald, Alan M. "Trotsky and American
     Intellectuals." **Cahiers Leon Trotsky [France]** 19
     (Sept. 1984).

     See items 448, 514-520, 555, 628, 1064, 1204, 1578,
     and 2004.

9

COMMUNISM AND THE AMERICAN LABOR MOVEMENT

GENERAL

* American Institute for Marxist Studies. "Lenin and the American Working-Class Movement." New York: American Institute for Marxist Studies, n.d. Cited as item 2083. Discusses Lenin's support for William Foster's strategy of 'boring from within' the AFL.

251. Babson, Steve, et al. **Working Detroit: The Making of a Union Town.** New York: Adama Books, 1984.

252. Barbash, Jack. "Communist Unionism -- Aims and Means." Unpublished manuscript, 1952.

253. Bernstein, Irving. **The Lean Years: A History of the American Worker, 1920-1933.** Boston: Houghton Mifflin, 1960. Discusses Communist dual union (Trade Union Unity League) activity and several major strikes involving Communist militants.

254. Bernstein, Irving. **Turbulent Years: A History of the American Worker, 1933-41.** Boston: Houghton Mifflin, 1970. Discusses Communist activity in the labor movement.

255. Boyer, Richard, and Herbert Morris. **Labor's Untold Story.** New York: United Electrical, Radio and Machine Workers, 1972. Sympathetic to those associated with the Communist Party.

256. Brecher, Jeremy. "Labor and the Left: The Long View from Below." **Political Power and Social Theory V. 4.** Howard Kimeldorf and Maurice Zeitlin, eds. Greenwich: JAI Press, 1984.

257. Brody, David. "Radical Labor History and Rank and File Militancy." **Labor History** 16 (Winter 1975).

258. Brody, David. "Radicalism and the American Labor
      Movement: From Party History to Social History."
      Political Power and Social Theory V. 4. Howard
      Kimeldorf and Maurice Zeitlin, eds. Greenwich:
      JAI Press, 1984.

259. Brooks, Thomas R. "Rewriting History: The Labor
      Myth." **The American Federationist** 85 (May 1978).
      Critical of those historians who criticize the
      expulsions of Communist-led unions from labor
      federations.

260. Chaison, Gary N. "Federation Expulsions and Union
      Mergers in the United States." **Relations
      Industrielles** 28 (1973).

261. Epstein, Albert, and Nathaniel Goldfinger.
      "Communist Tactics in American Unions." **Labor and
      Nation** 6 (1950).

262. Erickson, Herman. "WPA Strikes & Trials of 1939."
      Minnesota History 42,6 (1971). Notes Communist
      involvement in strikes by workers on federal work
      relief projects.

263. Deleted.

264. Galenson, Walter. "Communists and Trade Union
      Democracy." **Industrial Relations** 13,3 (Oct.
      1974).

265. Gerstle, Gary L. "The Pursuit of Legitimacy: Labor
      Militants and 'The Spirit of Americanism,' 1930-
      1948." Unpublished paper, 1981 Organization of
      American Historians annual meeting.

266. Gerstle, Gary L. "Founding Fathers and Powerful
      Proletarians: Illustrations of an American Labor
      Movement." Unpublished paper, 1981 Conference on
      New Deal Culture, Washington, D.C.

267. Gerstle, Gary L. "The Rise of Industrial Unionism:
      Class, Ethnicity and Labor Organization in
      Woonsocket, Rhode Island, 1931-1941." Ph.D.
      dissertation. Harvard University, 1982.
      Discusses the relationship of Americanism with
      union and political radicalism in the 1930s.

268. Glaberman, Martin. "Vanguard to Rearguard."
      Political Power and Social Theory V. 4. Howard
      Kimeldorf and Maurice Zeitlin, eds. Greenwich:
      JAI Press, 1984.

269. Green, James. "Working Class Militancy in the Depression." **Radical America** 6,6 (Nov.-Dec. 1972). Defends third period trade union policy and criticizes Popular Front labor policy.

270. Green, James. **The World of the Worker: Labor in Twentieth-Century America.** New York: Hill & Wing, 1980. Credits the Communist Party with setting the stage for and the initial successes of industrial unionism under the CIO. Highly critical of anti-Communist unionists of the postwar period.

271. Grob, Gerald N. **Workers and Utopia: A Study of Ideological Conflict in the American Labor Movement, 1865-1900.** Chicago: Northwestern University Press, 1969.

272. Haskett, William. "Ideological Radicals, the American Federation of Labor and Federal Labor Policy in the Strikes of 1934." Ph.D. dissertation. University of California, Los Angeles, 1957.

273. Healy, Dorothy. "False Consciousness and Labor Historians." **Political Power and Social Theory V. 4.** Howard Kimeldorf and Maurice Zeitlin, eds. Greenwich: JAI Press, 1984.

274. Howe, Irving, and B.J. Widick. "Communism and Trade Unions." **Industrial Relations** 14 (May 1975).

275. Laslett, John H.M. "Socialism and the American Labor Movement: Some New Reflections." **Labor History** 8 (Spring 1967).

276. Laslett, John H.M. **Labor and the Left: A Study of Socialist and Radical Influences in the American Labor Movement, 1881-1924.** New York: Basic Books, 1970.

277. Lens, Sidney. **Left, Right and Center: Conflicting Forces in American Labor.** Hinsdale: Regnery, 1949. Notes a Communist role in some unions.

278. Levenstein, Harvey. "Economism, Anti-economism and the History of the Communist Party." **Political Power and Social Theory V. 4.** Howard Kimeldorf and Maurice Zeitlin, eds. Greenwich: JAI Press, 1984.

279. Lichtenstein, Nelson. "The Communist Experience in American Trade Unions." [replies by Robert Zieger and Roger Keeran] **Industrial Relations** 19 (1980).

280. Marquart, Frank. "From a Labor Journal: Unions and Radicals in the Depression Era." **Dissent** 21 (1974).

281. Mikhailov, B.Y., et al. **Recent History of the Labor Movement in the United States, 1918-1939.** Moscow: Progress, 1977. Stresses the always correct and leading role of the American Communist Party.

282. O'Brien, F.S. "The 'Communist-Dominated' Unions in the United States Since 1950." **Labor History** 9,2 (Spring 1968).

283. Ozanne, Robert. "The Effects of Communist Leadership on American Trade Unions." Ph.D. dissertation. University of Wisconsin, 1954. Highly critical of the Communist role.

284. Prickett, James R. "Anti-Communism and Labor History." **Industrial Relations** 13 (Oct. 1974).

285. Prickett, James R. "Communists and the Communist Issue in the American Labor Movement, 1920-1950." Ph.D. dissertation. University of California, Los Angeles, 1975. Sympathetic examination of the Communist role in the International Ladies' Garment Workers Union, the National Maritime Union, and the United Electrical Workers; argues that the Communist Party did not dominate any CIO union, did not adjust trade union policy to accommodate Soviet foreign policy goals, and were more democratic than their opponents. Concludes that the Communist Party contribution of the labor movement was generally healthy whereas anti-Communists were largely destructive.

286. Prickett, James R. "New Perspectives on American Communism and the Labor Movement." **Political Power and Social Theory V. 4.** Howard Kimeldorf and Maurice Zeitlin, eds. Greenwich: JAI Press, 1984.

287. Saposs, David. **Left-Wing Unionism: A Study of Radical Policies and Tactics.** New York: International Publishers, 1926. Describes in a sympathetic fashion Communist Party activity in the union movement of the 1920s.

288. Saposs, David. **Communism in American Unions.** New
      York: McGraw-Hill, 1959. Unsympathetic survey of
      the role of the Communist Party in the trade
      union movement with emphasis on unions in
      Hollywood and the New York locals of the Hotel
      and Restaurant Workers.

289. Schneider, David Moses. "The Workers' (Communist)
      Party and American Trade Unions." Ph.D.
      dissertation. Johns Hopkins University, 1927.
      One of the earliest academic examinations of
      Communist activity.

290. Schneider, David M. **The Workers' (Communist) Party
      and American Trade Unions.** Johns Hopkins
      University Studies 46,2. Baltimore: The Johns
      Hopkins Press, 1928. Describes Communist Party
      activity in the trade union movement in the early
      1920s.

291. Sweeney, Eugene T. "The AFL's Good Citizen." **Labor
      History** 13,2 (1972). Notes the role of anti-
      Communism in the AFL's image of what constituted
      good citizenship in the 1920s and 1930s.

292. Taft, Philip. "Attempts to 'Radicalize' the Labor
      Movement." **Industrial and Labor Relations Review**
      (July 1948).

293. Taft, Philip. "Communism in Trade Unions." **Monthly
      Labor Review** 77,139 (1954).

294. Taft, Philip. **The AF of L in the Time of Gompers.**
      New York: Harper, 1957. Sympathetic discussion
      of Gompers' anti-Communism.

295. Taft, Philip. **The AF of L from the Death of
      Gompers to the Merger.** New York: Harper, 1959.
      Discusses the AFL's anti-Communist policy.

296. Zieger, Robert H. "The Popular Front Rides Again"
      Political Power and Social Theory V. 4. Howard
      Kimeldorf and Maurice Zeitlin, eds. Greenwich:
      JAI Press, 1984.

297. Zieger, Robert H. **American Workers, American
      Unions, 1920-1985.** Baltimore: Johns Hopkins
      University Press, 1986.

See items 355 and 1460.

COMMUNIST LABOR POLICY DURING WORLD WAR II

298. Freeman, Joshua B. "Delivering the Goods:
     Industrial Unionism During World War II." **Labor
     History** 19 (Fall 1978). Discusses the attitudes
     of Trotskyist and Communist union activists
     toward militant union tactics during the war.

299. Glaberman, Martin. Wartime Strikes: The Struggle
     Against the No-Strike Pledge in the UAW during
     World War II. Detroit: Bewick Editions, 1980.
     Part memoir, part history of wildcat strikes in
     World War II; notes the Communist role in
     opposing the wildcat movement. See item 2023.

300. Green, James. "Fighting on Two Fronts: Working
     Class Militancy in the 1940's." **Radical America** 9
     (July-Aug. 1975).

301. Jennings, Ed. "Wildcat! The Wartime Strike Wave in
     Auto." **Radical America** 9 (July-Aug. 1975).

302. Keeran, Roger. "'Everything for Victory':
     Communist Influence in the Auto Industry during
     World War II." **Science & Society** 63 (Spring
     1979). Examines and judges Communist policy
     toward industrial production and war policy to be
     justifiable.

303. Lichtenstein, Nelson. "Industrial Unionism Under
     the No-Strike Pledge: A Study of the CIO During
     the Second World War." Ph.D. dissertation.
     University of California, Berkeley, 1974.
     Discusses Communist opposition to disruptive
     labor militancy during the war.

304. Lichtenstein, Nelson. "Defending the No-Strike
     Pledge: CIO Politics during World War II."
     Radical America 9 (July-Aug. 1975).

305. Lichtenstein, Nelson. "Ambiguous Legacy: The Union
     Security Problem During World War II." **Labor
     History** 18 (1977).

306. Lichtenstein, Nelson. **Labor's War at Home: The CIO
     in World War II**. New York: Cambridge University
     Press, 1982.

307. Prickett, James R. "Communist Conspiracy or Wage
     Dispute?: The 1941 Strike at North American
     Aviation." **Pacific Historical Review** 50,2 (May
     1981). Asserts that the UAW strike at the North

American Aviation plant in Inglewood, California,
in 1941 was not promoted by Communist Party
unionists for political reasons.

308. Seidman, Joel. "Labor Policy of the Communist
Party During World War II." **Industrial and Labor
Relations Review** 4 (Oct. 1950).

309. Seidman, Joel. **American Labor from Defense to
Reconversion.** Chicago: University of Chicago
Press, 1953. Discusses the Communist Party's
trade union policy during World War II.

310. Weir, Stan. "American Labor on the Defensive: A
1940's Odyssey." **Radical America** 9 (July–Aug.
1975). Critical of the Communist Party's wartime
labor policies.

GOVERNMENT, UNION POLITICS, AND THE COMMUNIST PARTY

311. Auerbach, Jerold S. "The La Follette Committee:
Labor and Civil Liberties in the New Deal."
Journal of American History 61 (1964). Notes
that some committee staff were Communists.

312. Auerbach, Jerold S. **Labor and Liberty: The
La Follette Committee and the New Deal.** New York:
Bobbs-Merrill, 1966.

313. Barbash, Jack. "Unions, Government, and Politics."
Industrial and Labor Relations Review 1,1 (Oct.
1947). Discusses the role of Communists in the
union movement.

314. Blustain, Jonah. "The Treatment of the Collective
Bargaining Legislation of the New Deal by the
American Federation of Labor and the Communist
Party (USA), 1933–1939." Ph.D. dissertation. New
York University, 1954. Finds that Communist
Party predictions of the likely results of the
collective bargaining provisions of the 1933
National Industrial Recovery Act and the 1935
National Labor Relations Act were in error.

315. Daniel, Cletus E. **The ACLU and the Wagner Act: An
Inquiry into the Depression-Era Crisis of
American Liberalism.** Ithaca: Cornell University,
1980. Shows that in the early years of the
Depression, Roger Baldwin, head of the American
Civil Liberties Union, moved close to the
Communist Party and its allies; consequently, the

ACLU took a radical stance in opposing the
National Industrial Recovery Act and the Wagner
Act. This caused a reaction from a pro-Wagner
act faction in the ACLU. With the coming of the
Popular Front, the Communist Party embraced the
Wagner Act and the controversy ended.

316. Davin, Eric Leif, and Staughton Lynd. "Picket Line
and Ballot Box: The Forgotten Legacy of the Local
Labor Party Movement, 1932-1936." **Radical History
Review** 22 (Winter 1979-80). Argues that there was
widespread working-class interest in independent
labor and farmer-labor parties during 1932-36;
this movement was aborted by the CIO through its
organization of Labor's Non-Partisan League.
Berlin, New Hampshire is presented as a case
study.

317. Davis, Mike. "The Barren Marriage of American
Labour and the Democratic Party." **New Left Review**
124 (Nov.-Dec. 1980). Asserts that Communist
strategy in the mid-1930s and 1940s helped to
bring about the co-option of CIO militancy into
safe channels.

318. Daykin, Walter L. "The Operation of the Taft-
Hartley Act's Non-Communist Provisions." **Iowa Law
Review** 36,4 (Summer 1951).

319. Dzierba, Timothy R. "Organized Labor and the
Coming of the Second World War, 1937-1941." Ph.D.
dissertation. State University of New York,
Buffalo, 1984. Emphasizes that most labor
leaders regarded support for Roosevelt's foreign
policy as the reciprocal of Roosevelt's support
for labor's domestic goals.

320. Foster, James Caldwell. **The Union Politic: The CIO
Political Action Committee.** Columbia: University
of Missouri Press, 1975. In this history of CIO-
PAC, Foster argues that because of the refusal of
Communist Party unionists to support the CIO's
decision to back Truman (thereby endangering the
CIO's political standing) Philip Murray decided
to eliminate the Communist Party from the CIO.

321. Karsh, Bernard, and Phillips L. Garman. "The
Impact of the Political Left." **Labor and the New
Deal.** Milton Derber and Edwin Young, eds.
Madison: University of Wisconsin Press, 1957.

322. Koch, Lene. "Anti-Communism in the American Labor
     Movement: Reflections on the Communist Expulsions
     in 1949-50." **American Studies in Scandinavia**
     [Norway] 13,2 (1981). Discusses the link between
     the CIO's anti-Communism and its alliance with
     the Democratic Party.

323. Lipsitz, George. "A Rainbow at Midnight:
     Strategies of Independence in the Post War
     Working Class." Ph.D. dissertation. University of
     Wisconsin, 1979. Maintains that in 1946 mass
     popular general strikes broke out in five
     American cities. These strikes represented mass
     community revolt and broad worker solidarity.
     The strikes also won the support of small
     businessmen, clergy, and local politicians. The
     strikes, however, threatened the business,
     government and labor elite. The Cold War and
     Taft-Hartley were designed to suppress these
     popular revolts. Sees the attack on Communists
     in the labor movement as an excuse to smash rank
     and file militancy and create support for a
     foreign policy which would open up foreign
     markets for the U.S.

324. Lipsitz, George. **Class and Culture in Cold War**
     America: "A Rainbow at Midnight." South Hadley:
     J.F. Bergin, 1982.

325. Lipsitz, George. "Labor and the Cold War." **Working**
     for Democracy. Paul Buhle, and Alan Dawley, eds.
     Champaign: University of Illinois Press, 1986.

326. Lovin, Hugh T. "The Persistence of Third Party
     Dreams in the American Labor Movement, 1930-
     1938." **Mid-America** 58 (Oct. 1976).

327. Lovin, Hugh T. "The Ohio 'Farmer-Labor' Movement
     in the 1930s." **Ohio History** 87 (Autumn 1978).
     Notices a passing interest in a Farmer-Labor
     Party by Communist-aligned unions.

328. Lovin, Hugh T. "The Automobile Workers Unions and
     the Fight for Labor Parties in the 1930s."
     Indiana Magazine of History 77,2 (June 1981).
     Discusses the attitude of Indiana and Ohio UAW
     locals toward political action in the 1930s.

329. Lovin, Hugh T. "CIO Innovators, Labor Party
     Ideologues, and Organized Labor's Muddles in the
     1937 Detroit Elections." **Old Northwest** 8 (Fall
     1982). Notes Communist participation in labor
     political action in Detroit.

330. Lynd, Staughton. "A Chapter from History: the
     United Labor Party, 1946-1952." **Liberation** 18
     (Dec. 1973).

331. Nelson, Daniel. "The CIO at Bay: Labor Militancy
     and Politics in Akron, 1936-1938." **Journal of
     American History** 71,3 (Dec. 1984). Notes a
     Communist role in CIO and union political
     activity in Akron and the political use of anti-
     Communism by opponents of CIO-endorsed
     candidates.

332. Pratt, William C. "The Socialist Party, Socialist
     Unionists, and Organized Labor, 1936-1950."
     Political Power and Social Theory V. 4. Howard
     Kimeldorf and Maurice Zeitlin, eds. Greenwich:
     JAI Press, 1984.

333. Riker, William H. "The CIO in Politics, 1936-
     1946." Ph.D. dissertation. Harvard Univ., 1948.

334. Shair, David I. "How Effective is the Non-
     Communist Affidavit?" **Labor Law Journal** 1,12
     (Sept. 1950).

335. Shrake, Richard W., II. "Working Class Politics in
     Akron, Ohio, 1936: The Rubber Workers and the
     Failure of the Farmer-Labor Party." Master's
     thesis. University of Akron, 1974. Notes
     Communist Party involvement in the attempt to
     form a Farmer-Labor Party.

336. Spencer, Thomas T. "'Labor is with Roosevelt': The
     Pennsylvania Labor Non-partisan League and the
     Election of 1936." **Pennsylvania History** 46 (Jan.
     1979).

337. Taft, Philip. "Labor's Changing Political Line."
     Journal of Political Economy 45,5 (Oct. 1937).

     See items 97, 98, 100, 101, 133, 134, 137-142, 162,
     163, 176, 181, 184, 186, and 187.

LABOR, ANTI-COMMUNISM, AND FOREIGN POLICY

338. Abella, Irving. "The CIO, the Communist Party, and
     the Formation of the Canadian Congress of Labour,
     1936-1941." **Historical Papers [Canada]** 1969.

339. Abella, Irving. **Nationality, Communism and
     Canadian Labour: The CIO, the Communist Party and**

the **Canadian Congress of Labour, 1935-1956.**
Toronto: University of Toronto Press, 1973.

340. Berger, Henry. "Union Diplomacy: American Labor's
Foreign Policy in Latin America, 1932-1955."
Ph.D. dissertation. University of Wisconsin,
1966.

341. Berger, Henry. "Organized Labor and American
Foreign Policy." **The American Working Class
Today.** Irving Horowitz and John C. Leggett, eds.
New Brunswick: Transaction Books, 1979.

* Carew, Anthony. "The Schism within the World
Federation of Trade Unions: Government and Trade-
Union Diplomacy." **International Review of Social
History** 29,3 (1984). Cited as item 2049.

342. Carliner, Lewis. "The Dispute that Never Was."
Labor History 12,4 (Fall 1971). Essay review of
Alfred Hero and Emil Starr's **The Reuther-Meany
Foreign Policy Dispute** in which Carliner argues
that there was not a dispute of any significance
on the substance of foreign policy.

343. Carwell, Joseph. "The International Role of
American Labor." Ph.D. dissertation. Columbia
University, 1956.

344. Davies, Margaret. "The Role of American Trade
Union Representatives in the Aid to Greece
Program." Ph.D. dissertation. University of
Washington, 1960.

345. Godson, Roy. "The AFL Foreign Policy Making
Process from the End of World War II to the
Merger." **Labor History** 16,3 (Summer 1975).
Argues that the AFL's anti-Communist foreign
policy operations were based largely on
information gained from nongovernment sources,
chiefly the Free Trade Union Committee, and
decided upon independently of government
influence.

346. Godson, Roy. "Non-Governmental Organizations in
International Politics: The American Federation
of Labor, the International Labor Movement and
French Politics, 1945-1953." Ph.D. dissertation.
Columbia University, 1972.

347. Godson, Roy. **American Labor and European Politics:
The AFL as a Transnational Force.** New York:
Crane, Russak, 1976.

348. Godson, Roy. **The Kremlin and Labor: A Study in National Security Policy.** New York: Crane, Russak, 1977. Discusses Soviet and Communist policy toward the labor movement in the West.

349. Godson, Roy. **Labor in Soviet Global Strategy.** New York: Crase, Russak, 1984.

350. Gordon, Gerald R. "The AFL, the CIO, and the Quest for a Peaceful World Order, 1914-1946." Ph.D. dissertation. University of Maine, 1967. Discusses the role of anti-Communism in the foreign activities of the labor movement.

351. Hero, Alfred O., and Emil Starr. **The Reuther-Meany Foreign Policy Dispute.** New York: 1970. Discusses the split between Reuther and Meany over Cold War policy. See item 342.

352. Larson, Simeon. "Opposition to AFL Foreign Policy: A Labor Mission to Russia, 1927." **Historian** 43,3 (May 1981).

353. Lenburg, LeRoy Jones. "The CIO and American Foreign Policy, 1934-1955." Ph.D. dissertation. Pennsylvania State University, 1973. Finds the CIO divided into three foreign policy blocs: isolationists, the Left bloc, and the Right bloc. Isolationists under Lewis were a significant influence until Lewis challenged Roosevelt; American entry into the war finally shattered the isolationists. The Left bloc followed the foreign policy of the Soviet Union, shifting from interventionism prior to the Hitler-Stalin Pact to isolationism (1939-1941) and back to interventionism; the Cold War shattered the Left bloc. The Right bloc was the largest, was politically allied to the Democratic Party, followed Roosevelt's foreign policy lead, and tended to be internationalist because of a view that American prosperity was linked to foreign markets.

354. Levenstein, Harvey A. **Labor Organization in the United States and Mexico.** Westport: Greenwood, 1971. A comparative study which notes political influences in U.S. and Mexican unions.

355. Levenstein, Harvey A. "Leninists Undone by Leninism: Communism and Unionism in the United States and Mexico, 1935-1939." **Labor History** 22,2 (1981). Argues that the Communist Party's

authoritarian structure prevented it from exploiting the success of the Popular Front. The Communist Party's political leadership was largely restricted to survivors of the party's ideological purges, and the latter gave little power to successful Communist union leaders. The Communist Party's political leaders also intervened with generally disastrous results in trade union work. Attributes the collapse of the Communist Party's once strong position in the UAW to Browder's intervention and tendency to take a soft line against anti-Communists. Describes a similar pattern in the history of the Mexican Communist Party.

356. Lorin, Lewis. **The International Labor Movement.** New York: Harper, 1953. Discusses the involvement of American unions with pro- and anti-Communist international labor organizations.

357. McKee, Delber. "The American Federation of Labor and American Foreign Policy." Ph.D. dissertation. Stanford University, 1953.

358. Radosh, Ronald. **American Labor and U.S. Foreign Policy: The Cold War in the Unions from Gompers to Lovestone.** New York: Random House, 1969. Surveys the foreign policy activities of American unions, argues that the anti-Communist thrust of U.S. union activities was strongly influenced by government policy.

359. Sallach, David Louis. "Enlightened Self-Interest: The Congress of Industrial Organizations' Foreign Policy, 1935-1955." Ph.D. dissertation. Rutgers University, 1983.

360. Schonberger, Howard. "American Labor's Cold War in Occupied Japan." **Diplomatic History** 3,3 (1979). Discusses the work of American unions in 1945-52 to promote Japanese unions which were non-Communist and not export oriented.

361. Solomon, Lesley Lerner. "From Exclusion to Internationalism: The AFL-CIO as a Transnational Actor in the Far East." Ph.D. dissertation. University of Pennsylvania, 1981.

362. Sturmthal, Adolf. "The Crisis of the W.F.T.U." **Industrial and Labor Relations Review** 51 (July 1948).

363. Taft, Philip. **Defending Freedom: American Labor
      and Foreign Affairs.** Los Angeles: Nash Pub. 1973.
      Discusses American unions' involvement with
      foreign policy and their anti-Communist foreign
      activities.

364. Toth, C. "Samuel Gompers, Communism, and the Pan
      American Federation of Labor." **The Americas** 23,3
      (1967). Discusses the anti-Communist aims of
      Gompers' support for the Pan American Federation
      of Labor.

365. Toth, C. "Samuel Gompers, World Peace, and the Pan
      American Federation of Labor." **Caribbean Studies**
      7 (Oct. 1967).

366. Weiler, P. "The United States, International Labor
      and the Cold War: the Breakup of the World
      Federation of Trade Unions." **Diplomatic History** 5
      (Winter 1981).

367. Windmuller, John P. **American Labor and the
      International Labor Movement 1940-1953.** Ithaca:
      Cornell University Press, 1954.

      See item 2049.

ROMAN CATHOLICS AND ANTI-COMMUNISM IN THE LABOR MOVEMENT

368. Betten, Neil. "Urban Catholicism and Industrial
      Reform." **Thought** 44 (1969). Discusses the
      Association of Catholic Trade Unionists.

369. Betten, Neil. "The Great Depression and the
      Activities of the Catholic Worker Movement."
      Labor History 12,2 (Spring 1971). Notes that
      Father Charles Owen Rice and others later active
      in the Association of Catholic Trade Unionists
      were earlier associated with the Catholic Worker
      movement.

370. Betten, Neil. "Catholicism and the Industrial
      Worker During the Great Depression." Ph.D.
      dissertation. University of Minnesota, 1968.
      Notes that the Association of Catholic Trade
      Unionists was not very successful in its anti-
      Communist initiatives in the 1930s.

371. Betten, Neil. **Catholic Activism and the Industrial
      Worker.** Gainesville: University Presses of
      Florida, 1976. Examines the role of the anti-
      Communist Association of Catholic Trade Unionists

in the CIO. Judges that the effort to expel the Communist Party from the CIO in the 1940s also entailed a retreat from the radical Catholic social and economic goals of the 1930s.

372. Gerstle, Gary L. "Between Capitalism and Communism: The Church and Organized Labor in Rhode Island, 1934-1954." Unpublished paper, 1985 Organization of American Historians convention.

373. Harrington, Michael. "Catholics in the Labor Movement: A Case History." **Labor History** 1,3 (Fall 1960). Discusses the Association of Catholic Trade Unionists and its anti-Communist activities in the United Electrical Workers.

374. O'Brien, David. **American Catholics and Social Reform: The New Deal Years.** New York: Oxford University Press, 1968. Discusses the anti-Communism of the Association of Catholic Trade Unionists.

375. Schatz, Ronald. "Domesticating the Unions, Liberalizing the Church: The Catholic Labor Schools of Connecticut, 1942-1964." Unpublished paper, 1985 Organization of American Historians convention.

376. Seaton, Douglas P. "The Catholic Church and the Congress of Industrial Organizations: The Case of the Association of Catholic Trade Unionists, 1937-1950." Ph.D. dissertation. Rutgers University, 1975.

377. Seaton, Douglas P. **Catholics and Radicals: The Association of Catholic Trade Unionists and the American Labor Movement from Depression to Cold War.** Lewisburg: Bucknell University Press, 1981. Argues that the ACTU bears much of the guilt for driving the Communist Party out of the CIO.

378. Taft, Philip. "The Association of Catholic Trade Unionists." **Industrial and Labor Relations Review** 2 (Jan. 1949).

379. Ward, Roger J. "The Role of the Association of Catholic Trade Unionists in the Labor Movement." **Review of Social Economy** 14 (Sept. 1956).

380. Wattell, Harold. "The Association of Catholic Trade Unionists." Master's thesis. Columbia University, 1947.

See item 502.

COMMUNISM AND THE CIO: GENERAL

381. Cochran, Bert. **Labor and Communism: The Conflict
      that Shaped American Unions.** Princeton: Princeton
      University Press, 1977. Concentrates on the
      Communist role in the United Auto Workers with
      shorter sections on the United Electrical
      Workers, Transport, Longshore, and Mine, Mill.
      Finds that the Communist role in the UAW was
      significant but limited, and maintains that
      Walter Reuther manipulated opposition to the
      Communist Party's role to gain union leadership.
      Concludes that Communist subservience to Moscow
      tainted labor radicalism.

382. Emspak, Frank. "The Break-Up of the Congress of
      Industrial Organization (CIO), 1945-1950." Ph.D.
      dissertation. University of Wisconsin, 1972.
      Regards Communists as a positive force in the
      CIO; treats anti-Communists as aggressive
      opportunists who weakened the labor movement by
      changing it from a progressive and antiwar
      organization to a status quo body.

383. Galenson, Walter. **The CIO Challenge to the AFL: A
      History of the American Labor Movement, 1935-
      1941.** Cambridge: Harvard University Press, 1960.
      Discusses Communist Party influence in the CIO;
      regards Communists as illegitimate trade
      unionists.

384. Harris, Herbert. **Labor's Civil War.** New York:
      Greenwood, 1940. This early study of AFL and CIO
      conflict treats the Communist Party role in the
      CIO as conspiratorial and largely negative.

385. Kamp, Joe. **Join the C.I.O. and Help Build a Soviet
      America.** New York: Constitutional Education
      League, 1937. Far right-wing journalistic expose
      which presents the CIO as little more than a
      Communist Party plot.

386. Kampelman, Max. "The Communist Party vs. the
      C.I.O.: A Study in Political Power." Ph.D.
      dissertation. University of Minnesota, 1952.

387. Kampelman, Max. **The Communist Party vs. the
      C.I.O.: A Study in Power Politics.** New York: F.A.
      Praeger, 1957. Survey of Communist participation

in the CIO which sees the Communist role as
negative, conspiratorial, and manipulative.

388. Levenstein, Harvey A. **Communism, Anticommunism,
and the CIO.** Westport: Greenwood Press, 1981. A
account of the Communist role in the CIO that is
mostly sympathetic, although occasionally
critical. Critical of anti-Communist unionists.
See items 398 and 2024.

389. Levinson, Edward. **Labor on the March.** New York:
Harper & Brothers, 1938. Journalistic survey of
the union movement which discusses the Communist
role in the CIO.

390. Milton, David. "The Politics of Economism:
Organized Labor Fights its Way into the American
System Under the New Deal." Ph.D. dissertation.
University of California, Berkeley, 1980. Argues
that the CIO became incorporated in advanced
capitalism in 1940 (not 1949 when the "Left"
unions were expelled) when the Hillman-Murray
forces defeated the Left-Syndicalists under John
L. Lewis; places part of the blame on the
Communist Party for sharing the basic strategy of
the Hillman-Murray faction of an alliance with
Roosevelt arranged at the top.

391. Milton, David. "Class Struggle American Style."
Political Power and Social Theory V. 4. Howard
Kimeldorf and Maurice Zeitlin, eds. Greenwich:
JAI Press, 1984.

392. Morris, James O. **Conflict within the AFL: A Study
of Craft versus Industrial Unionism, 1901-1938.**
Ithaca: Cornell University Press, 1958. Notes
Communist involvement with the promotion of
industrial unionism.

393. Oshinsky, David. "Labor's Cold War: The CIO and
the Communists." **The Specter.** Robert Griffith and
Athan Theoharis, eds. New York: New Viewpoints,
1974.

394. Preis, Art. **Labor's Giant Step: Twenty Years of
the CIO.** New York: Pathfinder Press, 1964. Looks
at CIO Communists from a Trotskyist perspective.

395. Prickett, James R. "Some Aspects of the Communist
Controversy in the CIO." **Science and Society** 33,3
(Summer 1969). Discusses the assertion of CIO
anti-Communists that Communist Party trade
unionists supported Soviet foreign policy.

396. Stolberg, Benjamin. **The Story of the CIO.** New
     York: Viking Press, 1938. This early
     journalistic study sees the CIO as having been
     infiltrated by the Communist Party.

397. Urmann, Michael F. "Rank and File Communists and
     the CIO (Committee for Industrial Organization)
     Unions." Ph.D. dissertation. University of Utah,
     1981. Based upon eighteen oral interviews;
     maintains the Communist Party played a major role
     in the rapid growth of the CIO due to the
     activity of its union militants at the local
     level.

398. Zieger, Robert H. "Nobody Here But Us Trade
     Unionists: Communism and the CIO." **Reviews in
     American History** 10,2 (1982). Review-essay on
     Harvey Levenstein's **Communism, Anticommunism, and
     the CIO.**

399. Zieger, Robert H. "Toward the History of the CIO:
     A Bibliographical Report." **Labor History** 26,4
     (Fall 1985). Discusses historical treatment of
     CIO Communists.

     See items 568, 572, 573, 576, and 577.

COMMUNISM AND LABOR: BY UNION, INDUSTRY, AND REGION

Auto Industry and the United Auto Workers (UAW)

400. Andrew, William D. "Factionalism and Anti-
     Communism: Ford Local 600." **Labor History** 20,2
     (Spring 1979). Discusses the influence a 1952
     House Un-American Activities Committee hearing,
     along with a history of factionalism and anti-
     Reuther activity, had on the decision to impose
     an administrator on Local 600.

401. Barnard, John. **Walter Reuther and the Rise of the
     Auto Workers.** Boston: Little, Brown, 1983.

402. Baskin, Alex. "The Ford Hunger March - 1932."
     Labor History 13,3 (Summer 1972). Recounts the
     Communist-linked march in which four were killed
     and two dozen wounded by police. See item 434.

403. Blackwood, George D. "The United Automobile
     Workers of America, 1935-51." Ph.D. dissertation.
     University of Chicago, 1951.

404. Boryczka, Ray. "Seasons of Discontent: Auto Union
      Factionalism and the Motor Products Strike of
      1935-1936." **Michigan History** 61 (Spring 1977).

405. Boryczka, Ray. "Militancy and Factionalism in the
      United Auto Workers Union, 1937-1941." **Maryland
      Historian** 8,2 (Fall 1977). Concludes that work
      bench factionalism and militancy discouraged
      development of a politically radical rank-and-
      file labor movement.

406. Dahlheimer, Harry. **A History of the Mechanics
      Educational Society.** Detroit: Wayne State
      University Press, 1951.

407. Eaton, William J., and Frank Cormier. **Reuther.**
      Englewood Cliffs: Prentice-Hall, 1970.

408. Fine, Sidney. **The Automobile Under the Blue Eagle.**
      Ann Arbor: University of Michigan Press, 1963.
      This highly detailed and scholarly study notes
      the significant Communist presence in auto
      unionism in the period prior to the formation of
      the UAW-CIO.

409. Fine, Sidney. **Sit-Down.** Ann Arbor: University of
      Michigan Press, 1969. Discusses the key
      Communist Party role in the vital Flint UAW sit-
      down strike.

410. Fountain, Clayton. **Union Guy.** New York: Viking,
      1949. Discusses UAW factionalism.

411. Friedlander, Peter. **The Emergence of a UAW Local,
      1936-1939: A Study in Class and Culture.**
      Pittsburgh: University of Pittsburgh Press, 1975.

412. Glaberman, Martin. "A Note On Walter Reuther."
      Radical America 7 (Nov.-Dec. 1973). Suggests the
      Reuther may have been a Communist Party member
      for a short time in the 1930s.

413. Halpern, Martin. "The Disintegration of the Left-
      Center Coalition in the UAW, 1945-50." Ph.D.
      dissertation. University of Michigan, 1982.
      Finds that the Left caucus was destroyed by anti-
      Communist attack because of the role of the
      Communist Party in it, by Philip Murray's attacks
      on the Communist Party role in the CIO, by media
      hostility, and by the conclusion of many centrist
      union activists that, in view of the passage of
      Taft-Hartley, the political defenses of the labor

movement would best be served by the program of
the Reuther caucus.

*   Halpern, Martin. "Taft-Hartley and the Defeat of
the Progressive Alternative in the United Auto
Workers." **Labor History** 27,2 (Spring 1986).
Argues that the anti-Communist provisions of
Taft-Hartley strengthened the hand of the "right-
wing" Reuther faction in struggle with the "Left-
Progressive" faction. Cited as item 2052.

414.   Howe, Irving, and B.J. Widick. **The UAW and Walter
Reuther.** New York: Random House, 1949. Discusses
Communist and anti-Communist factional conflict
in the UAW.

415.   Keeran, Roger. "Communists and Auto Workers: The
Struggle for a Union, 1919-1941." Ph.D.
dissertation. University of Wisconsin, 1974.

416.   Keeran, Roger. "The Communists and UAW
Factionalism, 1937-39." **Michigan History** 60
(Summer 1976). Finds the Communist Party largely
innocent of aggression in factional conflict.

417.   Keeran, Roger. "Communist Influence in the
Automobile Industry, 1920-1933: Paving the Way
for an Industrial Union." **Labor History** 20,2
(Spring 1979). Discusses the pioneering role of
Communist Party militants in preparing the way
for unionism in the auto industry.

418.   Keeran, Roger. **The Communist Party and the Auto
Workers Unions.** Bloomington: Indiana University
Press, 1980. This detailed history finds the
Communist Party to have been a significant and
positive force in auto industry unionism.
Vindicates the Communist Party's trade union
tactics and political stance; highly critical of
anti-Communist union factions. See items 421,
2010, and 2023.

419.   Klehr, Harvey. "American Communism and the United
Auto Workers: New Evidence on an Old
Controversy." **Labor History** 24,3 (Summer 1983).
Reviews evidence of Communist involvement in UAW
wildcat and sit-down strikes and its role in
initiating factional conflict within the UAW.

420.   Kraus, Henry. **The Many and the Few: A Chronicle of
the Dynamic Auto Workers.** Los Angeles: Plantin
Press, 1947. Memoir by a UAW activist associated
with the Communist faction.

421. Laslett, John H.M. "Giving Superman a Human Face:
      American Communism and the Automobile Workers in
      the 1930s." **Reviews in American History** 9,1
      (1981). Review-essay of Keeran's **The Communist
      Party and the Auto Workers Union.**

422. Lichtenstein, Nelson. "Auto Worker Militancy and
      the Structure of Factory Life, 1937-1955."
      Journal of American History 67,2 (Sept. 1980).
      Notes that the UAW's Communist faction, along
      with all other union factions, was hostile to
      shop-floor syndicalism.

423. Lichtenstein, Nelson. "Life at the Rouge: A Cycle
      of Working Class Militancy 1940-1960." **Life and
      Labor: Dimensions of American Working Class
      History.** Charles Stephenson & Robert Asher, eds.
      1984. Discusses Communist and anti-Communist
      factionalism in a UAW local.

424. Meyer, Stephen, III. "Shop Culture, Shop Stewards,
      Shop Grievances: Sources of Labor Militancy at
      Allis-Chalmers in the 1930s and 1940s."
      Unpublished paper, 1982 Social Science History
      Conference.

425. Meyerowitz, Ruth Susan. "Organizing and Building
      the UAW: Women at the Ternstedt General Motors
      Part Plant, 1936-1950." Ph.D. dissertation.
      Columbia University, 1985. Notes Communist links
      of some women UAW militants.

426. Moore, Gilbert W. "Poverty, Class Consciousness,
      and Racial Conflict: The Social Basis of Trade
      Union Politics in the UAW-CIO, 1937-1955." Ph.D.
      dissertation. Princeton University, 1978. Finds
      that despite the growing threat of monopoly
      economic power to auto workers and the recurrent
      impoverishment of auto workers, the "Marxist"
      wing of the UAW was isolated and collapsed.
      Attributes the defeat of the Marxist wing to a
      few tactical errors by Marxists and the attack on
      the Marxists by an alliance of Roman Catholics,
      Socialist Party militants and Protestant
      fundamentalists. Racial conflict contributed to
      the ability of the latter alliance to defeat the
      formation of Marxist class consciousness.

427. Mortimer, Wyndham. **Organize, My Life as a Union
      Man.** Boston: Beacon Press, 1971. Autobiography
      by a Communist trade union figure prominent in
      organizing the UAW.

428. Prickett, James R. "Communism and Factionalism in
      the United Automobile Workers, 1939-1947."
      Science and Society 32,3 (Summer 1968).
      Attributes Reuther's eventual victory to the
      Communist faction's effort to conciliate non-
      Communists by refusing to take control of the
      union in 1939 when they were in a position to do
      so.

429. Prickett, James R. "Communists and the Automobile
      Industry in Detroit before 1935." **Michigan
      History** 57 (Fall 1973).

430. Reuther, Victor G. **The Brothers Reuther and the
      Story of the UAW: A Memoir.** Boston: Houghton
      Mifflin Co., 1976. Personal memoir by Victor
      Reuther regarding his role and those of his
      brothers Walter and Roy in the organization of
      the United Auto Workers. Discusses the conflict
      between Communist and non-Communist factions in
      the union, and the triumph of the anti-Communist
      Reuther faction under Walter's leadership.

431. Schwartz, Donald A. "The 1941 Strike at Allis
      Chalmers." Master's thesis. University of
      Wisconsin, 1943. Examines a strike with
      significant Communist leadership.

432. Skeels, Jack. "The Development of Political
      Stability Within the United Auto Workers Union."
      Ph.D. dissertation. University of Wisconsin,
      1957. Concludes that UAW factionalism was
      largely built around personalities and on
      organizational and bureaucratic rivalries and
      that the Communist Party presence in the Addes
      faction was one of the few substantive
      differences between it and the Reuther faction.

433. Skeels, Jack. "The Background of UAW
      Factionalism." **Labor History** 2,2 (Spring 1961).
      Finds that ideological factions such as
      Communists and Socialists were not a major source
      of factional disagreement.

434. Sugar, Maurice. **The Ford Hunger March.** Berkeley:
      Meiklejohn Civil Liberties Institute, 1980.
      Memoir by Detroit radical lawyer of the 1932
      march organized by the Communist Party-aligned
      Auto Workers Union of the TUUL and the Unemployed
      Council. Sugar, a lawyer for the Communist
      Party's International Labor Defense, defended
      those indicted after the march. Sugar attacks

most non-Communist Party groups involved in the
controversy, including the Socialist Party, the
Proletarian Party, and the Socialist Labor Party.
See item 402.

See items 381, 678, and 1546.

Needle Trades

435. Berman, Hyman. "Jewish Labor Movement." **American
     Jewish Historical Quarterly** 52 (1962).

436. Epstein, Melech. **Jewish Labor In U.S.A., Vol. II,
     1914-1952.** New York: Trade Union Sponsoring
     Committee, 1953. Discusses the Communist Party
     role in the needle trades unions.

437. Foner, Philip S. **The Fur and Leather Workers
     Union.** Newark: Nordan, 1950. Sympathetically
     recounts the dominant Communist role in the
     union.

438. Fraser, Steven C. "Sidney Hillman and the Origins
     of the 'New Unionism': 1908-1933." Ph.D.
     dissertation. Rutgers University, 1983.
     Discusses factionalism involving Communists in
     the Amalgamated Clothing Workers in the 1920s.

439. Gurowsky, David. "Factional Dispute Within the
     ILGWU, 1919-1928." Ph.D. dissertation. State
     University of New York, Binghamton, 1978.

440. Leiter, Robert D. "Fur Workers Union." **Industrial
     and Labor Relations Review** 3,2 (Jan. 1950).
     Discusses a union with a major Communist
     presence.

441. Morgan, J.W. "Communism in the Lather Labor
     Unions," "Combating Communism in Leather Unions,"
     and "Communist Tactics in the Leather Unions."
     Leather and Shoes (Aug. 14, Aug. 28, Sept. 11,
     1948).

442. Robinson, Donald. **Spotlight on a Union: The Story
     of the United Hatters, Cap and Millinery Workers
     International Union.** New York: Dial Press, 1948.
     Discusses Communist and Socialist Party
     factionalism in the union.

443. Seidman, Joel. **The Needle Trades.** New York: Farrar
     & Rinehart, 1942. Discusses the significant
     Communist Party role in the needle trades unions.

See items 570, 571, 574, 575, 580, and 1436.

Social Service Employees

444. Dawidowicz, Lucy. **The Social Service Employees
      Union: Communist Infiltration Through a Trade
      Union Movement.** New York: American Jewish
      Committee, March 6, 1951. Mimeographed study.

*   Haynes, John Earl. "Rank and File! The Rank and
      File Movement in Social Work, 1931-1941."
      Unpublished paper, Social Welfare History
      Archives, University of Minnesota, 1967. Cited
      as item 2084. Notes the leading role of
      Communists in attempts to organize public and
      private social workers into unions.

445. Haynes, John Earl. "The Rank and File Movement in
      Private Social Work." **Labor History** 16,1 (1975).
      Notes the role of Communists in organizing social
      work agencies into unions in the 1930s; discusses
      the Marxist analysis of social work advanced by
      the Rank and File movement; notes the shift of
      the Rank and File movement from harsh critic of
      the social work establishment and the New Deal
      before the Popular Front to friendly critic of
      the establishment and firm supporter of the New
      Deal after the Popular Front and back again after
      the Hitler-Stalin Pact.

446. Schriver, Joe M. "Harry Lawrence Lurie, A Rational
      Radical: His Contributions to the Development of
      Social Work, 1930-1950." Ph.D. dissertation.
      University of Iowa, 1984. Discusses Lurie's role
      in the Communist-influenced Rank and File
      movement among social workers in the 1930s.

447. Spano, Richard. "The Rank and File Movement in
      Social Work." Ph.D. dissertation. University of
      Minnesota, 1978. Notes a significant Communist
      role in the Rank and File movement.

Packinghouse Workers

448. Engelmann, Larry. "We Were the Poor People." **Labor
      History** 15,4 (1974). Notes that although some of
      the leaders of the successful strike at the
      Hormell plant in Austin, MN had an acquaintance
      with Trotskyism, there was little direct
      involvement by radical political bodies.

Furniture Workers

449. Arroyo, Luis Leobardo. "Industrial Unionism & the Los Angeles Furniture Industry, 1918-54." Ph.D. dissertation. University of California, Los Angeles, 1979. Recounts the rise of Communist-led locals of the United Furniture Workers (CIO) and the attack on the Communist leadership by an anti-Communist faction.

Longshore and Maritime

450. Bonthius, Andrew. "Origins of the International Longshoremen's and Warehousemen's Union." **Southern California Quarterly** 59,4 (Winter 1977). History of the origins of an important Communist-linked union.

451. Goldblatt, Louis (interview by Estolv Ethan Ward). **Working Class Leader in the ILWU, 1935-1977.** Berkeley: The Bancroft Library, Regional Oral History Office, 1980. Oral history interview with a one-time Communist Party militant who was the second ranking leader of the ILWU.

452. Goldberg, Joseph. **Maritime Story: A Study in Labor-Management Relations.** Cambridge: Harvard University Press, 1958.

453. Harris, Ed. "The Trouble with Harry Bridges." **International Socialist Review** 34 (Sept. 1973).

454. Kagel, John. "The Day the City Stopped: Memorable Scenes from San Francisco's 1934 General Strike." **California History** 63,3 (Summer 1984).

455. Lampman, Robert J. "The Rise and Fall of the Maritime Federation of the Pacific, 1935-1941." **Proceedings of the Pacific Coast Economic Association** (1950).

456. Larrowe, Charles. "The Great Maritime Strike of '34." **Labor History** 11,4 & 12,1 (Fall 1970 & Winter 1971). A detailed history of an important strike in which Communists participated.

457. Larrowe, Charles. **Harry Bridges: The Rise and Fall of Radical Labor in the United States.** Eastport: Lawrence Hill, 1972.

458. Mabon, David. "The West Coast Waterfront and Sympathy Strike of 1934." Ph.D. dissertation.

University of California, Berkeley, 1966. Finds
the Communist role in this important strike was
significant but not decisive.

459. Nelson, Joseph Bruce. "Maritime Unionism and
     Working-Class Consciousness in the 1930s." Ph.D.
     dissertation. University of California, Berkeley,
     1982. Analysis of the effect of maritime life on
     worker consciousness. Discusses the role of the
     Communist Party in exploiting grievances and in
     the Maritime Federation of the Pacific.

460. Nelson, Joseph Bruce. "'Pentecost' on the Pacific:
     Maritime Workers and Working-Class Consciousness
     in the 1930s." **Political Power and Social Theory**
     V. 4. Howard Kimeldorf and Maurice Zeitlin, eds.
     Greenwich: JAI Press, 1984.

461. Prickett, James R. "The NMU and the Ambiguities of
     Anti-Communism." **New Politics** 7 (Winter 1968).

462. Record, Jane. "The Rise and Fall of a Maritime
     Union." **Industrial and Labor Relations Review** 10
     (Oct. 1950). Discusses the destruction of the
     Communist-aligned National Union of Marine Cooks
     and Stewards.

463. Schmidt, Henry (interview by Miriam F. Stein and
     Estolv Ethan Ward). **Secondary Leadership in the**
     ILWU, 1933-1966. Berkeley: The Bancroft Library,
     Regional Oral History Office, 1983. Oral history
     interview with the longtime leader of the San
     Francisco local of the Communist-influenced ILWU.

464. Schwartz, Harvey. **The March Inland: Origins of the**
     ILWU Warehouse Division, 1934-1938. Los Angeles:
     Institute of Industrial Relations, University of
     California, L.A., 1978. History of the
     frustrated attempt of the Communist-linked ILWU
     to expand into warehouses and food-packing
     facilities outside its Bay Area base.

465. Schwartz, Harvey. "Harry Bridges and the Scholars:
     Looking at History's Verdict." **California History**
     59,1 (1980). Examines scholarly treatment of
     Harry Bridges and his leadership of the
     International Longshoreman's and Warehouseman's
     Union. Discusses his role in the longshoreman's
     strike and the San Francisco general strike of
     1934 and the repeated attempts of the U.S.
     government to deport Bridges. Notes that most
     scholars have found Bridges to be consistently

pro-Soviet and to work closely with the Communist Party. Suggests that Bridges relationship with the Communist Party is not an important question.

466. Shields, Art. "The San Pedro Waterfront Strike, 1923." **Political Affairs** (May, 1985).

467. Taft, Philip. "Unlicensed Seafaring Unions." **Industrial and Labor Relations Review** 3,2 (Jan. 1950). Discusses factional fighting in the National Maritime Union.

468. Toy, Eckard V., Jr. "The Oxford Group and the Strike of the Seattle Longshoremen in 1934." **Pacific Northwest Quarterly** 69 (Oct. 1978).

469. Ward, Estolv E. **Harry Bridges on Trial.** New York: Modern Age, 1940.

See items 381, 674, 684, 1665, and 1948.

Electrical and Machine

470. Cleland, Hugh. "The Political History of a Social Union: Local 601 of the CIO Electrical Workers Union." Ph.D. dissertation. Western Reserve University, 1957.

471. Cleland, Hugh. "The Communist Party and the Electrical Workers: Pittsburgh, 1935-1937." Unpublished paper, 1960 Mississippi Valley Historical Association meeting.

472. Filippelli, Ronald L. "The United Electrical Radio and Machine Workers of America, 1933-1949: The Struggle for Control." Ph.D. dissertation. Pennsylvania State University, 1970. Treats the UE Right as the aggressor in UE factionalism, attributes the UE's expulsion to anti-Communist hysteria, and finds that there was no evidence that the Communist Party exercised any inappropriate influence over the UE, and that even if it had, there is no evidence that the interests of workers were damaged by such influence.

473. Filippelli, Ronald L. "UE: The Formative Years, 1933-1937." **Labor History** 17,3 (Summer 1976). Discusses the coming together of company unions, IAM locals, Trade Union Unity League unions, and independent unions to form the UE.

474. Filippelli, Ronald L. "UE: An Uncertain Legacy."
      Political Power and Social Theory V. 4. Howard
      Kimeldorf and Maurice Zeitlin, eds. Greenwich:
      JAI Press, 1984.

475. Johnson, Ronald W. "Organized Labor's Post-War Red
      Scare: The UE in St. Louis." **North Dakota
      Quarterly** 48,1 (Winter 1980). Discusses the
      attack on the leadership of District 8 of the UE
      by antiradical and anti-Communist factions in the
      CIO.

476. Matles, James J., and James Higgins. **Them and Us,
      Struggles of a Rank and File Union.** Englewood
      Cliffs: Prentice-Hall, 1974. Memoir by a
      Communist Party-aligned leader of the UE. He
      does not acknowledge a significant Communist
      Party role in the UE.

477. Palladino, Grace. "Building a Union: The Early
      History of UE Local 610." **Western Pennsylvania
      Historical Magazine** 67 (1984).

478. Schatz, Ronald. "The End of Corporate Liberalism:
      Class Struggle in the Electrical Manufacturing
      Industry, 1933-1950." **Radical America** 9 (July-
      Aug. 1975).

479. Schatz, Ronald. "American Electrical Workers: Work,
      Struggles, Aspirations, 1930-1950." Ph.D.
      dissertation. University of Pittsburgh, 1977.
      Finds that the typical Communist union militant
      of the 1930s was a skilled veteran worker whereas
      most anti-Communist union activists of the late
      1940s were semiskilled and indifferent to
      ideology.

480. Schatz, Ronald. "Union Pioneers: The Founders of
      Local Unions at General Electric and
      Westinghouse, 1933-1937." **Journal of American
      History** 66,3 (Dec. 1979). Notes the role of
      Communist Party trade union militants in founding
      unions at several GE plants.

481. Schatz, Ronald. **The Electrical Workers: A History
      of Labor at General Electric & Westinghouse,
      1923-1960.** Urbana: University of Illinois, 1983.
      Discusses the rise and fall of the United
      Electrical Workers, the largest Communist-led
      union; tends to treat the Communist loyalties of
      some union militants as having no more historical
      significance than the Democratic and Republican
      Party preferences of other workers.

See items 373, 381, 674, 681, 1938, and 1943.

Mine, Mill and Smelter Workers

482. Beesley, David. "Communists and Vigilantes in the
     Northern Mines." **California History** 64,2 (Spring
     1985). Recounts how organized mobs broke up
     attempts to organize Nevada County gold miners
     into the International Union of Mine, Mill and
     Smelter Workers, CIO. Although the vigilantes
     charged the CIO with harboring Communists,
     Beesley notes no Communist influence in this or
     most other CIO organizing campaigns.

483. Huntley, Horace. "Iron Ore Miners and Mine Mill in
     Alabama: 1933-1952." Ph.D. dissertation.
     University of Pittsburgh, 1977. Highly
     sympathetic survey of Mine, Mill organizing in
     Alabama which treats charges that Mine, Mill was
     Communist influenced as the product of a witch
     hunt.

484. Huntley, Horace. "The Mine, Mill, and Smelter
     Workers in Birmingham." Unpublished paper, 1981
     Organization of American Historians annual
     meeting.

485. Jensen, Vernon. **Non-Ferrous Metal Industry
     Unionism 1932-1954.** Ithaca: Cornell University
     Press, 1954. Notes the significant role of the
     Communist Party in the Mine, Mill and Smelter
     Workers.

486. Keitel, Robert S. "The Merger of the International
     Union of Mine, Mill and Smelter Workers into the
     United Steel Workers of America." **Labor History**
     15,1 (Winter 1974). Finds that initial CIO raids
     on Mine, Mill on an anti-Communist political
     basis largely failed, but as Mine, Mill weakened
     in the 1950s and 1960s, Steelworker raids based
     on an economic appeal had success. Finally, with
     Mine, Mill organizationally weakened and with its
     radical political leadership attenuated, it
     agreed to merge in 1967.

See item 381.

Teachers' Unions

487. Eaton, William Edward. **The American Federation of
     Teachers.** Carbondale: Southern Illinois
     University Press, 1975. Stresses the importance

of the late 1930s when the union expelled
Communist influenced New York and Philadelphia
locals.

488. Hronicek, Francis Robert. "The Historical
      Development of Teachers' Unions in United States'
      Public Education." Ed.D. dissertation. Saint
      Louis University, 1980. Discusses the Communist
      role in teachers' unions.

489. Miller, Charles William. "Democracy in Education:
      A Study of How the American Federation of
      Teachers Met the Threat of Communist Subversion
      Through the Democratic Process." Ed.D.
      dissertation. Northwestern University, 1967.
      Concludes that there was a significant Communist
      presence in the AFT; finds that the impetus for
      their expulsion came from midwestern AFT locals
      and from William Green of the AFL.

490. Muraskin, L.D. "The Teachers Union of the City of
      New York from Inception to Schism, 1912-1935."
      Ph.D. dissertation. University of California,
      Berkeley, 1979. A sympathetic account of the
      local which came under Communist leadership in
      the 1930s.

491. Steinberg, Philip Arthur. "Communism, Education,
      and Academic Freedom: Philadelphia: A Case
      Study." Ph.D. dissertation. Temple University,
      1978. Discusses the firing (later reversed) of
      thirty-two teachers in connection with Communist
      activity; notes that the firings helped to
      destroy the radical teachers union and aided the
      growth of the liberal AFT local.

492. Zitron, Celia. The New York City Teachers Union,
      1916-1964. New York: Humanities Press, 1968.
      Discusses the lengthy fight within the teachers
      union over Communism.

United Steel Workers

493. Gordon, Max. "The Communists and the Drive to
      Organize Steel, 1936" Labor History 23,2 (Spring
      1982). Reviews the Communist Party's role in the
      labor movement and its participation in the Steel
      Workers' Organizing Committee's early organizing
      drives.

494. Hall, Gus. "Thirty Years of Struggle for a
      Steelworkers' Union and Working Class Ideology."

Political Affairs 53 (Sept. 1974). Hall, the dominant figure in the Communist Party from the mid-1960s to the present, worked as a organizer for the Steel Workers Organizing Committee.

495. Ingalls, Robert P. "The Flogging of Joseph Gelders: A Policeman's View." **Labor History** 20,4 (1979). Discusses documents dealing with the flogging of a Communist Party organizer and the links between the flogging and planned expansion of a U.S. Steel plant in Alabama.

496. Ingalls, Robert P. "Antiradical Violence in Birmingham during the 1930s." **Journal of Southern History** 47 (Nov. 1981). Notes attacks on Communist organizers.

497. Leab, Daniel J. "The Memorial Day Massacre." **Midcontinent American Studies Journal** 8 (Fall 1967).

498. Lynd, Staughton. "The Possibility of Radicalism in the Early 1930s: The Case of Steel." **Radical America** 6 (Nov.-Dec. 1972).

499. Sofchalk, Donald G. "The Little Steel Strike of 1937." Ph.D. dissertation. Ohio State University, 1961.

500. Sofchalk, Donald G. "The Chicago Memorial Day Incident: An Episode of Mass Action." **Labor History** 6,1 (Winter 1965). Notes charges of Communist leadership of the Memorial Day march were used to defend the police version of events.

501. Wilson, Joseph F. "Cold Steel: The Political Economy of Black Labor and Reform in the United Steelworkers of America (USWA)." Ph.D. dissertation. Columbia University, 1980. Discusses the role of anti-Communism in the Steelworkers elections in 1977.

See item 677.

Transport Workers' Union

502. Freeman, Joshua B. "Catholics, Communists, and Republicans: Irish Workers and the Organization of the Transport Workers Union." **Working Class America, Essays on Labor, Community, and American Society.** Michael Frisch & Daniel Walkowitz, eds. University of Illinois Press, 1983.

503.   Freeman, Joshua B. "The Transport Workers Union in
       New York City, 1933-1948." Ph.D. dissertation.
       Rutgers University, 1983. Surveys the Communist
       Party role in the TWU and Michael Quill's
       decision to eliminate the Communist Party
       presence in the union.

504.   McGinley, James J., S.J. **Labor Relations in the
       New York Rapid Transit Systems, 1904-1944.** New
       York: King's Crown, 1949. Discusses the
       Communist Party role in the TWU.

505.   Quill, Shirley. **Mike Quill - Himself.** New York:
       Devin-Adiar, 1984. Written by Mike Quill's
       second wife who was herself a union militant and
       a political aide to her husband.

506.   Whittemore, L.H. **The Man Who Ran the Subways: The
       Story of Mike Quill.** New York: Holt, Rinehart &
       Winston, 1968. Journalistic biography.

       See item 679.

Lumber and Wood

507.   Christie, Robert A. **Empire In Wood.** Ithaca:
       Cornell University Press, 1956. Notes the
       expulsion of a Communist faction from the
       carpenters union.

508.   Jensen, Vernon. **Lumber and Labor.** New York: Farrar
       and Rinehart, 1945. Surveys the role of the
       Communist Party in the International Woodworkers
       of America; sees the rank-and-file as
       predominately hostile to Communist leadership.

509.   Lembcke, Jerry. "The International Woodworkers of
       America: An Internal Comparative Study of Two
       Regions." Ph.D. dissertation. University of
       Oregon, 1978.

510.   Lembcke, Jerry. "Uneven Development, Class
       Formation and Industrial Unionism in the Wood
       Products Industry." **Political Power and Social
       Theory V. 4.** Howard Kimeldorf and Maurice
       Zeitlin, eds. Greenwich: JAI Press, 1984.

511.   Lembcke, Jerry, and William Tattam. **One Union In
       Wood.** New York: International Publishers, 1985.
       A history of the International Woodworkers of
       America (CIO) and its predecessors (including the
       Communist National Lumber Workers' Union)

emphasizing the positive contributions of
Communists and judging the role of anti-
Communists to be largely negative.

512. Zieger, Robert H. "Oldtimers & Newcomers: Change
      and Continuity in the Pulp, Sulphite Union in the
      1930s." **Journal of Forest History** 21 (Oct. 1977).

513. Zieger, Robert H. **Rebuilding the Pulp and Paper
      Workers' Union, 1933-1941.** Knoxville: University
      of Tennessee Press, 1984.

Trucking: the Teamsters

514. Dobbs, Farrell. **Teamster Rebellion.** New York:
      Monan Press, 1972. Memoir of a Trotskyist trade
      union leader. Discusses his role in the 1934
      Minneapolis Teamster strike which broke open-shop
      domination of the city.

515. Dobbs, Farrell. **Teamster Power.** New York: Monan
      Press, 1973. Discusses the growth of Teamster
      local 574 under Trotskyist leadership in the
      years 1934-1939.

516. Dobbs, Farrell. **Teamster Politics.** New York: Monan
      Press, 1975. Discusses political activity of
      Minneapolis Teamster Trotskyists in Minnesota
      politics, including their struggle with the
      Communist-led faction of the Farmer-Labor Party.

517. James, Ralph C., and Estelle James. **Hoffa and the
      Teamsters.** Princeton: Van Nostrand, 1965. Notes
      the influence of Trotskyists on Hoffa's tactics.

518. James, Ralph C., and Estelle James. "The Purge of
      the Trotskyites from the Teamsters." **Western
      Political Quarterly** 19,1 (1966). Reviews the
      rise and fall of Trotskyist power (1934-1941) in
      Minneapolis Teamsters locals and the Central
      States Drivers Council.

519. Mayer, George H. **The Political Career of Floyd B.
      Olson.** Minneapolis: University of Minnesota
      Press, 1951. Discusses the reaction of
      Minnesota's Farmer-Labor governor to the
      Trotskyist-led Teamster strike.

520. Walker, Charles Rumford. **American City: A Rank and
      File History.** New York: Farrar & Rinehart, 1937.
      Discusses the Trotskyist-led Teamster strike in
      Minneapolis.

Coal: United Mine Workers

521. Appalachian Movement Press. **Harlan and Bell Kentucky 1931-2: National Miner's Union.** Huntington: Appalachian Movement Press, 1972.

522. Appalachian Movement Press. **War in the Coal Fields.** Huntington: Appalachian Movement Press, 1972.

523. Buka, Tony. "The Harlan County Coal Strike of 1931." **Labor History** 11,1 (Winter 1970). Notes the role of the Communist aligned National Miners Union.

524. Cary, Lorin Lee. "The Reorganized United Mine Workers of America, 1930-1931." **Journal of the Illinois State Historical Society** 66 (Autumn 1973).

525. Draper, Theodore. "The Communists and the Miners, 1928-1933." **Dissent** 19 (Spring 1972).

526. Hevener, John W. **Which Side Are You On? The Harlan County Coal Miner, 1931-39.** Urbana: University of Illinois Press, 1978. Notes effort of Communist National Miners Union to organize Harlan mines in 1932.

527. Hudson, Harriet D. **The Progressive Mine Workers of America: A Study in Rival Unionism.** Urbana: University of Illinois Press, 1952. Discusses Communist involvement in mine worker factionalism.

528. Papanikolas, Helen Z. "Unionism, Communism, and the Great Depression: The Carbon County Coal Strike of 1933." **Utah Historical Quarterly** 41,3 (Summer 1973). Recounts the involvement of the Communist Party's National Miners Union in a violent strike eventually won by the United Mine Workers.

529. Singer, Alan J. "'Which Side Are You On?': Ideological Conflict in the United Mine Workers of America, 1919-1928." Ph.D. dissertation. Rutgers University, 1982. Discusses the Communist Party's National Miners' Union.

530. Wickersham, Edward Dean. "Opposition to the International Officers of the United Mine Workers of America: 1919-1933." Ph.D. dissertation.

Cornell University, 1951. Notes Communist
involvement in UMWA factionalism.

See item 567.

Textiles

531. Brooks, Robert R.R. "The United Textile Workers of
America." Ph.D. dissertation. Yale University,
1935. Notes internal conflict over Communism.

532. Cook, Sylvia. "Gastonia: The Literary
Reverberations of the Strike." **Southern Literary
Journal** 7,1 (1974). Discusses six novels based
on the 1929 North Carolina textile strike in
which Communists played an important role.

533. Draper, Theodore. "Gastonia Revisited." **Social
Research** (Spring 1971).

534. Gerstle, Gary L. "The Mobilization of the Working
Class Community: The Independent Textile Union in
Woonsocket, 1931-1946." **Radical History Review** 17
(Spring 1978).

535. Hood, Robin. "The Loray Mill Strike." Master's
thesis. University of North Carolina, 1932.

536. McCurry, Dan, and Carolyn Ashbaugh, eds.
"Gastonia, 1929: Strike at the Loray Mill."
Southern Exposure 1 (Winter 1973-74).

537. Pope, Liston. **Millhands and Preachers: Gastonia.**
New Haven: Yale University Press, 1942.
Discusses Communist involvement in several
Southern textile strikes.

538. Reeve, Carl. "The Great Gastonia Textile Strike."
Political Affairs 63,3 (March 1984). Reeve was a
veteran Communist organizer.

539. Reeve, Carl. "Gastonia: The Strike, The Frameup,
The Heritage." **Political Affairs** 63,4 (April
1984).

540. Santos, Michael W. "Community and Communism: The
1928 New Bedford Textile Strike." **Labor History**
26,2 (Spring 1985). Cited as item 2075.
Discusses the activities of the Communist Party's
Textile Mills committees.

541. Shields, Art. "Recollections of the Paterson
      Strike." **Political Affairs** 61,1 (1982). Memoir
      by a veteran Communist.

542. Siegel, Morton. "The Passaic Strike of 1925."
      Ph.D. dissertation. Columbia University, 1953.
      Notes the major Communist Party role in strike
      leadership.

543. Tippett, Tom. **When Southern Labor Stirs.** New York:
      Jonathan Cape & Harrison Smith, 1931. Discusses
      the leadership of several southern textile
      strikes by Communist-led unions in the late
      1920s.

544. Vorse, M.H. **Passaic Textile Strike, 1926-1927.**
      Passaic: General Relief Committee, 1927. Vorse
      was a writer often associated with the Communist
      Party.

545. Weisbord, Albert. **Passaic.** Chicago: Daily World
      Pub., 1926. Weisbord was one of the leading
      Communist organizers in this strike.

      See items 566 and 1461.

Culinary Unions

546. Josephson, Matthew. **Union House, Union Bar.** New
      York: Random, 1956. Notes a strong Communist
      presence in New York culinary unions.

Newspaper Guild

547. Kuczun, Sam. "History of the American Newspaper
      Guild." Ph.D. dissertation. University of
      Minnesota, 1970.

548. Leab, Daniel J. **A Union of Individuals: The
      Formation of the American Newspaper Guild: 1933-
      1936.** New York: Columbia University Press, 1970.
      Notes the significant role of Communists in
      organizing the ANG.

Shipbuilding

549. Bernard, Matthew Mergen. "A History of the
      Industrial Union of Marine and Shipbuilding
      Workers of America, 1931-1951." Ph.D.
      dissertation. University of Pennsylvania, 1968.
      Notes serious factionalism between anti-
      Communists and Communists in the union.

Labor in California

550. Perry, Louis B., and Richard S. Perry. **A History of the Los Angeles Labor Movement, 1911-1941.** Los Angeles: University of California Press, 1963. Notes some Communist success with the TUUL and greater success working through the CIO.

551. Selvin, David. **Sky Full of Storm: A Brief History of California Labor.** Berkeley: University of California Press, 1966. Discusses the Trade Union Unity League and the Communist Party.

Labor in Minnesota

552. Haynes, John Earl. "Communists and Anti-Communists in the Northern Minnesota CIO, 1936-1949." **Upper Midwest History** 1,1 (1981). Shows how factional fortunes were affected by the interplay of local politics, national and international political trends, and Communist goals.

553. Pinola, Rudolph. "Labor and Politics on the Iron Range of Northern Minnesota." Ph.D. dissertation. University of Wisconsin, 1957. Notes a Communist role in organizing Northern Minnesota unions in the 1930s.

554. Sofchalk, Donald G. "Organized Labor and the Iron Ore Miners of Northern Minnesota, 1907-1936." **Labor History** 12,2 (Spring 1971). Notes some National Miners Union organizing in the early 1930s.

555. Tselos, George Dimitri. "The Minneapolis Labor Movement in the 1930's." Ph.D. dissertation. University of Minnesota, 1970. Deals with the extensive Trotskyist and Communist role in Minneapolis unions in the 1930s.

See items 448, 514-516, and 518-520.

Labor in the Pacific Northwest

556. Lovin, Hugh T. "The CIO and That 'Damnable Bickering' in the Pacific Northwest 1937-1941." **Pacific History** 23,1 (1979). Discusses factional strife within Pacific Northwest CIO locals between the "Left" which was pro-Soviet and the "Opposition" or "rightists" who were anti-Communist.

Labor in Missouri

557.   Fink, Gary M. "The Unwanted Conflict: Missouri
        Labor and the CIO." **Missouri Historical Review** 54
        (July 1970). Notes the role of Communists in AFL
        versus CIO factionalism in Missouri.

        See item 475.

Labor in Wisconsin

558.   Ozanne, Robert. **The Labor Movement in Wisconsin: A
        History.** Madison: State Historical Society of
        Wisconsin, 1984. Discusses the struggle between
        Communists and anti-Communists to control key
        Wisconsin CIO locals and the state Industrial
        Union Council.

COMMUNISM AND THE UNEMPLOYED

559.   Kahn, Eleanor. "Organizations of the Unemployed as
        a Factor in the American Labor Movement."
        Master's thesis. University of Wisconsin, 1934.
        Notes little Communist success in organizing the
        unemployed in the 1920s despite considerable
        verbal commitment.

560.   Leab, Daniel J. "'United We Eat': The Creation and
        Organization of the Unemployed Councils in 1930."
        Labor History 8,3 (Fall 1967). Recounts the
        origins of the Communist Party's Unemployed
        Councils.

561.   Leab, Daniel J. "United We Eat, Divided We Starve:
        The Communist Party and the Unemployed."
        Unpublished paper, Fifth North American Labor
        History Conference, 1983.

562.   Prago, Albert. "The Organization of the Unemployed
        and the Role of Radicals 1929-1935." Ph.D.
        dissertation. Union Graduate School, 1976.
        Provides extensive and sympathetic coverage of
        Communist activity among the unemployed.

563.   Rosenzweig, Roy. "Radicals and the Jobless: the
        Musteites and the Unemployed Leagues, 1932-1936."
        Labor History 16,1 (Winter, 1975).

564.   Rosenzweig, Roy. "Organizing the Unemployed: The
        Early Years of the Great Depression, 1929-1933."
        Radical America 10 (July-August 1976).

565. Seymour, Helen. "Organization of the Unemployed."
      Master's thesis. Columbia University, 1940.
      Discusses the Communist Party's Unemployed
      Councils.

BIOGRAPHICAL MATERIAL

Beal, Fred

566. Beal, Fred. **Proletarian Journey: New England,
      Gastonia, Moscow.** New York: Hillman-Curl, 1937.
      Autobiography by a disillusioned Communist trade
      union figure.

Brophy, John

567. Brophy, John. **A Miner's Life.** Madison: University
      of Wisconsin Press, 1964. Brophy discusses some,
      but not all, of his contacts with Communist union
      activity in his career.

568. Mullay, Sr. M. Camilla. "John Brophy, Militant
      Labor Leader and Reformer: The CIO Years." Ph.D.
      dissertation. Catholic University of America,
      1966.

DeCaux, Len

569. DeCaux, Len. **Labor Radical: From the Wobblies to
      the CIO - A Personal History.** Boston: Beacon
      Press, 1970. Memoir by a Communist who managed
      press and public relations for the national CIO
      from its origin to the late 1940s.

Dubinsky, David

570. Danish, Max. **The World of David Dubinsky.**
      Cleveland: World Publishing Co., 1957.

571. Dubinsky, David, and A.H. Raskin. **David Dubinsky:
      A Life with Labor.** New York: Simon and Schuster,
      1977. Autobiography by a key leader of the anti-
      Communist wing of the labor movement and a
      leading figure in New York's American Labor Party
      and Liberal Party.

572. Stolberg, Benjamin. **Tailor's Progress.** New York:
      Doubleday Doran, 1944. Discusses Dubinsky's
      leadership of the anti-Communist wing of the New
      York union movement.

Germer, Adolph

573. Cary, Lorin Lee. "Adolph Germer: From Labor
     Agitator to Labor Professional." Ph.D.
     dissertation. University of Wisconsin, 1968.
     Critical of Germer's anti-Communist activity in
     the CIO.

574. Cary, Lorin Lee. "Institutionalized Conservatism
     in the Early C.I.O.: Adolph Germer, A Case
     Study." **Labor History** 13,4 (Fall 1972). Critical
     essay on Germer, a Socialist and anti-Communist
     union activist.

Hillman, Sidney

575. Josephson, Matthew. **Sidney Hillman, Statesman of
     Labor.** Garden City: Doubleday, 1952. Examines
     Hillman's relationship with the Communist Party.

Lewis, John L.

576. Dubofsky, Melvyn, and Warren Van Tine. **John L.
     Lewis: A Biography.** New York: Quadrangle-The New
     York Times Book Co., 1977. Discusses Lewis's
     decision to use Communist organizers in the early
     days of the CIO.

577. Wechsler, James. **Labor Baron, A Portrait of John
     L. Lewis.** New York: William Morrow and Co., 1944.
     Discusses Lewis's use of Communist Party
     organizers in the CIO.

Montgomery, David

578. Montgomery, David. "Once Upon a Shop Floor: An
     Interview with David Montgomery." **Radical History
     Review** 23 (1980). Interview with David
     Montgomery, a union organizer and Communist who
     later became a leading labor historian.

Nash, Al

579. Nash, Al. "A Unionist Remembers: Militant Unionism
     and Political Factions." **Dissent** 24 (Spring
     1977).

Pesotta, Rose

580. Pesotta, Rose. **Bread Upon the Waters.** New York:
     Dodd, Mead, 1944. Pesotta, a key organizer for
     the ILGWU, notes conflict with Communist Party
     dual unions in early 1930s.

notes conflict with Communist Party dual unions in the early 1930s.

Collective Biographies

581. Lynd, Staughton. "Personal Histories of the Early CIO." **Radical America** 5 (May–June 1971). Oral history interviews which include discussion of the Communist Party.

582. Lynd, Alice, and Staughton Lynd, eds. **Rank and File: Personal Histories by Working–Class Organizers.** Boston: Beacon, 1973. Edited interviews with radical labor organizers, including Communists and Trotskyists.

10

COMMUNISM, ETHNICITY, AND NATIONALITY

GENERAL

583. Klehr, Harvey. "Immigrant Leadership in the
Communist Party of the United States of America."
Ethnicity 6,1 (1979). Finds that until the late
1930s Communist leadership was predominately
foreign-born, disproportionately Eastern
European, and contained many Jews. Suggests that
the disproportionate immigrant leadership
hindered the Party's appeal to native Americans.

See items 207, 208, and 217.

CROATS

584. Prpic, George. "The Croats in America." Ph.D.
dissertation. Georgetown University, 1959. Notes
the significant role of the Communist Party in
several Croat organizations in the 1930s and
1940s.

FINNS

585. Ahola, David John. "Finnish-Americans and
International Communism (A study of Finnish-
American Communism from Bolshevization to the
Demise of the Third International)." Ph.D.
dissertation. Syracuse University, 1980. Based on
interviews with thirty first generation and
thirty second generation Finnish-American
Communists, this study examines the role of the
Finnish Workers' Federation in the Communist
Party and Communist Party pressure on what it
perceived as Social Democratic tendencies among
Finnish Communists.

586. Ahola, David John. **Finnish-Americans and
International Communism: A Study of Finnish-**

American Communism from Bolshevization to the demise of the Third International. Lanham: University Press of America, 1982.

587. Altenbaugh, Richard J., and Rolland G. Paulston. "Work People's College: A Finnish Folk High School in the American Labor College Movement." **Paedagogical History (Belgium)** 18,2 (1978).

588. Denison, Dave A. "O Pioneers: A North Country Elegy." **Progressive** 46,8 (Aug. 1982). Discusses the split between Finnish co-ops and the Communist Party.

589. Gedicks, Albert J. "Working Class Radicalism Among Finnish Immigrants in Minnesota and Michigan Mining Communities." Ph.D. dissertation. University of Wisconsin, 1979.

590. Halonen, Arne. "The Role of Finnish-Americans in the Political Labor Movement." Master's thesis. University of Minnesota, 1945.

591. Hoglund, A. William. **Finnish Immigrants in America: 1880-1920.** Madison: University of Wisconsin Press, 1960. Notes the radicalism of many Finnish immigrants.

592. Hummasti, Paul. "Finnish Radicals in Astoria, Oregon, 1904-1940: a Study in Immigrant Socialism." Ph.D. dissertation. University of Oregon, 1975. Discusses Socialist and Communist Finns.

593. Karni, Michael G. "Struggle on the Cooperative Front: The Separation of Central Cooperative Wholesale from Communism, 1929-30." **The Finnish Experience in the Western Great Lakes Region: New Perspectives.** Michael G. Karni, Matti E. Kaups, and Douglas J. Ollila, Jr., eds. Turku, Finland: Institute for Migration, 1975. Examines the conflict between the Communist Party and Communist Party-aligned Finnish-Americans over control of a large cooperative.

594. Karni, Michael G. "Yhteishyva-Or, For the Common Good: Finnish Radicalism in the Western Great Lakes Region, 1900-1940." Ph.D. dissertation. University of Minnesota, 1975. Estimates that 25% to 30% of Finnish immigrants were radicals and most of these joined the Communist Party after the Bolshevik revolution. Communist Finns

controlled most Finnish cooperatives, but when
the Communist Party insisted on more direct
control over the co-ops, many radical Finns
resisted and left the Communist Party.

595. Karni, Michael G., and D. Ollila, eds. **For the
Common Good, Finnish Immigrants and the Radical
Response to Industrial America.** Superior: Tyomies
Society, 1977.

596. Kercher, Leonard C., Vant W. Kebker, and Wilfred C.
Leland, Jr. **Consumers' Cooperatives in the North
Central States.** Roland S. Vaile, ed. Minneapolis:
University of Minnesota Press, 1941. Discusses
the Communist-led Finnish coops.

597. Kivisto, Peter. "The Decline of the Finnish
American Left, 1925-1945." **International
Migration Review** 17,1 (1983).

598. Kivisto, Peter. "Immigrant Socialists in the US:
The Case of Finns and the Left." Ph.D.
dissertation. New School for Social Research,
1982. Finds that 35% to 40% of immigrant Finns
maintained links with socialist and Communist
institutions.

599. Kivisto, Peter. **Immigrant Socialists in the United
States: The Case of Finns and the Left.**
Rutherford: Fairleigh Dickinson University Press,
1984. Discusses the decline of Finnish
membership in the Communist Party in the 1920s
and 1930s, the tragic results of "Karelia Fever,"
and the clash between the Communist Party and
Communist Finns over control of the Finnish
cooperative movement.

600. Kolehmainen, John I. **The Finns in America: A
Bibliographical Guide to Their History.** Hancock:
Suomi College, 1947.

601. Kolehmainen, John I. "The Inimitable Marxists: The
Finnish Immigrant Socialists." **Michigan History**
36 (1952). Discusses the attraction of
radicalism and Communism to Finnish immigrants.

602. Kolehmainen, John I., and George W. Hill. **Haven in
the Woods: The Story of the Finns in Wisconsin.**
Madison: State Historical Society of Wisconsin,
1951. Notes the Socialist and Communist
orientation of many Finnish immigrants.

603. Kostiainen, Auvo. "The Finns and the Crisis over
      'Bolshevization' in the Workers's Party, 1924-
      1925." **The Finnish Experience in the Western
      Great Lakes Region: New Perspectives.** Michael G.
      Karni, Matti E. Kaups, and Douglas J. Ollila,
      Jr., eds. Turku, Finland: Institute for
      Migration, 1975.

604. Kostiainen, Auvo. **The Forging of Finnish-American
      Communism, 1917-1924: A Study In Ethnic
      Radicalism.** Turku, Finland: Annales Universitatis
      Turkuensis, Ser. B. Part 147, 1978. Discusses
      the events leading the Finnish Socialist
      Federation to break with the Socialist Party and
      join the Communist Party and the reinforcement of
      Communist Finns by refugees fleeing the defeat of
      Red forces in the Finnish civil war.

605. Rintala, Harvin. "The Problem of Generations in
      Finnish Communism." **American Slavic and East
      European Review** 17 (1958). Discusses the
      tenacity of political orientation among Finnish
      generational cohorts.

606. Ross, Carl. **The Finn Factor in American Labor,
      Culture and Society.** New York Mills: Parta
      Printers, 1977. Discusses Finnish-American
      radicalism and Communism. Ross held key
      positions in the Young Communist League in the
      late 1930s and early 1940s and in the Communist
      Party in the late 1940s and early 1950s.

607. Tuomi, Kaarlo. "The Karelian Fever of the Early
      1930's: A Personal Memoir." **Finnish Americana** 3
      (1980). Memoir by a member of a Communist
      Finnish-American family who migrated to Soviet
      Karelia in the early 1930s to assist in the
      building of Communism. Relates the
      disillusionment of many Communist Finns with
      Soviet life and the imprisonment and execution of
      many migrants by the Soviet regime.

608. Turner, H. Haines. **Case Studies of Consumer's
      Cooperatives: Successful Cooperatives Started by
      Finnish Groups in the United States. Studies in
      Relation to Their Social and Economic
      Environment.** New York: Columbia University Press,
      1941. Discusses Communist-led Finnish
      cooperatives.

ITALIANS

609. Buhle, Paul. "Italian-American Radicals and Labor
      in Rhode Island, 1905-1930." **Radical History
      Review** 17 (Spring 1978). Notes some Communist
      activity among Italian-Americans in the early
      1920s.

JEWS

610. Aaron, Daniel. "Some Reflections on Communism and
      the Jewish Writer." **Salmagundi** 1 (1965).

611. Buhle, Paul. "Jews and American Communism: The
      Cultural Question." **Radical Historical Review** 23
      (Spring 1980). Discusses how the culture of
      those Jews who immigrated to the U.S. provided a
      basis for the emergence of a significant
      Communist Jewish minority.

612. Dennis, Peggy. "Am I a Jew? A Radical's Search for
      an Answer." **The Nation** (July 1980).

613. Epstein, Melech. **The Jew and Communism, 1919-1941.**
      New York: Trade Union Sponsoring Committee, 1959.
      Written by the former editor of the Jewish
      Communist journal **Freiheit** who left the Communist
      Party after the Hitler-Stalin Pact.

614. Fisch, Dov. "The Libel Trial of Robert Edward
      Edmonson: 1936-1938." **American Jewish History**
      71,1 (1981). Recounts the libel trial of an
      anti-Semitic publisher who saw the New Deal as a
      Jewish-Communist conspiracy.

615. Foster, Arnold. "American Radicals and Israel."
      **The Left Against Zion: Communism, Israel and the
      Middle East.** Robert S. Wistrich, ed. London:
      Ballentine, Mitchell, 1979.

616. Guttmann, Allen. "Jewish Radicals, Jewish
      Writers." **American Scholar** 32 (1963).

617. Guttmann, Allen. **The Jewish Writer in America:
      Assimilation and the Crisis of Identity.** New
      York: Oxford University Press, 1971.

618. Kagedan, Allan L. "American Jews and the Soviet
      Experiment: The Agro-Joint Project, 1924-1937."
      Jewish Social Studies 43,2 (1981).

619. Liebman, Arthur. "The Ties that Bind: The Jewish
      Support for the Left in the United States."
      American Jewish Historical Quarterly 66 (Dec.
      1976).

620. Liebman, Arthur. **Jews and the Left.** New York: John
      Wiley & Sons, 1979. Discusses Jews and the
      Communist Party.

621. Prago, Albert. "Jews in the International
      Brigades." **Jewish Currents** (Feb. 1979).

622. Schappes, Morris U. "The Jewish Question and the
      Left: Old and New." **Jewish Current Reprint.** New
      York: Jewish Currents, 1970. Discusses Jews and
      the Communist Party.

623. Shapiro, Edward S. "The World Labor Athletic
      Carnival of 1936." **American Jewish History** 74,3
      (March 1985). Notes Communist involvement in the
      sports festival organized by the Jewish Labor
      Committee in opposition to the Berlin Olympics.

624. Shuldiner, David P. "Of Moses and Marx: Folk
      Ideology within the Jewish Labor Movement in the
      United States." Ph.D. dissertation. University of
      California, Los Angeles, 1984. Discusses the
      syncretic class/ethnic world view of immigrant
      Jewish labor and political activists; based on
      oral history interviews.

625. Szajkowski, Zosa. **The Attitude of American Jews
      to World War I, the Russian Revolutions of 1917,
      and Communism (1914-1945): Jews, Wars, and
      Communism.** (Vol. 1) New York: Ktav Publishing
      House, 1973. Heavily documented survey.

626. Szajkowski, Zosa. **The Impact of the 1919-20 Red
      Scare on American Jewish Life: Jews, Wars, and
      Communism.** (Vol. 2) New York: Ktav Publishing
      House, 1974. Heavily documented survey.

627. Szajkowski, Zosa. "A Note on the American-Jewish
      Struggle Against Nazism and Communism in the
      1930's." **American Jewish Historical Quarterly**
      59,3 (1970). Discusses the problems created for
      spokesman for American Jewry by the Nazi tactic
      of couching anti-Jewish propaganda in anti-
      Communist rhetoric.

628. Wald, Alan M. "The Menorah Group Moves Left."
      Jewish Social Studies 38,3-4 (1976). Discusses

the activities of Jewish intellectuals associated
with **The Menorah Journal** in the 1920s. This
group (Elliot Cohen, Lionel Trilling, Herbert
Solow, and George Novack) became closely
associated with the Communist Party through the
National Committee for the Defense of Political
Prisoners. By the latter part of the 1930s most
had broken with the Communist Party and moved
toward Trotskyism or other positions.

629. Zuker, Bat-Ami. "Radical Jewish Intellectuals and
      the New Deal." **Bar-Ilan Studies in History.**
      Edited by Pinhas Artzi. Ramat-Gan, Israel: Bar-
      Ilan University Press, 1978. Advances the view
      that Jewish radicals in the 1930s were largely
      second generation Jews facing an alienation
      crisis because of their transition from poverty
      to prosperity. Roosevelt's New Deal, however,
      reconciled many radicals to American society.

      See items 435-443, 635, 759, 845, 1057, 1430-1432,
      and 1449.

MEXICANS

630. Monroy, Douglas. "Mexicanos in Los Angeles, 1930-
      1941: An Ethnic Group in Relation to Class
      Forces." Ph.D. dissertation. University of
      California, Los Angeles, 1978. Notes the lack of
      relevance of Communist ideology to Mexican-
      Americans in the 1930s.

631. Monroy, Douglas. "La Costura en Los Angeles, 1933-
      1939: The ILGWU and the Politics of Domination."
      **Mexican Women in the United States: Struggles
      Past and Present.** Magdalena Mora and Adelaida R.
      Del Castillo, eds. Los Angeles: 1980. Notes that
      Communist dual unions were unable to defeat the
      ILGWU for the loyalty of Mexican workers in the
      southern California women's wear industry.

632. Monroy, Douglas. "Anarquismo y Communismo: Mexican
      Radicalism and the Communist Party in Los Angeles
      during the 1930s." **Labor History** 24,1 (1983).
      Argues that the Communist Party failed to made
      significant progress among Mexicans in southern
      California because it failed to accommodate
      Mexican nationalist and anarco-syndicalist
      traditions.

      See items 355, 756, 809, 813, and 814.

SWEDES

633. Brook, Michael. "Radical Literature in Swedish-
      America: A Narrative Survey." **Swedish Pioneer
      Historical Quarterly** 20,3 (1969). Surveys
      Swedish immigrant radical journalism; although
      largely socialist in orientation, some Swedish
      radicals turned to Communism after the Bolshevik
      revolution.

11

COMMUNISM AND BLACK AMERICANS

GENERAL

* Bone, Robert. **The Negro Novel in America.** New Haven: Yale University Press, 1968. Cited as item 2066. Sees Communist influence on black writers as having promoted racial nationalism.

634. Brandt, Joe, ed. **Black Americans in the Spanish People's War Against Fascism 1936-1939.** New York: New Outlook, 1981.

635. Cruse, Harold. **Crisis of the Negro Intellectual.** New York: William Morrow and Co., 1967. A former Communist criticizes the Communist Party and the role of Jews in it from a black nationalist perspective.

636. Foner, Philip S. **American Socialism and Black Americans: From the Age of Jackson to World War II.** Westport: Greenwood Press, 1978. Asserts that prior to the Bolshevik Revolution, the Socialist Party's right-wing was racist. After the Revolution, unions led by anti-Communist Socialist were racists. Praises Communist-aligned groups such as the National Negro Congress.

637. Geschwender, James A. "League of Revolutionary Black Workers: Problems Confronting Black Marxist-Leninist Organizations." **Journal of Ethnic Studies** 2 (Fall 1974).

638. Graves, John. "Reaction of Some Negroes to Communism." Ph.D. dissertation. Teachers College, Columbia University, 1955. Survey of Harlem blacks which indicates significant support for Communism.

639. Korstad, Robert. "Black Women in the Tobacco Factories of Winston-Salem." Unpublished paper, 1982 Southern Labor Studies Conference.

640. Kosa, John, and Clyde Z. Nunn. "Race, Deprivation
      and Attitude toward Communism." **Phylon** 25,4
      (1964). Finds that Negro college students are
      more intolerant of Communists than are white
      students.

641. Naison, Mark. "Marxism and Black Radicalism in
      America." **Radical America** 5 (May-June 1971).

642. Nolan, William A. "Communist Propaganda and
      Tactics Among Negroes in the United States."
      Ph.D. dissertation. Fordham University, 1949.

643. Nolan, William A. **Communism Versus the Negro.**
      Chicago: Regnery, 1951.

644. Record, Wilson. **The Negro and the Communist Party.**
      Chapel Hill: University of North Carolina Press,
      1951.

645. Record, Wilson. **Race and Radicalism, The NAACP and
      the Communist Party in Conflict.** Ithaca: Cornell
      University Press, 1964. Discusses rivalry
      between the National Association for the
      Advancement of Colored People and the Communist
      Party.

646. Robinson, Cedric J. **Black Marxism: The Making of
      the Black Radical Tradition.** London: Zed Press,
      1983. Discusses the political and intellectual
      development of W.E.B. DuBois, C.L.R. James, and
      Richard Wright.

647. Sanford, Delacy W., Jr. "Congressional
      Investigation of Black Communism, 1919-1967."
      Ph.D. dissertation. State University of New York,
      Stony Brook, 1973. Surveys the testimony and
      deliberations of Congressional investigations of
      radical activity among Blacks.

648. Simama, Jabari Onaje. "Black Writers Experience
      Communism: An Interdisciplinary Study of
      Imaginative Writers, Their Critics, and the
      CPUSA." Ph.D. dissertation. Emory University,
      1978. Finds that the Communist Party hindered
      Black Communist writers who attempted to
      articulate themes which the Communist Party did
      not endorse; concludes that the Communist Party's
      Black Republic and Black Self-Determination
      themes were largely propaganda devices; notes
      that the Communist Party used its Black members
      to attack Black writers who attempted self-

expression; remarks that the Communist Party was successful in American society at large only when it was successful in the Black community.

649. Solomon, Mark. "Red and Black: Negroes and Communism, 1929-1932." Ph.D. dissertation. Harvard University, 1972.

650. Stein, Judith. "Black, Red . . . and Sometimes Green." **Reviews in American History** 7,2 (1979). Review article prompted by Haywood's **Black Bolshevik** and Wright's **American Hunger.**

651. Sullivan, William C. "Communism and the American Negro." **Religion in Life** 37,4 (1968). Finds that Communists have failed to attract significant Negro membership despite major efforts.

652. Taylor, Brennen. "UNIA and American Communism in Conflict 1917-1928: An Historical Analysis in Negro Social Welfare." Ph.D. dissertation. University of Pittsburgh, 1984. Argues that the Communist Party's program for blacks significantly advanced black social welfare; attributes passage of the Social Security Act of 1935 in part to Communist agitation.

653. William, Henry. **Black Response to the American Left: 1917-1929.** Princeton: Princeton University Department of History, 1973. Survey of the response of black intellectuals and community leaders to socialism and Communism in the 1920s.

*   Young, James O. **Black Writers of the Thirties.** Baton Rouge: Louisiana State University Press, 1973. Cited as item 2067. Judges that the Communist Party stifled black writers associated with it.

COMMUNISM AND BLACKS IN NEW YORK CITY AND HARLEM

*   Hickey, Neil, and Ed Edwin. **Adam Clayton Powell and the Politics of Race.** New York: Fleet Pub., 1965. Cited as item 2075. Discusses Powell's complex and ambiguous relationship with the Communist Party.

654. Lewinson, Edwin R. **Black Politics in New York City.** New York: Twayne Publishers, 1974. Notes the role of Ben Davis and other black Communists in black city politics in the 1940s.

655.   Naison, Mark. "Communism and Black Nationalism in
        the Depression: the Case of Harlem." **Journal of
        Ethnic Studies** 2,2 (Summer 1974). Examines the
        long history of ideological struggle between
        black nationalism (race consciousness) and class
        consciousness. Examines the conflict between
        Communists and Garveyists in the African Blood
        Brotherhood in the 1920s and the greater success
        of the Communist Party in the 1930s when themes
        of black-white working class solidarity had
        greater appeal.

656.   Naison, Mark. "The Communist Party in Harlem:
        1928-1936." Ph.D. dissertation. Columbia
        University, 1976.

657.   Naison, Mark. "The Communist Party in Harlem in
        the Early Depression Years: A Case Study in the
        Reinterpretation of American Communism." **Radical
        History Review** 3 (Fall 1976).

658.   Naison, Mark. "Harlem Communists and the Politics
        of Black Protest." **Marxist Perspectives** 1,3 (Fall
        1978). Finds that Communist Party protests
        against economic conditions and support for black
        causes attracted significant black support in the
        1930s.

659.   Naison, Mark. "Historical Notes on Blacks and
        American Communism: The Harlem Experience."
        Science & Society 42,3 (Fall 1978). Finds that
        the Communist Party was more successful than the
        Socialist Party in attracting black support due
        to its support for black nationalism, its
        internal policy against white racism, and its
        frequent support for black causes. However,
        Communist Party subordination to Moscow and
        ideological rigidity alienated many blacks.

660.   Naison, Mark. "Communism and Harlem Intellectuals
        in the Popular Front: Anti-Fascism and the
        Politics of Black Culture." **Journal of Ethnic
        Studies** 9,1 (Spring 1981). Examines the
        Communist Party's approach to black community
        leaders during the Popular Front. The greatest
        success came when class struggle themes were
        dropped and black issues emphasized through such
        organizations as the National Negro Congress.

661.   Naison, Mark. **Communists in Harlem During the
        Depression.** Urbana: University of Illinois Press,
        1983. Well researched and well written history

of the Communist Party's role in Harlem and its
relationship with non-Communist and anti-
Communist black leaders. See items 2010 & 2011.

662. Walter, John C., and Jill Louise Ansheles. "The
Role of the Caribbean Immigrant in the Harlem
Renaissance." **Afro-Americans in New York Life and
History** 1,1 (1977). Notes that Cyril Briggs and
Otto Huiswoud, Caribbean immigrants, introduced
the Communist Party into Harlem.

THE NATIONAL NEGRO CONGRESS

663. Hughes, Cicero A. "Toward a Black United Front:
National Negro Congress Movement." Ph.D.
dissertation. Ohio University, 1982. Surveys the
history of the Negro Sanhedrin, the Negro
Industrial League, Joint Committee on National
Recovery, Howard University Conference, and
National Negro Congress.

664. Streater, John B., Jr. "The National Negro
Congress, 1936-1947." Ph.D. dissertation.
University of Cincinnati, 1981. Sympathetic
history of the NNC.

665. Wittner, Lawrence. "The National Negro Congress: A
Reassessment." **American Quarterly** 22,4 (Winter
1970). Finds that the Congress had some early
success in promoting local agitation against
discrimination but was crippled by the pressure
for left-wing sectarianism.

See items 636 and 728.

SOVIET AND COMINTERN POLICY TOWARD BLACK AMERICANS

666. American Institute for Marxist Studies. "Lenin,
National Liberation, and the United States." New
York: American Institute for Marxist Studies,
n.d. Discusses Lenin's views on black Americans.
Contains material on the Garvey movement, W.E.B.
DuBois, W.A. Domingo, Claude McKay, Edwin Brooks,
Paul Robeson, Langston Hughes and Richard Wright.

667. Dewitt, Anthony Price. "Attitudes and Tactics of
the Soviet and American Communist Parties towards
Nationalist Manifestations in North America --
Two Case Studies: the Black Nationalist and Civil
Rights Movements, the Puerto Rican Independence

Movement." Ph.D. dissertation. Fletcher School of
Law and Diplomacy, Tufts University, 1980.

668. Hooker, James. **Black Revolutionary: George
Padmore's Path from Communism to Pan-Africanism.**
New York: Praeger, 1967.

669. Kanet, Roger. "The Comintern and the 'Negro
Question': Communist Policy in the United States
and Africa, 1921-1941." **Survey** 19 (Autumn 1973).

670. Padmore, George. **How Russia Transformed Her
Colonial Empire.** London: Dobson, 1946. Discusses
the Comintern's influence on the American
Communist Party's approach to the black question.

671. Padmore, George. **Pan-Africanism or Communism?**
London: Dobson, 1956.

672. Record, Wilson. "The Development of the Communist
Position on the Negro Question in the United
States." **The Phylon Quarterly** 19,3 (Fall 1958).

673. Van Zanter, John W. "Communist Theory and the
American Negro Question." **Review of Politics** 29
(1967).

BLACKS AND COMMUNIST-LED UNIONS

*   Citron, Alice. "An Answer to John Hatchett."
Jewish Currents (Sept. 1968). Cited as item
2074. Discusses the relationship of Communist-
led unions and blacks.

674. Critchlow, Donald C. "Communist Unions and Racism:
A Comparative Study of the Responses of United
Electrical Radio and Machine Workers and National
Maritime Union to the Black Question During World
War II." **Labor History** 17,2 (Spring 1976). UE
national officers and most local officers gave
only lip-service to the problems of integrating
black workers into the electrical industry. In
contrast, the NMU had a policy of gradual but
firm integration of blacks into the industry.

675. Foner, Philip S. **Organized Labor and the Black
Worker, 1619-1973.** New York: Praeger Publishers,
1974. Survey of black-white relations in the
labor movement that exalts the Communist Party
and Communist-aligned labor bodies.

676. Honey, Michael. "The Labor Movement and Racism in the South: A Historical Overview." **Racism and the Denial of Human Rights.** Berlowitz & Edari, eds. Minneapolis: MEP Publications, 1983.

677. Hudson, Hosea. "Struggle Against Philip Murray's Racist Policies in Birmingham." **Political Affairs** 53 (Sept. 1974). Memoir of Communist involvement in Steel Workers' Organizing Committee work.

678. Meier, August, and Elliott Rudwick. **Black Detroit and the Rise of the UAW.** New York: Oxford University Press, 1979. Notes the participation of the UAW's Communist faction in building a working alliance between the UAW and blacks. See item 2023.

679. Meier, August, and Elliott Rudwick. "Communist Unions and the Black Community: the Case of the Transport Workers Union, 1934-1944." **Labor History** 23,2 (Spring 1982). Finds that the TWU stressed integrationist rhetoric but did little, except when under strong pressure from the Black community. TWU leadership was fearful of the prejudice of its mostly white membership and of the use of racism by employers and rival unions.

680. Olson, James S. "Organized Black Leadership and Industrial Unionism: The Racial Response, 1936-1945." **Labor History** 10,3 (Summer 1969).

681. Purcell, Theodore V., and Daniel P. Mulvey. **The Negro in the Electrical Manufacturing Industry.** Philadelphia: University of Pennsylvania Press, 1971. Discusses the attitude of the Communist-led UE toward black issues.

682. Rosen, Sumner. "The CIO Era." **The Negro and the American Labor Movement.** Garden City: Anchor, 1968. Argues that during World War II, Communist CIO unionists subordinated black concerns to the war effort to a greater extent than did non-Communist unionists.

683. Spero, Sterling D., and Abram L. Harris. **The Black Worker: The Negro and the Labor Movement.** New York: Atheneum, 1972. Originally published in 1931, discusses the lack of success of the Communist Party in recruiting Blacks in the 1920s.

684.   Swift, William S. "The Negro in the Offshore
        Maritime Industry." **Negro Employment in the
        Maritime Industries.** William S. Swift, _et al._
        Philadelphia: University of Pennsylvania Press,
        1974. Discusses the policy of the Communist-
        aligned NMU toward blacks.

SCOTTSBORO, INTERNATIONAL LABOR DEFENSE AND THE CIVIL
        RIGHTS CONGRESS

685.   Carter, Dan. **Scottsboro: A Tragedy of the American
        South.** New York: Oxford University Press, 1971.
        Discusses the Communist Party's leading role in
        the Scottsboro case.

686.   Emerson, Thomas I. "Southern Justice in the
        Thirties." **Civil Liberties Review** 4,1 (1977).
        Review-essay of Martin's **The Angelo Herndon Case.**

687.   Martin, Charles H. **The Angelo Herndon Case And
        Southern Justice.** Baton Rouge: Louisiana State
        University Press, 1976. Discusses the harassment
        of Communist organizers throughout the South as
        well as the Georgia's prosecution of a black
        Communist organizer for incitement to
        insurrection. See item 686.

688.   Martin, Charles H. "Communists and Blacks: The ILD
        and the Angelo Herndon Case." **Journal of Negro
        History** 64,2 (Spring 1979). Discusses the role
        of the Communist-aligned International Labor
        Defense in defending Herndon against insurrection
        charges. Concludes that contradictory ILD
        actions in other Southern cases during the 1930s
        prevented the Communist Party from gaining
        continued support from Southern blacks.

689.   Martin, Charles H. "The Civil Rights Congress and
        the Second Red Scare." Unpublished paper, 1984
        Organization of American Historians annual
        meeting.

690.   Martin, Charles H. "The International Labor
        Defense and Black Americans." **Labor History** 26,2
        (Spring, 1985).

691.   Martin, Charles H. "Race, Gender, and Southern
        Justice: The Rosa Lee Ingram Case." **American
        Journal of Legal History** 29 (July 1985).
        Discusses a case handled by the Civil Rights
        Congress.

692. Moon, Henry Lee. **Balance of Power: The Negro Vote.**
      New York: Garden City, 1948. Discusses the ILD's
      entrance into the Scottsboro case.

693. Murray, Hugh T., Jr. "The NAACP versus the
      Communist Party: the Scottsboro Rape Cases, 1931-
      1932." **Phylon** 28 (1967).

694. Van West, Carroll. "Perpetuating the Myth of
      America: Scottsboro and its Interpreters." **South
      Atlantic Quarterly** 80 (1981).

695. Deleted.

      See item 881.

BIOGRAPHICAL MATERIAL

Crosswaith, Frank R.

696. Seabrook, John Howard. "Black and White Unite: The
      Career of Frank R. Crosswaith." Ph.D.
      dissertation. Rutgers University, 1980.
      Biography of Crosswaith, a Socialist Party
      figure, ILGWU organizer, New York political
      figure, head of the Negro Labor Committee, and
      strong anti-Communist.

697. Walter, John C. "Frank R. Crosswaith and the Negro
      Labor Committee in Harlem, 1925-1939." **Afro-
      Americans in New York Life and History** 3 (July
      1979).

698. Walter, John C. "Frank R. Crosswaith and Labor
      Unionization in Harlem, 1939-1945." **Afro-
      Americans in New York Life and History** 7 (July
      1983).

Davis, Benjamin J.

699. Davis, Benjamin J. **Communist Councilman from
      Harlem.** New York: International Publishers, 1969.

*   Greenberg, Ken. "Benjamin Jefferson Davis, Jr., in
      the City Council: Harlem's Reaction to Communism
      During the 1940's." Master's thesis. Columbia
      University, 1970. Cited as item 2073.

DuBois, W.E.B.

700. Drake, Willie Avon. "From Reform to Communism: the
      Intellectual Development of W.E.B. DuBois." Ph.D.

dissertation. Cornell University, 1985. Argues
that a socialist vision underlay DuBois thought
throughout his life.

701. DuBois, Shirley Grahm. **His Day Is Marching On: A
Memoir of W.E.B. DuBois.** Philadelphia:
Lippincott, 1971.

702. DuBois, W.E.B. **The Autobiography of W.E.B. DuBois.**
New York: International Publishers, 1968.

703. Green, Dan. "W.E.B. DuBois: Black Yankee."
Connecticut Review 6 (Oct. 1972).

704. Horne, Gerald C. "Black and Red: W.E.B. Du Bois
and the Cold War, 1944-1963." Ph.D. dissertation.
Columbia University, 1984. Sympathetic
biography.

705. Horne, Gerald C. **Black and Red: W.E.B. Du Bois and
the Afro-American Response to the Cold War, 1944-
1963.** Albany: SUNY Press, 1986.

706. Lester, Julius, ed. **The Seventh Son -- The Thought
and Writings of W.E.B. DuBois.** New York: Random
House, 1971.

See items 646 and 666.

Hayden, Robert

707. Williams, Pontheolla Taylor. "A Critical Analysis
of the Poetry of Robert Hayden Through his Middle
Years." Ed.D. dissertation. Columbia University
Teachers College, 1978. Notes the early
radicalism and later rejection of Communism by
Hayden, an Afro-American poet.

Haywood, Harry

708. Goldfield, Michael. "The Decline of the Communist
Party and the Black Question in the U.S.: Harry
Haywood's **Black Bolshevik.**" **Review of Radical
Political Economics** 12,1 (Spring 1980). Review-
essay of Haywood's autobiography and its analysis
of Communist strategy toward racism and
revolution.

709. Haywood, Harry. **Black Bolshevik, Autobiography of
an Afro-American Communist.** Chicago: Liberator
Press, 1978. Autobiography by one of the
Communist Party's chief black leaders of the 1930s

and 1940s. Haywood was expelled in 1959 and
became associated with Maoist organizations. See
item 2009.

Hudson, Hosea

710. Hudson, Hosea. **Black Worker in the Deep South.** New
     York: International Publishers, 1972.

711. Painter, Nell Irvin. "Hosea Hudson: A Negro
     Communist in the Deep South." **Radical America**
     11,4 (July-Aug. 1977). Edited autobiographical
     oral history interview.

712. Painter, Nell Irvin. **The Narrative of Hosea
     Hudson, His Life as a Negro Communist in the
     South.** Cambridge: Harvard University Press, 1979.
     Edited autobiographical oral history interview.
     See item 2009.

Hurston, Zora Neale

713. Hemenway, Robert E. **Zora Neal Hurston: A Literary
     Biography.** Urbana: University of Illinois Press,
     1977.

714. Holt, Elvin. "Zora Neale Hurston and the Politics
     of Race: A Study of Selected Nonfictional Works."
     Ph.D. dissertation. University of Kentucky, 1983.
     Notes anti-Communist themes in Hurston's
     writings.

James, C.L.R.

715. MacKenzie, Alan J. "Radical Pan-Africanism in the
     1930s: A Discussion with C.L.R. James." **Radical
     History Review** 24 (Fall 1980). Discusses the
     role of Communists in Black politics in the
     1930s.

716. Robinson, Cedric J. "C.L.R. James and the Black
     Radical Tradition." **Review** 6 (Winter 1983).

     See item 646.

King, Martin Luther

717. Briendel, Eric M. "King's Communist Associates."
     The New Republic (Jan. 30, 1984). Discusses the
     links to the Communist Party of some aides to
     Martin Luther King, Jr.

718. Fairclough, Adam. "Was Martin Luther King a
      Marxist?" History Workshop Journal [Great
      Britain] 15 (1983).

719. Garrow, David J. The FBI and Martin Luther King,
      Jr.: From "Solo" to Memphis. New York: Norton,
      1981. Notes that initial FBI interest in King
      was due to his relationship with Stanley Levison,
      a former Communist. The FBI's concern about
      Levison was based on information from a double
      agent inside the Communist Party.

720. Spruill, Larry Hawthorne. "Southern Exposure:
      Photography and the Civil Rights Movement, 1955 -
      1968." Ph.D. dissertation. State University of
      New York, Stony Brook, 1983. Notes the use of
      photos of Martin Luther King, Jr. at the
      Highlander Folk School in a campaign to link King
      to Communism.

McKay, Claude

721. Cooper, Wayne F. "Claude McKay as a Communist."
      Unpublished paper, 1985 Organization of American
      Historians convention.

722. Donohue, Charles T. "The Making of a Black Poet: A
      Critical Biography of Claude McKay for the Years
      1889-1922." Ph.D. dissertation. Temple
      University, 1972. Concludes that McKay's
      political radicalism was largely emotional.

723. McKay, Claude. A Long Way from Home. New York:
      Furman, 1937. Discusses his experiences in the
      Communist Party of the 1920s.

724. McKay, Claude. Harlem. New York: Dutton, 1940.
      Discusses social relations among blacks and
      Communists.

725. Tillery, Tyrone. "Claude McKay: Man and Symbol of
      the Harlem Renaissance, 1880-1948." Ph.D.
      dissertation. Kent State University, 1981.

726. Tillery, Tyrone. "Claude McKay: from Radical to
      Racial Chauvinist." Unpublished paper, 1985
      Organization of American Historians convention.

727. Warren, Stanley. "Claude McKay as an Artist."
      Negro History Bulletin 40 (1977).

      See item 666.

Patterson, William L.

*   Patterson, William L. **The Man Who Cried Genocide**
       New York: International Publishers, 1971. Cited
       as item 2063. Memoir by a prominent black
       Communist leader.

Randolph, A. Philip

728.   Anderson, Jervis. **A. Philip Randolph: A
       Biographical Portrait.** New York: Harcourt Brace
       Jovanovich, 1972. Discusses Randolph's
       experiences in and disillusionment with the
       Communist-aligned National Negro Congress.

729.   Brooks, T.R., and A.H. Raskin. "A. Philip
       Randolph, 1889-1979." **New Leader** 62 (June 4,
       1979). Biographical essay.

730.   Garfinkel, Herbert. **When Negroes March.** Glencoe:
       Free Press, 1959. Notes the changing Communist
       attitude to A. Philip Randolph's March on
       Washington Movement in World War II.

731.   Harris, William H. "A. Phillip Randolph as a
       Charismatic Leader, 1925-1941." **Journal of Negro
       History** 64 (Spring 1979).

732.   Henderson, Jeff. "A. Philip Randolph and the
       Dilemmas of Socialism and Black Nationalism in
       the United States, 1917-1941." **Race & Class** 20
       (Autumn 1978).

733.   Marable, Manning. "A. Philip Randolph and the
       Foundation of Black American Socialism." **Radical
       America** 14 (March-April 1980).

Robeson, Paul

734.   Brown, Lloyd L. "Paul Robeson Rediscovered."
       American Institute for Marxist Studies
       [occasional paper] 19 (1976).

735.   Cunningham, Earl L. "PBS to Air Play About Paul
       Robeson." **Rutgers Alumni Magazine** (Sept. 1979).
       Discusses controversy regarding a play about
       Robeson.

736.   Davis, Lenwood G. **A Paul Robeson Research Guide: A
       Selected Annotated Bibliography.** Westport:
       Greenwood Press, 1982.

737. Graham, Shirley. **Paul Robeson: Citizen of the
      World**. New York: Messner, 1946.

738. Hoyt, Edward. **Paul Robeson: The American Othello**.
      Cleveland: World Pub., 1967.

739. Marshall, Herbert. **Bulletin of the Center for
      Soviet and East European Studies**. (1976).
      Discusses Robeson's meeting with Itzik Fefer in
      1949.

740. Robeson, Paul. **Here I Stand**. New York: Othello
      Associates, 1958.

741. Robeson, Paul, Jr. "How My Father Last Met Itzik
      Fefer." **Jewish Currents** (Nov. 1981). Paul
      Robeson's son asserts that his father met the
      Soviet Jewish poet Itzik Fefer, an old friend, in
      1949 in Moscow, learned of Stalin's anti-Semitic
      campaign, but chose to keep the information
      private.

742. Seton, Marie. **Paul Robeson**. London: Dobson, 1958.

743. Smith, Ronald A. "The Paul Robeson-Jackie Robinson
      Saga and a Political Collision." **Journal of Sport
      History** 6,2 (1979). Discusses the decision of
      Jackie Robinson (the first black major league
      baseball player) to criticize Paul Robeson's
      statement that blacks should not fight for the
      U.S. in a war with the Soviet Union. Treats
      Robinson's criticism, made at the request of the
      House Committee on Un-American Activities, as an
      example of Cold War hysteria.

744. Tygiel, Jules. **Baseball's Great Experiment: Jackie
      Robinson and His Legacy**. New York: Oxford
      University Press, 1983.

745. Wright, Charles. **Robeson: Labor's Forgotten
      Champion**. Detroit: Balamp Publishing, 1975.
      Surveys Robeson's Communist and left-wing
      political activity.

      See item 666.

Rustin, Bayard

746. Viorst, Milton. **Fire in the Streets**. New York:
      Simon and Schuster, 1979. Notes that Bayard
      Rustin broke with the Communist Party in 1941 due
      to its rapid change of line.

Wright, Richard

747. Davis, Jane Maria. "This Peculiar Kind of Hell:
     The Role of Power in the Novels of Richard
     Wright." Ph.D. dissertation. Stanford University,
     1984. Discusses Wright's perception of Communist
     Party pressure on his writings as the use of
     power against him.

*   Fabre, Michel. **The Unfinished Quest of Richard
     Wright.** New York: Morrow, 1973. Cited as item
     2069.

*   Gayce, Addison. **Richard Wright: Ordeal of a Native
     Son.** Garden City: Doubleday, 1980. Cited as item
     2070.

748. Hurst, Catherine Daniels. "A Survey of the
     Criticism of Richard Wright's Fiction." Ph.D.
     dissertation. University of Alabama, 1979.
     Discusses Wright's association with the Communist
     Party and how that association influenced
     criticism of his writings.

749. Kinnamon, Keneth. **The Emergence of Richard Wright:
     A Study in Literature and Society.** Urbana:
     University of Illinois Press, 1972. Discusses
     his involvement with Communism.

750. Kumasi, Kandi Baba. "The Critical Reputation of
     Richard Wright's **Native Son** (1940-1975)." Ph.D.
     dissertation. University of Detroit, 1980.
     Discusses how Wright's break with the Communist
     Party affected Left and liberal literary
     criticism of **Native Son.**

751. Naison, Mark. "Richard Wright & the Communist
     Party." **Radical America** 13,1 (1979). Examines
     American Hunger, Richard Wright's autobiographical
     novel which deals with his experiences as a black
     intellectual within the Communist Party.

*   Web, Constance. **Richard Wright: A Biography.** New
     York: Putnam's, 1968. Cited as item 2071.

*   Wright, Richard. **Native Son.** New York: Harper and
     Brothers, 1940. Cited as item 2072.
     Autobiographical.

752. Wright, Richard. **American Hunger.** New York: Harper
     & Row, 1944, 1977. Autobiographical: discusses
     Wright's experiences as a black intellectual in
     the Communist Party of the 1930s.

753. Wright, Richard. "With Black Radicals in Chicago."
      Dissent 24,2 (1977). Excerpt from **American
      Hunger.**

      See items 646, 650, 666, and 1031.

12

THE COMINTERN AND INTERNATIONAL AFFAIRS

GENERAL

754. American Institute for Marxist Studies. "Lenin, National Liberation, and the United States." New York: American Institute for Marxist Studies, n.d. An appendix describes the Russian-American Industrial Corp. which raised funds from American workers for investment in the Soviet clothing industry.

755. Brown, Anthony Cave, and Charles B. MacDonald. **On a Field of Red: The Communist International and the Coming of World War II.** New York: Putnam, 1981. Journalistic expose of the Comintern; discusses Comintern involvement with the American Communist Party.

756. Christopulos, Diana K. "American Radicals and the Mexican Revolution, 1900-1925." Ph.D. dissertation. State University of New York at Binghamton, 1980. Notes that some American Communists attempted to influence Mexican revolutionary groups.

757. Corey, Esther. "Footnote on Lenin and Some American Writers." **The Antioch Review** (Winter 1958). Discusses Lenin's views on John Reed and Louis C. Fraina.

758. Drachkovitch, Milorad, and Branko Lazitch, eds. **The Comintern: Historical Highlights.** New York: Praeger, 1966. Discusses the Comintern relations with the American Communist Party.

759. Farsoun, Karen, Samih Farsoun, and Alex Ajay. "Mid-East Perspectives from the American Left." **Journal of Palestine Studies [Lebanon]** 4,1 (1974). Recounts the shift of the Communist Party and other American Leftist groups from a pro-Israeli to a pro-Arab position after the Six-Day War.

760. Keiser, John H., ed. "An American Communist
     Reports from Russia, November, 1922." **Illinois
     State Historical Society Journal** 60 (1967).

761. Ra'anan, Gavriel David. "Factions and their
     'Debates' over International Policy during the
     Zhdanovshchina Ramifications for Ruling and Non-
     ruling Communist Parties." Ph.D. dissertation.
     Fletcher School of Law and Diplomacy, Tufts
     University, 1980.

762. Stokes, Melvyn. "American Progressives and the
     European Left." **Journal of American Studies** 17
     (April 1983).

     See items 618 and 1122.

THE KUZBAS PROJECT

763. Morray, J. P. **Project Kuzbas: American Workers In
     Siberia, 1921-1926.** New York: International
     Publishers, 1982.

764. Smith, William Thomas. "The Kuzbas Colony, Soviet
     Russia, 1921-1926: An American Contribution to
     the Building of a Communist State." D.A.
     dissertation. University of Miami, 1977.
     Recounts the history of industrial complex in
     Siberia where American Communists and Wobblies
     provided the managerial and technical staff for
     an early Soviet industrial project.

THE SPANISH CIVIL WAR

765. Eby, Cecil. **Between the Bullet and the Lie:
     American Volunteers in the Spanish Civil War.** New
     York: Holt, Rinehart & Wilson, 1969. Describes
     the American Communist Party's Lincoln Battalion.

766. Gerassi, John. **The Premature Antifascists: North
     American Volunteers in the Spanish Civil War, An
     Oral History.** New York: Praeger, 1986.

767. Guttmann, Allen. **The Wound in the Heart: America
     and the Spanish Civil War.** New York: Free Press
     of Glencoe, 1962.

768. Johnston, Verle. **Legions of Babel: The
     International Brigades in the Spanish Civil War.**
     University Park: Pennsylvania State University

Press, 1967. Discusses the American Communist
Party's Lincoln battalion.

769. Landis, Arthur. **The Abraham Lincoln Brigade.** New
     York: Citadel Press, 1967.

770. Lovin, Hugh T. "The American Communist Party and
     the Spanish Civil War, 1936-1939." Ph.D.
     dissertation. University of Washington, 1963.
     Finds that Communist Party propaganda themes on
     the Spanish war paralleled those of the USSR;
     notes only limited Communist success in
     penetrating and controlling other pro-loyalist
     bodies and the Communist Party had almost no
     success influencing the labor movement or
     Roosevelt.

771. McIntyre, Edison. "The Abraham Lincoln Battalion:
     American Volunteers Defend the Spanish Republic."
     American History Illustrated 18,1 (1983).

772. Richardson, R. Dan. "The International Brigades as
     a Comintern Propaganda Instrument." **Canadian
     History** 9 (1974).

773. Richardson, R. Dan. **Comintern Army: The
     International Brigades and the Spanish Civil War.**
     Lexington: University Press of Kentucky, 1982.

774. Rolfe, Edwin. **The Lincoln Battalion.** New York:
     Haskell House, 1939, 1974. Written by the
     battalion's historian.

775. Rosenstone, Robert A. "The Men of the Abraham
     Lincoln Battalion: Soldiers and Veterans, 1937-
     1965." Ph.D. dissertation. University of
     California, Los Angeles, 1965.

776. Rosenstone, Robert A. "The Men of the Abraham
     Lincoln Battalion." **Journal of American History**
     54,2 (1967). Finds that men serving with the
     Lincoln Battalion were acquainted with labor
     activism, politically radical, sympathetic to
     Communism, and apathetic toward religion.

777. Rosenstone, Robert. **Crusade on the Left: The
     Lincoln Battalion in the Spanish Civil War.** New
     York: Pegasus, 1969.

778. Sessions, John. "American Communists and the Civil
     War in Spain." Unpublished manuscript in
     possession of Harvey Klehr.

779. Taylor, Frederick J. **The United States and the Spanish Civil War.** New York: Bookman Asoc., 1956.

See items 621 and 634.

13

COMMUNISM, FARMERS, AND FARM WORKERS

GENERAL

780. Dann, Jim. "In the Great Depression -- 1930-1940: Communists Try to Organize 'Factories in the Fields.'" **PL: Progressive Labor** 6 (Feb. 1969).

*   Dyson, Lowell. "The Milk Strike of 1939 and the Destruction of the Dairy Farmers Union." **New York History** (Oct. 1970). Cited as item 2056. After the DFU, which had a significant element of Communist leadership, led a successful milk strike, anti-Communism was used to discredit and destroy it.

781. Dyson, Lowell K. "Radical Farm Organizations and Periodicals in America, 1920-1960." **Agricultural History** 45,2 (April 1971).

782. Dyson, Lowell K. "The Red Peasant International In America." **Journal of American History** 58 (March 1972). Discusses the difficulty Communists had in deciding upon a strategy for approaching American farmers.

*   Dyson, Lowell. "The Farmer and the Left: The Influence of Radical Farm Organizations." **Farmers, Bureaucrats, and Middlemen.** Trudy H. Peterson, ed. Washington, D.C.: Howard University Press, 1981. Cited as item 2057. Discusses the importance of Communist farm organizations in the late 1920s and early 1930s.

783. Dyson, Lowell K. **Red Harvest, The Communist Party and American Farmers.** Lincoln: University of Nebraska Press, 1982. Well written and well researched history of the Communist Party's efforts, largely unsuccessful, to organize farmers in the 1920s and 1930s. Emphasizes the period prior to the Popular Front. See item 2031.

2

12 COMMUNISM AND ANTI-COMMUNISM IN THE UNITED STATES

* Dyson, Lowell, ed. **Agrarian Periodicals in the United States, 1920–1960.** Westport: Greenwood, 1984. Cited as item 2055. Microfilm guide to radical farm journals, pamphlet material and some manuscript collections.

784. Harris, Lement. **Harold Ware (1890–1935) Agricultural Pioneer, USA and USSR.** New York: American Institute of Marxist Studies, 1978. Biography of the Party's pioneering agricultural specialist by another of the Party's agricultural specialists.

NATIONAL FARMERS UNION

785. Crampton, John A. **National Farmers Union.** Lincoln: University of Nebraska Press, 1965. Briefly discusses factionalism in the NFU involving those close to the Communist Party.

786. Crampton, John A. "'Yours for Humanity . . .': The Role of Ideology in the Farmers Union." Ph.D. dissertation. University of California, 1962.

787. Mast, Charles Anthony. "Farm Factionalism over Agricultural Policy: The National Farmers Union, 1926–1937." Master's thesis. University of Maryland, 1967. Notes Communist attempts to influence agricultural organizations.

788. Pratt, William C. "The National Farmers Union and the Cold War." Unpublished paper, 1980 Northern Great Plains History Conference, Duluth, MN. Discusses the elimination of Popular Front elements from the NFU in the early 1950s.

See item 815.

COMMUNISM AND SOUTHERN AGRICULTURE

789. Auerbach, Jerold S. "Southern Tenant Farmers: Socialist Critics of the New Deal." **Labor History** 7 (1966).

790. Cobb, William H., and Donald H. Grubbs. "Arkansas' Commonwealth College and the Southern Tenant Farmers' Union." **Arkansas Historical Quarterly** 25 (Winter 1966).

791. Cobb, William H. "From Utopian Isolation to
      Radical Activism: Commonwealth College, 1925-
      1935." **Arkansas Historical Quarterly** 32 (1973).

792. Conrad, David Eugene. **The Forgotten Farmers: The
      Story of Sharecroppers in the New Deal.** Urbana:
      University of Illinois Press, 1965.

793. Dyson, Lowell K. "The Southern Tenant Farmers
      Union and Depression Politics." **Political Science
      Quarterly** 34 (1973).

794. Grubbs, Donald H. "Gardner Jackson, That
      'socialist' Tenant Farmers' Union, and the New
      Deal." **Agricultural History** 42 (1968).

795. Grubbs, Donald H. **Cry From the Cotton: The
      Southern Tenant Farmers' Union and the New Deal.**
      Chapel Hill: University of North Carolina Press,
      1971. Notes the Communist role in the STFU.

796. Mitchell, H.L. "Founding and Early History of the
      Southern Tenant Farmers' Union." **Arkansas
      Historical Quarterly** 32 (1973). Memoir by a key
      STFU leader noting Communist involvement.

797. Mitchell, H.L. **Mean Things Happening in This Land.**
      Montclair: Allancheld, Osmun & Co, 1979.
      Discusses the Communist Party's attempt to take
      control of the Southern Tenant Farmers' Union.

798. Naison, Mark. "Great Depression: the Threads of a
      Lost Tradition." **Journal of Ethnic Studies** I
      (Fall 1973). Discusses the affiliation of the
      Southern Tenant Farmers' Union with the CIO's
      UCAPAWA.

799. Naison, Mark. "All God's Dangers and Oral
      History." **Journal of Ethnic Studies** 4,4 (1977).
      Review article prompted by Theodore Rosengarten's
      All God's Dangers. Discusses the Communist-
      linked Alabama Sharecroppers union.

800. Rosen, Dale. "The Alabama Share Croppers Union."
      Honors essay. Radcliffe College, 1969.

801. Rosen, Dale, and Theodore Rosengarten. "Shoot-Out
      at Reeltown: The Narrative of Jess Hull, Alabama
      Tenant Farmer." **Radical America** 6,6 (Nov.-Dec.
      1972). Discusses the Alabama Sharecroppers
      Union, a Communist-aligned organization active in
      the early 1930s.

802. Rosengarten, Theodore. **All God's Dangers.** New York: Alfred Knopf, 1974. Edited oral history memoir of Nate Shaw, an activist in the Alabama Sharecropper's Union in 1931. See item 799.

803. Thrasher, Sue, and Leah Wise. "The Southern Tenant Farmers' Union." **Southern Exposure** I (Winter 1973/74). Interviews with union participants.

COMMUNISM AND WEST COAST AGRICULTURE

804. Daniel, Cletus E. "Labor Radicalism in Pacific Coast Agriculture." Ph.D. dissertation. University of Washington, 1972. Scholarly examination of the success and failures of the Communist Party's Cannery and Agricultural Workers Industrial Union (Trade Union Unity League) in 1930-1934 as well as of earlier efforts by the Industrial Workers of the World.

805. Daniel, Cletus E. "Radicals on the Farm in California." **Agricultural History** 49 (Oct. 1975).

806. Daniel, Cletus E. **Bitter Harvest: A History of California Farmworkers, 1870-1941.** Ithaca: Cornell University Press, 1981. Thoroughly researched and comprehensive history which includes coverage of Communist activity.

807. Holcomb, Ellen Lois. "Efforts to Organize the Migrant Workers by the Cannery and Agricultural Workers Industrial Union in the 1930's." Master's thesis. California State University, Chico, 1963.

808. Jamieson, Stuart. **Labor Unionism in American Agriculture.** Washington: Department of Labor, 1945. Notes a Trade Union Unity League role in several California farm worker strikes in the 1930s.

809. Lopez, Ronald W. "The El Monte Berry Strike of 1933." **Aztlan** (1970). Notes Communist involvement in a strike by Mexican-American workers.

810. Matthews, Glenna. "Fruit Workers of the Santa Clara Valley: Alternative Paths to Union Organization during the '30s." **Pacific History Review** 54,1 (Feb. 1985). Discusses Communist organizing among farm and cannery workers under the TUUL, the AFL, and the CIO.

811. McWilliams, Carey. **Factories in the Fields.**
Boston: Little, Brown, 1939. Notes Communist
role in several California farm worker strikes.

812. Monfross, John. "The Associated Farmers of
California." Unpublished paper, 1976 Southwest
Labor Studies Conference. Discusses the
antiunion and anti-Communist activities in the
1930s of the Associated Farmers, a group largely
financed by corporate interests.

813. Ruiz, Vicki Lynn. "UCAPAWA, Chicanas, and the
California Food Processing Industry, 1937-1950."
Ph.D. dissertation. Stanford University, 1982.

814. Wollenberg, Charles. "Race and Class in Rural
California: The El Monte Berry Strike of 1933."
California Historical Quarterly 51 (1972).

COMMUNISM AND MIDWESTERN AGRICULTURE

815. Chambers, Steven A. "Relations between Leaders of
the Iowa and National Farmers Union
Organizations, 1941 to 1950." Honors essay.
University of Iowa, 1961. Notes the leadership
of the Iowa Farmers Union by Popular Front
adherents in the 1940s.

816. Dyson, Lowell K. "The Farm Holiday Movement."
Ph.D. dissertation. Columbia University, 1968.

817. Haynes, John Earl. "Farm Co-ops and the Election
of Hubert Humphrey to the Senate." **Agricultural
History** 57,2 (Fall 1983). Notes the role of farm
co-ops in aiding Humphrey's anti-Communist faction
in its fight to control Minnesota's Democratic-
Farmer-Labor Party in 1948.

818. Mathews, Allan. "The History of the United Farmers
League in South Dakota, 1923-1936: A Study in
Farm Radicalism." Master's thesis. University of
South Dakota, 1972.

819. Mathews, Allan. "Agrarian Radicals: The United
Farmers League of South Dakota." **South Dakota
History** 3,4 (1973). Recounts the brief
popularity of the Communist-linked United Farmers
League in northeastern South Dakota in the early
1930s.

820. Pratt, William C. "The Decline of Agrarian
     Radicalism in the Upper Midwest." Unpublished
     paper, Third University of Wyoming American
     Studies Conference, 1982. Notes occasional
     Communist Party participation in midwestern farm
     agitation.

821. Rowley, William D. "'Grass Roots' and Imported
     Radicalism in Nebraska, 1932-1934." Master's
     thesis. University of Nebraska, 1963.

822. Shover, John. "The Communist Party and the Midwest
     Farm Crisis of 1933." **Journal of American History**
     51 (Sept. 1964).

823. Shover, John. "The Farmers' Holiday Association
     Strike, August 1932." **Agricultural History** 39
     (1965).

824. Shover, John. "The Penny-Auction Rebellion:
     Western Farmers Fight Against Foreclosure, 1932-
     1933." **American West** 2 (Fall 1965).

825. Shover, John. **Cornbelt Rebellion: The Farmers'
     Holiday Association.** Champagne: University of
     Illinois Press, 1965. Notes Communist Party role
     in the FHA protests of the early 1930s.

826. Vindex, Charles. "Radical Rule in Montana."
     Montana: The Magazine of Western History 18 (Jan.
     1968). Reviews the political activity of "Red
     Flag" Charley Taylor, editor of a rural Montana
     newspaper and longtime Communist Party member.

14

COMMUNISM AND WOMEN

827. De Grazia, Victoria. "Women and Communism in
Advanced Capitalist Societies: Readings and
Resources." **Radical History Review** 23 (Spring
1980). Bibliography of primary and secondary
material.

828. Dennis, Peggy. "A Response to Ellen Kay
Trimberger's Essay, 'Women in the Old and New
Left.'" **Feminist Studies** 5,3 (1979). Dennis
asserts that Trimberger did not understand the
nature of a total commitment to Communism.

829. Dixler, Elsa Jane. "The Woman Question: Women and
the American Communist Party, 1929-1941." Ph.D.
dissertation. Yale University, 1974. Finds that
the Communist Party was not a feminist
organization, tended to follow traditional
patterns of male-female relations, and in the
Popular Front period the Communist Party
glorified traditional women's roles of mother,
housewife, and consumer.

830. Foner, Philip S. **Women and the American Labor
Movement: From World War I to the Present.** New
York: Free Press, 1980. Finds that Communists
nearly always acted correctly toward women and
the labor movement whereas anti-Communist
unionists nearly always did the wrong thing.

831. Gordon, Linda, and Allen Hunter. "Feminism,
Leninism & the U.S.: A Comment." **Radical America**
13,5 (1979).

832. Shaffer, Robert. "Women and the Communist Party,
1930-1940." **Socialist Review** (May-June 1979).

833. Strom, Sharon Hartmen. "Challenging Woman's Place:
Feminism, the Left, and Industrial Unionism in
the 1930s." **Feminist Studies** 9 (1983).

834. Tax, Meridith. "Women's Councils in the Thirties."
      Unpublished paper, 1984 Berkshire Conference on
      the History of Women. Discusses the role of
      Communist Party women's councils in Communist
      Party cultural and political activities in New
      York.

835. Trimberger, Ellen Kay. "Women in the Old and New
      Left: The Evolution of a Politics of Personal
      Life." **Feminist Studies** 5,3 (1979). Compares
      Dennis's **The Autobiography of an American
      Communist** with the memoir of Elinor Langer, a
      1960s New Leftist feminist. See item 828.

      See item 1417.

COMMUNISM AND THE CHURCHES

GENERAL

836. Centola, Kathleen Gefell. "The American Catholic Church and Anti-Communism, 1945-1960: An Interpretive Framework and Case Studies." Ph.D. dissertation. State University of New York, Albany, 1984. Attributes Catholic anti-Communism to reflection of general American social frustration that broke out in irrational anti-Communism and to Catholic use of anti-Communism to assert an American identity.

837. Drakeford, John W. "The Implications of Communism for Religious Education." Ph.D. dissertation. Southwestern Baptist Theological Seminary, 1956.

838. Feldblum, Esther. "On the Eve of a Jewish State: American-Catholic Responses." **American Jewish Historical Quarterly** 64,2 (1974). Notes that fear of Communism spreading to the Middle East was one of several factors contributing to American Catholic reservations about the creation of Israel.

839. Gustafson, Merlin. "Church, State, and the Cold War, 1945-1952." **Church and State** (Winter 1965).

840. Gustafson, Merlin. "The Church, the State and the Military in the Truman Administration." **The Rocky Mountain Social Science Journal** 2 (Oct. 1966).

841. Karmarkovic, Alex. "American Evangelical Responses to the Russian Revolution and the Rise of Communism in the Twentieth Century." **Fides et History** 4,2 (1972). After initial indifference, most evangelical Christians perceived Communism and the Soviet Union as violent, antireligious spiritual threats to Christianity and the US.

842.   Kyser, John L.   "The Deposition of Bishop William
       Montgomery Brown in New Orleans, 1925." **Louisiana
       History** 8,1 (1967).   Recounts the career of
       Bishop Brown, who was expelled from office by the
       Episcopal Church in 1925 after he moved from
       extreme religious Modernism into open heresy and
       membership in the Communist Party.

843.   Lefever, Ernest W.   **Amsterdam to Nairobi: The World
       Council of Churches and the Third World.**
       Washington, D.C.: Ethics and Public Policy, 1979.
       Finds the WCC leadership hostile to capitalism
       and desiring accommodation with Soviet Communism.

844.   Marshall, Paul, and Mike Welton.   "A Guide to
       Christian-Marxist Dialogue." **Canadian Dimension**
       13,5 (1979).   Bibliography of sources on the
       attraction of many recent theologians to
       Communism.

845.   Maurer, Marvin.   "Quakers and Communists: Vietnam
       and Israel." **Midstream** 25,9 (1979).   Compares the
       campaign of Communists, Quakers, and others to
       undermine American support of Israel in the 1970s,
       with a similar effort regarding South Vietnam in
       the 1960s.

846.   Muravchik, Joshua.   "The National Council of
       Churches and the U.S.S.R." **This World** 9 (Fall
       1984).   Discusses the habit of NCC officials of
       finding justification for Soviet regulation of
       churches.

847.   Murphy, Richard J.   "The Canonico-Juridical Status
       of a Communist." Ph.D. dissertation. Catholic
       University of America, 1959.

848.   O'Hearn, Michael James.   "Political Transformation
       of a Religious Order." Ph.D. dissertation.
       University of Toronto (Canada), 1983.   Discusses
       the transformation of the Catholic Scarboro
       Foreign Mission Society from anti-Communism to
       anticapitalism.

849.   Roy, Ralph L.   **Communism and the Churches.** New
       York: Harcourt, Brace and Co., 1960.   Using
       legalistic standards of evidence, notes some
       Communist influence among clergymen; finds much
       criticism of Communism in the churches to be
       irresponsible or unproven.

850. Smyle, Robert F. "The U.S. and the USSR: Religious
     Liberty as a Human Right." **Worldview** 20,9 (1977).
     Discusses changes over time in American attitudes
     toward Soviet religious policy.

851. Touchet, Francis H. "The Social Gospel and the
     Cold War: The Melish Case." Ph.D. dissertation.
     New York University, 1981. Sees the Rev. Dr.
     John Melish and Rev. William Melish, who were
     forced from a Brooklyn Heights, NY Episcopal
     church in the 1950s, as victims of Cold War
     hysteria and Right Wing opportunism because of
     their 'progressive' attitudes and 'friendship'
     for the Soviet people.

852. West, Charles C. "Recent Theological Encounters
     with Communism." Ph.D. dissertation. Yale
     University, 1955.

853. Yablonsky, Mary Jude. "A Rhetorical Analysis of
     Selected Television Speeches of Archbishop
     Fulton J. Sheen on Communism - 1952-1956." Ph.D.
     dissertation. Ohio State University, 1974.

854. Deleted.

ANTI-COMMUNISM, THE SPANISH CIVIL WAR, AND CATHOLICISM

855. Crosby, Donald F. "Boston's Catholics and the
     Spanish Civil War: 1936-1939." **New England
     Quarterly** 44,1 (1971). Finds that the near
     unanimous backing of Franco in the Spanish Civil
     War derived from fear of Communism. The
     association of Communism with the violent
     repression of the church in Mexico in the 1920s
     played a large role in the vehemence of the
     Catholic fear of Communism.

856. Valaik, J. David. "American Catholics and the
     Second Spanish Republic, 1911-1936." **Journal of
     Church and State** 10,1 (1968). Finds that
     American Catholics accepted the conspiratorial
     explanations of Spanish anticlericalism offered
     by the church leadership due to their ignorance
     of Spanish history.

857. Valaik, J. David. "American Catholic Dissenters
     and the Spanish Civil War." **Catholic Historical
     Review** 53 (1968).

858. Valaik, J. David. "In the Days before Ecumenism:
     American Catholics, anti-Semitism, and the

Spanish Civil War." **Journal of Church and State**
13,3 (1971). Discusses the feud between American
Catholic leaders and Jewish spokesmen over the
Spanish Civil War, with Catholics seeing the
conflict as a fight against Communism whereas
Jews saw it as a fight against anti-Jewish
Fascism.

BIOGRAPHICAL MATERIAL

Hargis, Billy James

859. Rededip, John H. **American Far Right: A Case Study
of Billy James Hargis and Christian Crusade.**
Grand Rapids: W.B. Eerdmans, 1968.

860. Seaman, John. "Dilemma: The Mythology of Right and
Left." **Journal of Human Relations** 17,1 (1969).
Examines the anti-Communism of Billy James
Hargis, a Protestant evangelical minister who
lectured and wrote about the Communist threat.

Matthews, Mark Allison

861. Soden, Dale Edward. "Mark Allison Matthews:
Seattle's Southern Preacher." Ph.D. dissertation.
University of Washington, 1980. Discusses the
popular anti-Communism of a influential
Presbyterian minister in Seattle, 1902-1940.

Pierce, Bob

862. Hamilton, John Robert. "An Historical Study of Bob
Pierce and World Vision's Development of the
Evangelical Social Action Film." Ph.D.
dissertation. University of Southern California,
1980. Finds that the early strong anti-Communism
of World Vision mellowed over time.

Ward, Harry F.

863. Duke, David Nelson. "Christianity and Marxism in
the Life and Thought of Harry F. Ward." Ph.D.
dissertation. Emory University, 1980.
Sympathetic analysis of Ward's reconciliation of
Christianity to Soviet Communism.

864. Fennero, Matthew John. "Social Gospelers and
Soviets, 1921-1926." **Journal of Church and State**
19,1 (1977). Discusses the support of Soviet
religious policy by Harry F. Ward and other
prominent American social gospel proponents.

865. Link, Eugene P. "Latter Day Christian Rebel: Harry
      F. Ward." **Mid-America** 56 (1974).

866. Link, Eugene P. **Labor-Religion Prophet: The Times
      and Life of Harry F. Ward.** Boulder: Westview,
      1984. Biography of a prominent advocate of
      social Christianity and a political friend of the
      Soviet Union.

16

FRIENDS OF COMMUNISM AND THE SOVIET UNION

GENERAL

867. Caute, David. **The Fellow-Travelers: A Postscript to the Enlightenment**. New York: Macmillan, 1973. Extensive discussion of the attraction to Communism of a segment of Western liberals and radicals. See item 868.

868. Feuer, Lewis S. "The Fellow-Travellers." **Survey [Great Britain]** 20,2-3 (1974). Argues that fellow travelers often felt that the Soviet ruling class was "their kind" of an intellectual elite; reviews David Caute's **The Fellow Travellers**.

869. Harrington, Michael. "A Time to Think." **Worldview** 17,9 (1974). Discusses the attitude of the New Left of the 1960's toward Communism.

870. Hollander, Paul. "Reflection on Anti-Americanism in Our Times." **Worldview** (June 1978).

871. Hollander, Paul. "Selective Affinities." **The New Republic** (Oct. 18, 1982). Discusses the ability of some longtime friends of Communism to resist all revision of their views.

872. Lowenfish, Lee. "American Radicals and Soviet Russia, 1917-1940." Ph.D. dissertation. University of Wisconsin, 1968. Discusses the attitude of radicals toward the Soviet Union. Sees the initial admirers as lyrical radicals such as John Reed, Max Eastman, and Raymond Robins. These were followed by realistic relativists who admired Soviet planning and economic dynamism and who did not mind the human cost. The latter included Rexford Tugwell, Stuart Chase, Louis Fischer, Walter Duranty, George Soule, Walter Frank, Samuel Harper, and Edmund Wilson.

* Rossi, John. "Farewell to Fellow Traveling: The Waldorf Peace Conference of March 1949."

Continuity 10 (Spring 1985). Cited as item 2085.
See item 211.

873. Shaw, Peter, and Seymour Martin Lipset. "Two
      Afterthoughts on Susan Sontag." **Encounter [Great
      Britain]** (June-July 1982).

874. Sontag, Susan. "Communism and the Left." **The
      Nation** (Feb. 27, 1982). Comments on illusions
      about Communism over time. See item 873.

ORGANIZATIONS ASSOCIATED WITH COMMUNISM

875. Bailey, Percival R. "Progressive Lawyers: A
      History of National Lawyers Guild, 1936-1958."
      Ph.D. dissertation. Rutgers University, 1979.
      Examines the NLG and the Communist role in it;
      concludes that the NLG's policies were humane and
      progressive and the Communist role was benign.

876. Bailey, Percival R. "The Case of the National
      Lawyers Guild, 1939-1958." **Beyond the Hiss Case.**
      Athan Theoharis, ed. Philadelphia: Temple
      University Press, 1982.

877. Dunbar, Anthony P. **Against the Grain: Southern
      Radicals and Prophets, 1929-1959.**
      Charlottesville: University Press of Virginia,
      1981. Some of those discussed associated at some
      point with the Communist Party.

878. Finison, Lorenz. "Unemployment, Politics, and the
      History of Organized Psychology." **American
      Psychologist** (Nov. 1976). Notes the role of the
      Communist Party in forming the Psychologists'
      League in the 1930s.

879. Finison, Lorenz. "Radical Professionals in the
      Great Depression, An Historical Note: The
      Interprofessional Association." **Radical History
      Review** 4 (1977). Discusses the Communist-
      influenced IPA.

880. Finison, Lorenz. "The Psychological Insurgency,
      1936-1940." **Journal of Social Issues** 42,1 (1986).

881. Goldsmith, William. "The Theory and Practice of
      the Communist Front." Ph.D. dissertation.
      Columbia University, 1971. Examines in detail
      the International Labor Defense, the World
      Committee Against War and Fascism, and the
      International Workers Order.

882. Harris, Benjamin. "Reviewing Fifty Years of the
      Psychology of Social Issues." **Journal of Social
      Issues** 42,1 (1986).

883. Kreuger, Thomas. **And Promises to Keep: The
      Southern Conference for Human Welfare, 1938-1948.**
      Nashville: Vanderbilt University Press, 1967.
      Discusses the Communist Party's largely secret
      role in this liberal southern organization.

884. Lamont, Corliss (ed.). **The Trial of Elizabeth
      Gurley Flynn by the ACLU.** New York: Horizon
      Press, 1968. Deals with Flynn's expulsion from
      the ACLU.

885. Muravchik, Joshua. "The Think Tank of the Left."
      New York Times Magazine (April 26, 1981).
      Discusses the pro-Soviet orientation of the
      Institute for Policy Studies.

886. Walker, Thomas J. "The International Workers
      Order: A Unique Fraternal Body." Ph.D.
      dissertation. University of Chicago, 1983.
      History of a Communist-aligned fraternal
      insurance organization that was dissolved in the
      what the author sees as the "tyrannical" McCarthy
      era.

AMERICAN VISITORS TO COMMUNIST SOCIETIES

887. Crowl, James William. **Angels in Stalin's Paradise:
      Western Reporters in Soviet Russia, 1917 to 1937,
      a Case Study of Louis Fischer and Walter Duranty.**
      Lanham: University Press of America, 1982.

888. Enzensberger, Hans Magnus. "Tourists of the
      Revolution." **The Consciousness Industry: On
      Literature, Politics and the Media.** New York:
      Seabury Press, 1974.

889. Feuer, Lewis S. "American Travelers to the Soviet
      Union, 1917-1932: The Formation of a Component of
      New Deal Ideology." **American Quarterly** (Summer
      1962).

890. Hollander, Paul. **Political Pilgrims: Travels of
      Western Intellectuals to the Soviet Union, China,
      and Cuba, 1928-1978.** New York: Oxford University
      Press, 1981. Discusses Western intellectuals who
      visit and praise Communist societies. Concludes
      that their hostility to their own societies and

their need to believe in the possibility of
social perfection caused them not to notice the
oppressive nature of Communist states.

891. Hollander, Paul. "Pilgrims on the Run: Ideological
      Refugees from Paradise Lost." **Encounter [Great
      Britain]** 57,4 (1981).

892. Pauluch, Peter. "Spiking the Ukrainian Famine,
      Again." **National Review** (April 11, 1986).
      Discusses the suppression of news of the
      Ukrainian famine under Stalin by Walter Duranty,
      an American reporter stationed in the Soviet
      Union.

      See item 872.

THE MOSCOW TRIALS

893. Gilder, Peggy Allen. "American Intellectuals and
      the Moscow Trials." Thesis. Smith College, 1960.

894. Hook, Sidney. "Bert Brecht, Sidney Hook and
      Stalin." (letter) **Encounter [Great Britain]**
      (March 1978). Discusses Western reaction to the
      Moscow purges and trials.

895. Hook, Sidney. "Memories of the Moscow Trials."
      Commentary 73,3 (1984). Recounts his experiences
      as a Left intellectual when news of the trials
      reached the U.S.

896. Libbey, James K. "Liberal Journals and the Moscow
      Trials of 1936-38." **Journalism Quarterly** 52
      (Spring 1975).

897. Watson, George. "Were the Intellectuals Duped?"
      Encounter [Great Britain] (Dec. 1973). Discusses
      Western reaction to the Stalin's purge trials of
      the 1930s.

JOURNALS OF OPINION AND THE PRESS

898. Rees, John. "Infiltration of the Media by the KGB
      and its Friends." Accuracy in Media Conference,
      Washington, DC, April 20, 1978. Rees, a far
      Right researcher and journalist, synthesizes
      testimony regarding Soviet security service
      operations aimed at influencing U.S. media.

899. Tyson, James L. **Target America: The Influence of
      Communist Propaganda on US Media.** Chicago:
      Regnery Gateway, 1981. Journalistic expose of
      pro-Soviet advocacy groups in the US.

900. Warren, Frank A., III. "American Liberalism in the
      1930's: Its Relation to Communism." Ph.D.
      dissertation. Brown University, 1962. A detailed
      look at the attitude toward Communism and the
      Soviet Union taken by three leading liberal
      journals: **The New Republic, The Nation,** and
      Common Sense. Discusses the nature of the
      Popular Front relationship between liberals and
      Communists.

901. Warren, Frank A., III. **Liberals and Communism, The
      "Red Decade" Revisited.** Bloomington: Indiana
      University Press, 1966. Discusses the nature of
      the Popular Front relationship between some
      Liberals and Communism. Suggests that the
      relationship was ambiguous, informal, and not
      essentially conspiratorial. See item 61.

Monthly Review

902. Clecak, Peter. **"Monthly Review:** An Assessment."
      Monthly Review 20 (Nov. 1968).

National Guardian

903. Belfrage, Cedric, and James Aronson. **Something to
      Guard: The Stormy life of The National Guardian,
      1948-1967.** New York: Columbia University Press,
      1978. Story of a radical journal sympathetic to
      the Soviet Union and Communism.

904. Munk, Michael. **"The Guardian** from Old to New
      Left." **Radical America** 2 (March-April 1968).

      See items 911 and 1495.

The Nation

*   Redlich, Norman. "McCarthy's Global Hoax." **The
      Nation** (Dec. 2, 1978). Cited as item 2034. A
      defense of the history of **The Nation**'s editorial
      policy regarding McCarthyism and Communism.

905. Rozakis, Laurie E. "How the Division within the
      Liberal Community Was Reflected in **The Nation,**
      1930-1950." Ph.D. dissertation. State University

of New York, Stony Brook, 1984. Regards the
split between anti-Communist liberals and those
who cooperated with the Communist Party as
decisive in shaping the direction of American
artistic life; sees the political needs of the
Communist Party as a significant influence on
literary life.

See items 900, 901, and 2034.

The New Republic

906. Bliven, Bruce. **Five Million Words Later.** New York:
J. Day Co., 1970. Memoir by one of **The New
Republic's** editors of the 1930s.

907. Diggins, John P. **"The New Republic & Its Times."**
The New Republic December 10, 1984. Discusses
the attitude of **The New Republic** toward American
Communism in the course of reviewing the
magazine's history.

908. Fothergill, Garland Wayne. "Stalinist Communism
and Fascism: A Study in the Ambivalences of 'New
Republic' Liberalism." Ph.D. dissertation.
University of Minnesota, 1966. Argues that in
the 1920's **The New Republic** became an apologist
for Soviet totalitarianism.

909. Seideman, David. **THE NEW REPUBLIC: A Voice of
Modern Liberalism.** New York: Praeger, 1986.

See items 900, and 901.

BIOGRAPHICAL MATERIAL

Baldwin, Roger

910. Baldwin, Roger. "Recollections of a Life in Civil
Liberties-II: Russia, Communism, and United
Fronts, 1920-1940." **Civil Liberties Review,** 2,4
(1975). Memoir stressing his painful experiences
when cooperating with Communists. See item 315.

Belfrage, Cedric

911. Belfrage, Cedric. **The Frightened Giant: My
Unfinished Affair with America.** London: Secker &
Warberg, 1957. Discusses his deportation from
the United States due to his Communist links.

Frank, Waldo

912. Trachtenberg, Alan, ed. **Memoirs of Waldo Frank.**
     Amherst: University of Massachusetts Press, 1973.

Hellman, Lillian

913. Falk, Doris V. **Lillian Hellman.** New York: Ungar,
     1978.

914. Glazer, Nathan. "An Answer to Lillian Hellman."
     Commentary 61,6 (1976). Disagrees with Lillian
     Hellman's criticism of intellectuals who did not
     defend her and others who refused to testify to
     the House Un-American Activities Committee.
     Judges that had responsible intellectuals written
     openly about the Communist Party in the 1940s and
     1950s, congressional investigations would have
     been unnecessary.

915. Hellman, Lillian. **An Unfinished Woman.** Boston:
     Little, Brown and Co., 1969.

916. Hellman, Lillian. **Scoundrel Time.** Boston: Little,
     Brown, 1976. Hellman, a longtime friend of the
     Communist Party, discusses her experiences with
     the House Un-American Activities Committee;
     expresses contempt for ex-Communists who publicly
     repudiate their experiences in the Communist
     Party; hostile to anti-Communist liberals.

917. Hook, Sidney. "Lillian Hellman's **Scoundrel Time.**"
     Encounter [Great Britain] (Feb. 1977). Critical
     review-essay.

918. Howe, Irving. "Lillian Hellman and The McCarthy
     Years." **Dissent** (Fall 1976).

919. Kakutani, Michiko. "Hellman-McCarthy Libel Suit
     Stirs Old Antagonisms." **New York Times** (March 19,
     1980). Discusses Lillian Hellman's libel suit
     against Mary McCarthy for her remarks regarding
     Scoundrel Time.

920. Kazin, Alfred. "The Legend of Lillian Hellman."
     Esquire (Aug. 1977).

921. Kramer, Hilton. "The Life and Death of Lillian
     Hellman." **The New Criterion** 3,2 (1984). Critical
     review of Hellman's political history.

922. Mailer, Norman. "An Appeal to Lillian Hellman and
      Mary McCarthy." **New York Review of Books** (May 11,
      1980). Exchange of letters regarding the Hellman
      libel suit against McCarthy. Other letters in
      the issue of June 15, 1980.

923. McCracken, Samuel. "'Julia' & Other Fictions by
      Lillian Hellman." **Commentary** 77,6 (1984).

924. McPherson, Michael L. "Lillian Hellman and Her
      Critics." Ph.D. dissertation. University of
      Denver, 1976.

925. Phillips, William. "What Happened in the Fifties."
      Partisan Review 43,3 (1976). Essay critical of
      Lillian Hellman's **Scoundrel Time** and defending
      Left anti-Communism.

Lamont, Corliss

926. Lamont, Corliss. **Voice in the Wilderness:
      Collected Essays of Fifty Years.** Buffalo:
      Prometheus Books, 1975. Lamont was a longtime
      friend of the Communist Party and the Soviet
      Union.

*   Lamont, Corliss. **Yes to Life: Memoirs of Corliss
      Lamont.** New York: Horizon Press, 1981. Cited as
      item 2082.

Matthews, J.B.

927. Matthews, J.B. **Odyssey of a Fellow-Traveller.** New
      York: Mount Vernon Publishers, 1938.
      Autobiography of a close friend of the Communist
      Party who became a harsh anti-Communist.

Williams, Claude

928. Belfrage, Cedric. **South of God.** New York: Modern
      Age Books, 1941. Sympathetic biography of the
      Rev. Claude Williams, a Southerner closely
      associated with the Communist Party.

929. Belfrage, Cedric. **A Faith to Free the People.** New
      York: Dryden Press, 1944. Slightly revised
      version of item 928.

930. Naison, Mark. "Claude and Joyce Williams: Pilgrims
      of Justice." **Southern Exposure** 1 (Winter
      1973/74).

17

COMMUNISM, EDUCATION, AND YOUTH

GENERAL

931. Brickman, William W. "Communism and American
      Education." **School and Society** (March 25, 1950).
      Bibliographic essay.

932. Campbell, Katherine Moos. "An Experiment in
      Education: The Hessian Hills School, 1925-1952."
      Ph.D. dissertation. Boston University, 1984.
      Finds that Communism shaped much of the
      philosophy of this private progressive school
      near New York in the 1930s; however, after the
      Hitler-Stalin Pact liberal parents controlling
      the school forced the resignation of its pro-
      Communist director.

933. Iversen, Robert W. **The Communists and the Schools.**
      New York: Harcourt, Brace and Co., 1959. Survey
      of Communist involvement in American educational
      institutions.

934. Marden, David L. "The Cold War and American
      Education." Ph.D. dissertation. University of
      Kansas, 1975. Finds that education responded to
      the Cold War by ideological emphasis on
      democracy, the American way, citizenship and
      anti-Communism. Educators also sought to find
      ways to cooperate with defense needs. Regards
      Korea as a decisive event in prompting educators
      to adjust their plans to Cold War needs.

935. Mirel, Jeffrey Edward. "Politics and Public
      Education in the Great Depression: Detroit, 1929-
      1940." Ph.D. dissertation. University of
      Michigan, 1984. Notes that despite attacks on
      local radical teachers by the American Legion and
      the Dies Committee, the Detroit School Board
      refused to take action; discusses the radical
      politics of the local teachers' union.

936. Ryan, Leo J. "The Implications of Paradise." **California Social Science Review** 4,1 (1964). Charges that self-appointed censors with little education and shallow patriotism unjustly accused teachers of Communism in the city of Paradise.

See items 67, and 487-492.

TEACHING ABOUT COMMUNISM IN SECONDARY SCHOOLS

937. Barron, James S. "Teaching about Communism in California Public Secondary Schools." **California Social Science Review** 4,2 (1965). Surveys the extent of teaching about Communism.

938. Berman, Marvin Herschel. "The Treatment of the Soviet Union and Communism in Selected World History Textbooks, 1920-1970." Ph.D. dissertation. University of Michigan, 1975.

939. Burkhardt, Richard. "The Teaching of The Soviet Union in American School Social Studies." Ph.D. dissertation. Harvard University, 1952.

940. Eversull, Le Roi Eldridge. "The Americanism Versus Communism Unit in the Public Secondary Schools of Louisiana." Ed.D. dissertation. The Louisiana State University and Agricultural and Mechanical Col., 1963.

941. Gray, Roland F. "Teaching about Communism: A Survey of Objectives." **Social Education** 28,2 (1964). Finds that state public education programs on Communism are biased toward anti-Communism.

942. Hainsworth, Jerome Child. "Teaching About Communism in the American Secondary Schools." Ed.D. dissertation. Brigham Young University, 1967.

943. Herz, Martin F. "How the Cold War is Taught." **Social Education** 43,2 (1979). Finds that secondary school textbooks are critical of America's role in the Cold War and tend to justify Soviet actions.

944. Lomis, Dean Constantine. "The Relationships Among Instructional Programs About Communism in Selected Texas High Schools." Ph.D. dissertation. East Texas State University, 1967.

945. O'Leary, Richard James. "A Comparison of the
      Opinions of Lay and Professional Groups
      Concerning Generalizations and Understandings
      about Communism that should be Examined in High
      School Classes." Ed.D. dissertation. Boston
      University, 1968.

946. Perdew, Richard M. "Source Materials for Teaching
      About Communism." **Social Education** 28,2 (1964).
      Lists books, documents, articles, films and
      filmstrips available to help secondary teachers
      deal with Communism.

947. Peters, Norma Jean. "A Study of Pressures and
      Influences on Social Studies Curriculum: The
      Virginia Unit for Teaching about Communism, 1959-
      1964." Ed.D. dissertation. Virginia Polytechnic
      Institute and State University, 1977.

948. Sistrunk, Walter Everett. "The Teaching of
      Americanism Versus Communism in Florida Secondary
      Schools." Ed.D. dissertation. University of
      Florida, 1966.

949. Swearingen, Rodger. "Teaching about Communism in
      the American Schools." **Social Education** 28,2
      (1964). Discusses and evaluates approaches used
      to teach about Communism in public schools.

950. Wirsing, Marie Emilia. "What An American Secondary
      School Student Should Know About Communism."
      Ph.D. dissertation. University of Denver, 1966.

COMMUNISM, ANTI-COMMUNISM, AND HIGHER EDUCATION

951. Allen, R.B., et al. "Communism and Academic
      Freedom." **American Scholar** 18 (1949).

952. Cohen, Robby. "Professor William Parry, HUAC and
      the University of Buffalo." Unpublished paper,
      n.d.

953. Coulton, Thomas Evans. **A City College in Action.**
      New York: Harper, 1955. Contains a chapter on
      Communism at Brooklyn College.

954. Davis, Jerome. **Character Assassination.** New York:
      Philosophical Library, 1950. Discusses his
      dismissal from Yale due to his pro-Soviet views.

955. Diamond, Sigmund. "The Arrangement: the FBI and
     Harvard University in the McCarthy Period."
     Beyond the Hiss Case. Athan Theoharis, ed.
     Philadelphia: Temple University Press, 1982.

956. Downing, Lyle A., and Jerome J. Salomone.
     "Professors of the Silent Generation." **Trans-
     Action** 6,8 (1969). Based on a survey of faculty,
     the authors relate the degree of opposition to
     the war in Vietnam to the period when attitudes
     toward Communism were formed.

957. Fischel, Jacob Robert. "Harry Gideonse: The Public
     Life." Ph.D. dissertation. University of
     Delaware, 1973. Biography of the anti-Communist
     liberal president of Brooklyn College (1939-1966)
     who eliminated much of the Communist Party
     influence in the college and who as a leader of
     Freedom House also opposed Joseph McCarthy.

958. Gardner, David P. **The California Oath Controversy.**
     Berkeley and Los Angeles: University of
     California Press, 1967.

959. Gardner, David P. "By Oath and Association: The
     California Folly." **Journal of Higher Education**
     40,2 (1969). Critical recounting of the
     dismissal of thirty-six University of California
     faculty for failure to sign loyalty oaths.

960. Gettleman, Marvin E. "Communists in Higher
     Education: CCNY and Brooklyn College on the Eve
     of the Rapp-Coudert Investigation, 1935-1939."
     Unpublished paper, 1977 Organization of American
     Historians annual meeting.

961. Gettleman, Marvin E. "Rehearsal for McCarthyism:
     The New York State Rapp-Coudert Committee and
     Academic Freedom, 1940-41." Unpublished paper,
     1982 American Historical Association annual
     meeting.

962. Gettleman, Marvin E. "'Granted?': American
     Communist Recruitment Propaganda in an Academic
     Setting During the Popular Front Era."
     Unpublished paper. Examines the recruitment
     techniques and political arguments of Communist
     Party faculty units at New York City colleges in
     the mid-1930s.

*   Hook, Sidney. "Communists in the Classroom." **The
     American Spectator** (Aug. 1986). Cited as item

2053.   Reviews the controversy in the 1940s and
        1950s regarding the conflict between the
        professional responsibility of college faculty
        and Communist Party membership.

963.   Hughes, H. Stuart. "Why We Had No Dreyfus Case."
       American Scholar (Fall 1961). Argues that
       academics were seriously intimidated by
       McCarthyism.

964.   Lazarsfeld, Paul, and Wagner Thielens, Jr. **The**
       Academic Mind. Glencoe: Free Press, 1958.
       Surveys academic faculty and finds them
       apprehensive about McCarthyism.

965.   Lydenberg, John, ed. "Political Activism and the
       Academic Conscience: The Harvard Experience 1936-
       1941." Hobart and William Smith Colleges, 1975.

966.   McDougall, Daniel J. "McCarthyism and Academia:
       Senator Joe McCarthy's Political Investigations
       of Educators, 1950-1954." Ph.D. dissertation.
       Loyola University, 1977.

967.   Morgan, Alda Clarke Marsh. "Academic Freedom in
       Higher Education: An Historical and Theological
       Examination of its Place and Function in the
       Light of Five Cases." Ph.D. dissertation.
       Graduate Theological Union, 1984. Discusses
       several academic freedom cases involving
       Communists or those close to the Communist Party.

968.   Johnson, Oakley C. "Campus Battles for Freedom in
       the Thirties." **Centennial Review** 3 (1970).
       Johnson, a secret Communist at the time,
       remembers protests regarding his firing by City
       College of New York in the early 1930s.

969.   Nass, Deanna R. "The Image of Academic Freedom
       Conveyed by Select Scholarly Journals of the
       McCarthy Era." Ph.D. dissertation. Columbia
       University, 1979. A survey and analysis of
       journal articles.

970.   Ollman, Bertell, and Edward Vernoff. **The Left**
       Academy. New York: McGraw-Hill, 1982. Discusses
       the growing role of Marxists in American colleges
       and how that growth can be assisted and used to
       promote Marxist goals.

971.   Pyle, Gordon Bruce. "The Communist Issue and Due
       Process on the Campus." Ph.D. dissertation. The

Ohio State University, 1958. Examines and discusses issues involved in the position of faculty Communists.

972. Reutter, E. Edmund, Jr. **The School Administration and Subversive Activities.** New York: Teachers College, Columbia, 1951. Surveys legislation and practices.

973. Sanders, Jane. **Cold War on the Campus: Academic Freedom at the University of Washington, 1946–1954.** Seattle: University of Washington Press, 1979. Recounts the turmoil at the University of Washington regarding the denial of tenure to faculty with Communist Party links and several state and federal investigations of subversive activities; treats opposition to Communism as hysterical and irrational.

974. Sargent, S. Stansfeld, and Benjamin Harris. "Academic Freedom, Civil Liberties, and SPSSI." **Journal of Social Issues** 42,1 (1986). Discusses the defense of psychologists for subversive views by the Society for the Psychological Study of Social Issues.

975. Schrecker, Ellen. "The House Marxists." **The Nation** (Jan. 27, 1979). Discusses the growing role of Marxists in the academic world of the 1970s.

976. Schrecker, Ellen. "Academic Freedom and the Cold War." **Antioch Review** 38,3 (1980). Maintains that many colleges and universities unjustly denied jobs to Communists or those who would not deny Communist Party links from 1940 into the 1950s.

977. Schrecker, Ellen. "An Obligation of Candor: The Academy's Response to Congressional Investigating Committees." Unpublished paper, 1982 American Historical Association annual meeting.

978. Schrecker, Ellen. "An Obligation of Candor." **New York University Education Quarterly** (Summer 1983).

979. Schrecker, Ellen. "'In the Camp of the People': Academics and the Communist Party in the 1930s and 1940s." Unpublished paper, Fifth North American Labor History Conference, 1983.

980. Schrecker, Ellen. "The Missing Generation: Academics and the Communist Party from the

Depression to the Cold War." **Humanities in Society** 6 (Spring-Summer 1983). Finds that academic Communists kept their politics out of their classrooms, prized objectivity, and generally acted in accordance with the best traditions of the academy. Suggests that academics adversely affected by their Communist sympathies were heroic victims of a witch-hunt.

*   Schrecker, Ellen W. **No Ivory Tower: McCarthyism and the Universities.** New York: Oxford University Press, 1986. Detailed and thorough.

981. Van Den Haag, Ernest. "McCarthyism and the Professors." **Commentary** (Feb. 1959). Maintains that much of the academic apprehension about McCarthyism was baseless and contained a significant element of self-glorification.

982. Zimring, Fred R. "Academic Freedom and the Cold War: The Dismissal of Barrows Dunham from Temple University, A Case Study." Ed.D. dissertation. Columbia University Teachers College, 1981. Regards the 1954 dismissal of Dunham, a Marxist-Leninist and one time Communist Party member, from Temple University as an act of political repression; finds that the university administration and faculty redefined academic freedom to exclude political dissenters.

983. Zimring, Fred R. "Cold War Compromises: Albert Barnes, John Dewey, and the Federal Bureau of Investigation." **The Pennsylvania Magazine** 106,1 (1984). Notes that John Dewey discouraged use of his endorsement of a philosophy book when he learned that its author was sympathetic to Henry Wallace.

YOUTH AND STUDENTS

984. Brax, Ralph S. **The First Student Movement: Student Activism in the United States During the 1930s.** Port Washington: Kennikat, 1981. Notes the influence of the Communist Party on some student movement leaders.

985. Draper, Hal. "The Student Movement of the Thirties." **As We Saw the Thirties.** Rita J. Simon, ed. Urbana: University of Illinois Press, 1967. Notes the Communist role in various student organizations.

986.   Eagan, Eileen. "The Student Peace Movement in the
       U.S., 1930-1941." Ph.D. dissertation. Temple
       University, 1979. Sees the peace movement
       growing out of the Marxist, radical and reformist
       atmosphere of campuses in the 1930s. The
       movement was strongly pacifist and reached its
       peak in 1936. It was fractured by divisions over
       the Spanish civil war, the Hitler-Stalin Pact,
       and American entry into the war, but it left a
       pacifist legacy to inspire future generations.
       Notes a Communist role.

987.   Eagan, Eileen. **Class, Culture, and the Classroom:
       The Student Peace Movement of the 1930s.**
       Philadelphia: Temple University Press, 1981.

988.   Glaberman, Martin, and George Rawick. "The
       Champion of Youth: An Introduction and
       Appraisal." **Labor History** 11,3 (Summer 1970).
       Discusses a Young Communist League journal.

989.   Gordon, Max. "Seeds of Student Conflicts, A Memoir
       of 50 Years Ago." **The City College Alumnus** (Oct.
       1981). Gordon was later a Communist official.

990.   Gower, Calvin W. "Conservatism, Censorship, and
       Controversy in the CCC, 1930s." **Journalism
       Quarterly** 52,2 (1975). Notes exclusion of
       Communist youth publications from Civilian
       Conservation Corps camps.

991.   Lash, Joseph. **Eleanor Roosevelt, A Friend's
       Memoir.** Garden City: Doubleday and Co., 1956.
       Lash discusses his relationship with the
       Communist Party as a student leader in the 1930s.
       See item 2004.

992.   Miller, Michael H. "The American Student Movement
       of the Depression, 1931-1941: A Historical
       Analysis." Ph.D. dissertation. Florida State
       University, 1981. Studies the Student League for
       Industrial Democracy, the National Student
       League, American Student Union, National Student
       Federation of America, American Youth Congress,
       and the United Student Peace Committee. Notes
       that disagreements about collective security, the
       Hitler-Stalin Pact, and World War II disrupted
       the student movement.

993.   Phelps, Marianne Ruth. "The Response of Higher
       Education to Student Activism, 1933-1938." Ph.D.
       dissertation. George Washington University, 1980.

Studies in detail the reaction of administrations at George Washington University, Swarthmore, and the University of Wisconsin to student radicalism.

994. Rawick, George P. "The New Deal and Youth: The Civil Conservation Corps, the National Youth Administration and the American Youth Congress." Ph.D. dissertation. University of Wisconsin, 1957. Discusses the Communist Party's role in the AYC and the NYA.

995. Schlatter, Richard. "On Being a Communist at Harvard." **Partisan Review** 44,4 (1977). Memoir of Schlatter's experiences in the Communist Party while a student in the 1930s.

996. Schnell, Rodolph L. "National Activist Student Organizations in American Higher Education, 1905-1944." Ph.D. dissertation. University of Michigan, 1975. Notes the Communist role in the student organizations of the 1930s.

997. Stern, Sol. "A Short Account of International Student Politics and the Cold War with Particular Reference to the NSA, CIA, Etc." **Ramparts** (March 1967). Journalistic expose.

998. Wandersee, Winifred D. "Why Not Youth: The New Deal and the American Youth Movement, 1936-1943." Unpublished paper, 1985 Organization of American Historians convention.

999. Wechsler, James A. **Revolt on the Campus.** New York: Convici-Friede, 1935. Notes the role of the Communist Party in the student Left of the early 1930s.

1000. Wechsler, James A. **The Age of Suspicion.** New York: Random House, 1953. Discusses his experiences in the leadership of the Young Communist League.

See item 2004.

18

COMMUNISM, INTELLECTUALS, AND CULTURE

1001. Aaron, Daniel. "The Thirties - Now & Then."
American Scholar 35,3 (Summer 1966).

1002. Aaron, Daniel, and R. Bendiner, eds. **The Strenuous
Decade: A Social and Intellectual Record of the
1930s.** Garden City: Anchor Books, 1970.

1003. Bell, Daniel. "The Mood of Three Generations: The
Once-Born, the Twice-Born and the After-Born."
The End of Ideology. Daniel Bell. New York: The
Free Press, 1961. Discusses the political mood
of three generations of American Leftists.

1004. Clecak, Peter. **Radical Paradoxes, Dilemmas of the
American Left: 1945-1970.** New York: Harpers,
1973. Discusses the attitude of major non-
Communist radical intellectuals toward
Communism.

1005. de Toledano, Ralph. **Lament for a Generation.** New
York: Farrar, Straus and Cudahy, 1960.

1006. Dickstein, Morris. "Cold War Blues: Notes on the
Culture of the Fifties." **Partisan Review** 41,1
(1974). Discusses the cultural stance of
intellectuals in the 1950s.

* Greeley, Andrew. **The Most Distressful Nation.**
Chicago: Quadrangle, 1972. Cited as item 2076.

1007. Hicks, Granville. "How Red Was the 'Red Decade'?"
Harper's 207 (1953).

1008. Howe, Irving. "A Memoir of the Thirties." **Steady
Work: Essays on the Politics of Democratic
Radicalism 1953-1966.** Irving Howe, ed. New York:
Harcourt, Brace & World, 1966.

1009. Howe, Irving. "The New York Intellectuals: A
Chronicle and a Critique." **Commentary** (Oct.
1968). Discusses and defends the role of anti-
Communist intellectuals in the 1930s and 1940s.

1010. Howe, Irving. "On 'The Middle of the Journey.'"
       The New York Times Book Review (Aug. 22, 1976).

1011. Howe, Irving. "The New York Intellectuals."
       Decline of the New. Irving Howe, ed. New York:
       Harcourt Brace Jovanovich, 1970.   Discusses
       radicalism and anti-Communism among
       intellectuals. See item 1586.

1012. Howe, Irving. **A Margin of Hope.** New York:
       Harcourt Brace Jovanovich, 1982.

1013. Josephson, Matthew. **Infidel in the Temple: A
       Memoir of the Nineteen-Thirties.** New York:
       Knopf, 1967.   Discusses the attitude of
       intellectuals to Communism.

1014. Kazin, Alfred. **A Walker in the City.** New York:
       Harcourt, Brace, 1951.   Discusses the radical
       tone on intellectual-literary life in the 1930s.

1015. Kazin, Alfred. **On Native Grounds, An
       Interpretation of Modern American Prose
       Literature.** New York: Reynal & Hitchock, 1942.

1016. Kazin, Alfred. **Starting Out in the Thirties.**
       Boston: Little, Brown, 1965.

1017. Kazin, Alfred. **New York Jew.** New York: Knopf,
       1978.   See item 1586.

1018. Kempton, Murray. **Part of Our Time: Some Ruins and
       Monuments of the Thirties.** New York: Delta
       Books, 1967.   Discusses some of the
       personalities involved in Communist and anti-
       Communist activity.

1019. Laqueur, Walter, and George L. Mosse, eds. **The
       Left-Wing Intellectuals Between the Wars, 1919-
       1939.** New York: Harper & Row, 1966.

1020. Ninkovich, Frank A. "The New Criticism and Cold
       War America." **Southern Quarterly** 20 (Fall 1981).

1021. Peeler, David P. "America's Depression Culture:
       Social Art and Literature of the 1930s." Ph.D.
       dissertation. University of Wisconsin, 1980.
       Argues that artists and writers were largely
       ambivalent or opposed to Communism despite their
       bitter indictment of American capitalism.

1022. Pells, Richard H. **Radical Visions and American Dreams: Culture and Social Thought in the Depression Years.** New York: Harper & Row, 1973. Analysis of the reaction of intellectuals associated with the Left to the Depression. Discusses acceptance by some of conformity of Communist Party cultural themes, the obsession with proletarian culture, and intellectual shifts required by the Popular Front. Argues that the patriotism aroused by World War II diminished the appeal of radicalism and established the basis for postwar elitist anti-Communism.

1023. Pells, Richard H. **The Liberal Mind in a Conservative Age: American Intellectuals in the 1940s and 1950s.** New York: Harper and Row, 1985. Sees intellectuals after the war as weary of Marxism and mistrustful of mass political movements; unsympathetic to anti-Communist liberalism.

1024. Podhoretz, Norman. **Making It.** New York: Random House, 1967. Podhoretz, a prominent literary critic and editor of **Commentary,** discusses radical and anti-Communist intellectuals in New York.

1025. Podhoretz, Norman. **Breaking Ranks: A Political Memoir.** New York: Harper & Row, 1979. Discusses politics in New York intellectual circles and Podhoretz's shift from the Left to a 'neoconservative' stance.

1026. Sussman, Warren. "The Thirties." **The Development of an American Culture.** Stanley Coben and Lorman Ratner, eds. Englewood Cliffs: Prentice-Hall, 1970. Discusses the relationship of the Popular Front to intellectual-cultural currents.

1027. Trilling, Diana. **We Must March My Darlings: A Critical Decade.** New York: Harcourt Brace Jovanovich, 1977. Defends liberal anti-Communism and discusses the Popular Front.

1028. Wald, Alan M. "Marxism and Intellectuals in the United States: Some Lessons from the Past and Perspectives for the Future." **Changes** 6,11 (Nov.-Dec. 1984).

19

COMMUNISM, WRITERS, AND LITERATURE

GENERAL

1029. Aaron, Daniel. "Communism and the American
Writer." **The Newberry Library Bulletin** 5 (Aug.
1959).

1030. Aaron, Daniel. **Writers on the Left: Episodes in
American Literary Communism.** New York: Harcourt,
Brace and World, 1959. Discusses the influence
of Communism on writers in the 1930s and 1940s.

1031. Crossman, Richard, ed., **The God That Failed.** New
York: Harper and Row, 1949. Contains essays by
Richard Wright, black writer, and Louis Fischer,
journalist, regarding their experiences with
Communism. See items 872 and 1039.

1032. Davis, Earle. "Howard Hunt and the Peter Ward-CIA
Spy Novels." **Kansas Quarterly** 10,4 (1978).
Discusses the treatment of Communism in the
novels of Watergate figure Howard Hunt.

1033. Diggins, John P. **Up From Communism; Conservative
Odysseys in American Intellectual History.** New
York: Harper & Row, 1975. Discusses the
evolution of Max Eastman, John Dos Passos, Will
Herberg, and James Burnham from association with
Communism to firm anti-Communism.

1034. Deleted

1035. Hein, Virginia H., and Joseph O. Baylen.
"American Intellectuals and the 'Red Decade.'"
Studies in History and Society 2,1-2 (1977).
Examines the appeal of Communism and the Soviet
Union to American intellectuals, particularly
literary figures. Notes that sympathy for
Communism and the Soviet Union peaked in the
Popular Front period and declined drastically
after the Hitler-Stalin Pact in 1939. Surveys
the literary production of those associated with
the Communist Party and discusses the American

Writers' Congress and the League of American Writers.

* Knight, Rolf. **Traces of Magma: An Annotated Bibliography of Left Literature.** Vancouver, Canada: Draegerman, 1983. Cited as item 2038.

1036. Laqueur, Walter, and George L. Mosse, eds. **Literature and Politics in the Twentieth Century.** New York: Harper & Row, 1967.

1037. Latham, Earl. "From Left to Right." **Reviews in American History** 5,1 (1977). Review article prompted by Diggins's **Up From Communism.** See item 1033.

1038. Olster, Stacey Michele. "'Subjective Historicism' in the Post-Modern American Novel: A Study of Norman Mailer, Thomas Pynchon, and John Barth." Ph.D. dissertation. University of Michigan, 1981. Discusses the role of disillusion with Communism and the Soviet Union in shaping the world view of several major writers.

1039. Podhoretz, Norman. "Why **The God That Failed** Failed." **Encounter [Great Britain]** 60,1 (1983). Argues that intellectually the position of the ex-Communist writers of **The God That Failed** failed because they continued to believe in utopian reform although they rejected Communism due to its oppressive nature.

1040. Rideout, Walter B. **The Radical Novel in the United States, 1900-1954: Some Interrelations of Literature and Society.** Cambridge: Harvard University Press, 1956.

1041. Rossi, John P. "America's View of George Orwell." **Review of Politics** 43,4 (1981). Recounts the shifting attitude toward Orwell among American literary figures. During the 1930s he was ignored because he attacked Communism as well as Fascism, after World War II he became popular among anti-Communist liberals and Leftists, and in the 1950s he was a favorite of conservatives.

1042. Roth, Henry, and John S. Friedman. "On Being Blocked and Other Literary Matters." **Commentary** 64,2 (1977). Notes that Roth was a member of the Communist Party for a period.

1043.   Rothweiler, Robert Liedel. "Ideology and Four
        Radical Novelists: The Response to Communism of
        Dreiser, Anderson, Dos Passos, and Farrell."
        Ph.D. dissertation. Washington University, 1960.

1044.   Sanders, David Scott. "Pattern of Rejection:
        Three American Novelists and the Communist
        Literary Line, 1919-1949." Ph.D. dissertation.
        University of California, Los Angeles, 1956.

1045.   Schwartz, Lawrence H. "The C.P.U.S.A.'s Approach
        to Literature in the 1930's: Socialist Realism
        and the American Party's 'Line' on Literature."
        Ph.D. dissertation. Rutgers University, 1977.
        Concludes that the Communist Party never
        developed a coherent literary program; nor did
        it attempt to impose a Soviet model on American
        culture, with the possible exception of some
        effort in the 1933-35 period.

1046.   Schwartz, Lawrence H. **Marxism and Culture: The
        CPUSA and Aesthetic in the 1930s.** Port
        Washington: Kennikat, 1980.

1047.   Winegarten, Renee. **Writers and Revolution: The
        Fatal Lure of Action.** New York: New Viewpoints,
        1974.

1048.   Winter, Ella. **And Not to Yield.** New York:
        Harcourt, Brace, 1963. Memoir by a close
        literary friend of the Communist Party. Winter
        was also the wife of Lincoln Steffens and, after
        Steffens death, the playwright and secret
        Communist Party member Donald Ogden Stewart.

        See items 610, 616, 617, 648, .650, 666, 714, 747-
        753, 906, 2066 and 2067.

ORGANIZED WRITERS

1049.   Aaron, Daniel, ed. "Thirty Years Later: Memories
        of the First American Writers' Congress."
        American Scholar 35,3 (1966). Comments by
        Kenneth Burke, Malcolm Cowley, Granville Hicks,
        and William Phillips.

*   Mangione, Jerre. **The Dream and the Deal: The
        Federal Writers' Project, 1935-1943.** Boston:
        Little, Brown, 1972. Cited as item 2079.

1050. Penkower, Monty Noam. **The Federal Writers'
       Project: A Study in Government Patronage of the
       Arts.** Urbana: University of Illinois, 1977.
       Notes the activities of the Communist-aligned
       Writers Union among those employed by the New
       York FWP and the reaction of conservative
       politicians to that activity.

1051. Smiley, Sam. "Friends of the Party: The American
       Writers' Congresses." **Southwest Review** 54
       (1969).

1052. Wolfe, Thomas Kennerly, Jr. "The League of
       American Writers: Communist Organizational
       Activity among American Writers, 1929-1942."
       Ph.D. dissertation. Yale University, 1956.
       Finds that the League of American Writers was
       successful in guiding and manipulating the
       literary community in New York City in the 1937-
       1940 period, but the rapid shifts of the Hitler-
       Stalin Pact in late 1939 and the Nazi invasion
       of Russia in 1941 crippled the organization's
       effectiveness.

       See item 1035.

PROLETARIAN LITERATURE

1053. Alexandre, Laurie Ann. "John Reed Clubs: An
       Historical Reclamation." Master's thesis.
       California State University at Northridge, 1976.

1054. Ferrari, Arthur C. "Proletarian Literature: A
       Case of Convergence of Political and Literary
       Radicalism." **Cultural Politics.** Jerold Starr,
       ed. New York: Praeger, 1985.

1055. Homberger, Eric. "Proletarian Literature and the
       John Reed Clubs 1929-1935." **Journal of American
       Studies [Great Britain]** 13,2 (1979). Discusses
       the shifting Communist attitude toward
       Prolecult, the theory that artistic and
       intellectual ideals were latent in the masses.
       Michael Gold and the John Reed Clubs were the
       principal advocates of Prolecult. Notes that
       the Communist Party required the Clubs to follow
       the ultrarevolutionary "third period" literary
       line from 1930 to 1935 and then forced a swift
       shift to a Popular Front stance.

1056.   Peck, David R.   "The Development on an American
        Marxist Literary Criticism: the Monthly **New
        Masses**." Ph.D. dissertation. Temple University,
        1968.   Defends the Marxist criticism developed
        by those associated with the **New Masses**;
        maintains that anti-Marxist historians have
        distorted and ignored the significant
        contributions of Marxists to American literary
        life.

        See items 532 and 2038.

Mike Gold

1057.   Berman, Paul.   "East Side Story: Mike Gold, the
        Communists and the Jews." **Radical America** 17,4
        (July/Aug. 1983).   Treats Gold as a
        representative figure of a generation of Jewish
        radicals.

1058.   Brogna, John J.   "Michael Gold: Critic and
        Playwright." Ph.D. dissertation. University of
        Georgia, 1982.

1059.   Folsom, Michael.   **Mike Gold: A Literary Anthology**.
        New York: International Publishers, 1972.   See
        item 1063.

1060.   Hertz, Howard Lee.   "Writer and Revolutionary: The
        Life and Works of Michael Gold, Father of
        Proletarian Literature in the United States."
        Ph.D. dissertation. University of Texas, 1974.
        Literary biography of Gold and analysis of
        proletarian literature.   Sees the literary
        promise of **Jews Without Money** and the
        proletarian literary movement as having been
        killed by the Communist Party's capitulation to
        liberal capitalism when it adopted Popular Front
        policies.

1061.   Naficy, Azar.   "The Literary Wars of Mike Gold, A
        Study in the Background and Development of Mike
        Gold's Literary Ideas, 1920-1941." Ph.D.
        dissertation. University of Oklahoma, 1979.
        Sympathetic literary biography; notes the
        dangers of sectarianism in Gold's proletarian
        literature.

1062.   Pyros, John.   **Mike Gold: Dean of American
        Proletarian Writers**. Tarpon Springs: Dramatika
        Press, n.d.

1063. Wald, Alan M. "Mike Gold and the Radical Literary
       Movement of the 1930's." **International Socialist
       Review** 34,3 (1973). Review-essay on Michael
       Folsom's **Mike Gold: A Literary Anthology.**

       See item 1132.

BIOGRAPHICAL MATERIAL

Abel, Lionel

1064. Abel, Lionel. **The Intellectual Follies: A Memoir
       of the Literary Venture in New York and Paris.**
       New York: W.W. Norton, 1984. Memoir of a
       Trotskyist intellectual.

Adamic, Louis

1065. Adamic, Louis. **My America.** New York: Harper &
       Brothers, 1938. Adamic, a writer, was
       associated with many Communist and left-wing
       causes during his career.

Anderson, Sherwood

1066. Carlson, G. Bert, Jr. "Sherwood Anderson's
       Political Mind: The Activist Years." Ph.D.
       dissertation. University of Maryland, 1966.
       Finds that Anderson's commitment to Communism in
       the early 1930s was timid and that he welcomed
       the New Deal as an alternative to radicalism.
       See item 1043.

Brooks, Van Wyck

1067. **The Van Wyck Brooks -- Lewis Munford Letters.** New
       York: Dutton, 1970. Some letters discuss the
       relationship of Left intellectuals with
       Communism in the 1930s. See item 1132.

Cowley, Malcolm

1068. Cowley, Malcolm. **Exile's Return: A Literary
       Odyssey of the 1920's.** New York: Viking Press,
       1951. Discusses radical political currents
       among intellectuals in the 1920s and 1930s.
       Cowley was a leading liberal intellectual ally
       of the Communist Party in the 1930s.

1069. Cowley, Malcolm. "A Remembrance of the Red
       Romance." **Esquire** (March 1964).

1070. Cowley, Malcolm. **And I Worked at the Writer's
       Trade: Chapters of Literary History 1918-1978.**
       New York: Penguin Books, 1979.

1071. Cowley, Malcolm. **The Dream of the Golden
       Mountains: Remembering the 1930s.** New York:
       Viking Press, 1980. Discusses radical and
       Popular Front cultural affairs; events in which
       Cowley, often close to the Communist Party,
       participated.

1072. Hazlett, John D. "Conversion, Revisionism, and
       Revision in Malcolm Cowley's **Exile's Return.**"
       South Atlantic Quarterly 82,2 (1983). Discusses
       the shift in attitude toward Communism and
       Marxism between Cowley's 1934 and his 1951
       autobiographical narratives.

1073. Lynn, Kenneth S. "Malcolm Cowley Forgets." **The
       American Spectator** (Oct. 1980). Critical
       commentary on Cowley's **The Golden Mountains** for
       distorting the record of Cowley's support for
       Communist causes in the 1930s.

Dos Passos, John

*   Carr, Virginia Spencer. **Dos Passos: A Life.**
       Garden City: Doubleday, 1984. See item 2051.
       Detailed biography.

1074. Dos Passos, John. "Reminiscences of a Middle-
       Class Radical." **National Review** (Jan. 18, 1956).

1075. Dos Passos, John. **The Theme Is Freedom.** New York:
       Dodd, Mead, 1956.

1076. Ludington, Townsend. **John Dos Passos: A Twentieth
       Century Odyssey.** New York: E. P. Dutton, 1980.
       Relates Dos Passos' shift from close ally of the
       Communist Party to firm anti-Communist.

       See items 1033, 1043, 1132 and 2051.

Eastman, Max

1077. Diggins, John P. "Getting Hegel Out of History:
       Max Eastman's Quarrel with History." **American
       Historical Review** 79 (1974).

1078. Eastman, Max. **Love and Revolution: My Journey
       Through an Epoch.** New York: Random House, 1964.
       Discusses his association with Trotsky and other
       Communist leaders.

1079. O'Neill, William L. **The Last Romantic: The Life of Max Eastman.** New York: Oxford University Press, 1978. Eastman moved from Bohemian and literary radicalism to Communism and, in the end, to anti-Communism.

See item 872.

Farrell, James T.

1080. Wald, Alan M. **James T. Farrell: The Revolutionary Socialist Years.** New York: New York University Press, 1978. Discusses Farrell's break with the Communist Party in the 1930s.

See item 1043.

Fast, Howard

1081. Fast, Howard. **The Naked God: The Writer and the Communist Party.** New York: Praeger, 1957.

1082. Wald, Alan M. "The Legacy of Howard Fast." **Radical America** 17,1 (1983).

Herberg, Will

1083. Gnall, Janet Marita. "Will Herberg, Jewish Theologian: A Biblical-Existential Approach to Religion." Ph.D. dissertation. Drew University, 1983. Discusses Herberg's early Communism and its influence on his later thinking. See item 1033.

Herbst, Josephine

1084. Langer, Elinor. **Josephine Herbst: The Story She Could Never Tell.** Boston: Little Brown, 1984. Biography of a literary friend of the Communist Party.

1085. Rubinstein, Annette. "Fiction of the Thirties: Josephine Herbst." **Science & Society** 49 (Spring 1985).

Hicks, Granville

1086. Hicks, Granville. **Where We Came Out.** New York: Viking, 1954.

1087. Hicks, Granville. **Part of the Truth: An Autobiography.** New York: Harcourt, Brace and World, 1965.

Hofstadter, Richard

1088. Baker, Susan Stout. "Out of the Engagement.
          Richard Hofstadter: The Genesis of a Historian."
          Ph.D. dissertation. Case Western Reserve
          University, 1982. Discusses Hofstadter's
          association with Communism.

1089. Baker, Susan Stout. **Radical Beginnings: Richard
          Hofstadter and the 1930s.** Westport: Greenwood,
          1985.

1090. Singal, Daniel Joseph. "Beyond Consensus: Richard
          Hofstadter and American Historiography."
          American Historical Review 89,4 (Oct. 1984).
          Notes Hofstadter's involvement with Communism
          and with intellectuals close to **Partisan Review.**

          See item 1549.

Josephson, Matthew

1091. Shi, David E. **Matthew Josephson, Bourgeois
          Bohemian.** New Haven: Yale University Press,
          1981.

Matthiessen, F.O.

1092. Levin, Harry. "The Private Life of F.O.
          Matthiessen." **New York Review of Books** (July 20,
          1978).

1093. Lynn, Kenneth S. "Teaching: F.O. Matthiessen."
          American Scholar (Winter 1976-1977).

1094. Sweezy, Paul M., and Leo Huberman, eds. **F.O.
          Matthiessen: A Collective Portrait.** New York:
          1950. Sympathetic essays on a leading literary
          intellectual and close friend of the Communist
          Party.

1095. White, George Abbott. "Ideology and Literature:
          American Renaissance and F.O. Matthiessen."
          Literature in Revolution. George Abbot White and
          Charles Newman, eds. New York: Holt, Rinehart
          & Winston, 1972.

Olsen, Tillie.

1096. Orr, Miriam Elaine Neil. "Tillie Olsen's Vision:
          A Different Way of Keeping Faith." Ph.D.
          dissertation. Emory University, 1985. Discusses
          the Communist influences on Olsen's writings.

Sandoz, Mari.

1097. Bancroft, Caroline. "Two Women Writers: Caroline
       Bancroft Recalls Her Days with Mari Sandoz."
       Colorado Heritage 1 (1982). Notes that Sandoz
       admired Communism for a period.

Steffens, Lincoln

1098. Palermo, Patrick F. **Lincoln Steffens.** Boston:
       Twayne, 1978.

1099. Steffens, Lincoln. **The Autobiography of Lincoln
       Steffens.** New York: Harcourt, Brace, 1931.
       Notes his observations on Communists and
       Communism.

1100. Whitfield, Stephen J. "Muckraking Lincoln
       Steffens." **Virginia Quarterly Review** 54,1
       (1978). Analyzes Steffens' writings, including
       his attitude toward Communism.

       See item 1048.

Trilling, Lionel

1101. Anderson, Quentin. "On the Middle of the
       Journey." **Art, Politics and Will: Essays in
       Honor of Lionel Trilling.** Quentin Anderson,
       Stephen Donadio and Steven Marcus, eds. New
       York: Basic Books, 1977.

1102. Trilling, Lionel. **The Middle of the Journey.**
       Garden City: Doubleday, 1957. An influential
       novel depicting the literary-cultural life of
       the 1930s and 1940s.

Wilson, Edmund

1103. Wilson, Edmund. **Edmund Wilson: Letters on
       Literature and Politics 1912-1972.** Elena Wilson,
       ed. New York: Farrar, Straus & Giroux, 1977.
       Contains letters discussing the attitude of
       Wilson and other liberal intellectuals toward
       Communism in the 1930s. See items 872 and 1595.

20

COMMUNISM AND POETS

1104. Fabre, Michel. "Walt Whitman and the Rebel Poets:
A Note on Whitman's Reputation Among Radical
Writers During the Depression." **Walt Whitman
Review** 12 (1966).

1105. Guttmann, Allen. "Walter Lowenfels' Poetic
Politics." **Massachusetts Review** 6 (1965).

1106. Hall, Tim. "Henry George Weiss, Rebel Poet."
Struggle [Marxist-Leninist Party, Detroit] 1,1
(1985). Discusses some of the poems of Weiss,
who published in Communist Party journals until
1935 when he was criticized for left-wing
sectarianism.

1107. Hall, Tim. "W.S. Stacy, Poet of the Working-Class
Struggle." **Struggle** [Marxist-Leninist Party,
Detroit] 1,2 (1985). Discusses the work of a
little-known Communist poet of the early 1930s.

1108. Novak, Estelle G. "Proletarian Poetry in the
United States: Theory and Practice from 1926 to
1939." Ph.D. dissertation. University of
California, Los Angeles, 1968. Sympathetic
survey of Marxist-Leninist poetics in the 1930s;
finds significant contributions to American
poetry by Marxism and Marxist poets.

1109. Santora, Patricia Bridget. "The Poetry and Prose
of Kenneth Flexner Fearing." Ph.D. dissertation.
University of Maryland, 1982. Notes that
Fearing's poetry was praised by Communists in
the 1920s, but he responded passively.

1110. Wald, Alan M. "The Pilgrimages of Sherry Mangan:
From Aesthete to Revolutionary Socialist."
Pembroke Magazine 8 (1977).

1111. Wald, Alan M. "Erasing the Thirties: Boston's
Forgotten Marxist Poets." **New Boston Review** 6,1
(1981).

1112. Wald, Alan M. "From Antinomianism to
       Revolutionary Marxism: John Wheelwright and the
       New England Rebel Tradition." **Marxist
       Perspectives** 3 (1980).

1113. Wald, Alan M. **The Revolutionary Imagination: The
       Poetry and Politics of John Wheelwright and
       Sherry Mangan.** Chapel Hill: University of North
       Carolina Press, 1983.

See item 707.

21

COMMUNISM AND ART

*   Baigell, Matthew, and Julia Williams, eds.
      **Artists Against War and Fascism: Papers of the
      First American Artists' Congress.** New
      Brunswick: Rutgers University Press, 1986.
      Cited as item 2084. Papers from the 1936
      meeting of this Popular Front organization along
      with a sympathetic commentary by the editors.

1114. Bongartz, Roy. "Who Was This Man: and Why did He
      Paint such Terrible Things about Us." **American
      Heritage** 29,1 (1978). Discusses the art of the
      Mexican Communist Diego Rivera and the
      controversy regarding his propagandistic mural
      in Rockerfeller Center.

1115. Fitzgerald, Richard. **Art and Politics:
      Cartoonists of the Masses and Liberator.**
      Westport: Greenwood, 1973.

1116. Gahn, Joseph A. "The America of William Gropper,
      Radical Cartoonist." Ph.D. dissertation.
      Syracuse University, 1966. Biography of a
      leading **New Masses** cartoonist and social protest
      artist.

*   Kramer, Hilton. "The Big Red Paintpot." **The New
      York Times Book Review** April 27, 1986. Cited as
      item 2975. Essay-review of **Artists Against War
      and Fascism** (Matthew Baigtell and Julia
      Williams, eds.) highly critical of the American
      Artists' Congress. See item 2084.

1117. Lawless, Ken. "'Continental Imprisonment':
      Rockwell Kent and the Passport Controversy."
      Antioch Review 38,3 (1980). Describes Kent's
      successful legal action regarding the refusal of
      the U.S. government in 1950 to issue a passport
      to him because of the artist's relationship with
      the Communist Party.

1118. Mathews, Jane DeHart. "Art and Politics in Cold
       War America." **American Historical Review** 81,4
       (1976). Discusses the controversy around
       federal cultural exchange programs of the late
       1940s and 1950s involving charges of Marxist
       influence. Suggests that the hostility toward
       modern art by right-wing anti-Communists
       reflected the preservationist character of the
       latter.

1119. McCoy, Garnett. "Poverty, Politics and Artists,
       1930-1945." **Art in America** 53 (Aug.-Sept. 1965).

1120. McDonald, William F. **Federal Relief
       Administration and the Arts.** Columbus: Ohio
       State University Press, 1969. Notes controversy
       about Communist involvement in some FRA art
       projects.

1121. McKinzie, Richard D. **The New Deal for Artists.**
       Princeton: Princeton University Press, 1973.
       Notes controversy regarding charges of Communist
       involvement in some New Deal art projects.

1122. Monroe, Gerald M. "The American Artists Congress
       and the Invasion of Finland." **Archives of
       American Art Journal** 15 (1975).

1123. Monroe, Gerald M. "The 1930's: Art, Ideology and
       the WPA." **Art in America** 63,6 (1975). Notes
       controversy over links of some WPA artists to
       the Communist Party.

1124. Starr, Jerold M. "Revolutionary Art versus Art
       for the Revolution: Dadaists and Leninists,
       1916-1923." **Cultural Politics.** Jerold Starr, ed.
       New York: Praeger, 1985.

22

COMMUNISM, RADICALISM, AND DRAMA

1125. Bentley, Eric. "Broadway's Missing Communists: Theatre Without Candor." **Commentary** 22 (Sept. 1956). Notes that a number of Communist Broadway personalities prefer to keep their loyalties secret.

1126. Clurman, Harold. **The Fervent Years: The Story of the Group Theatre and the Thirties.** New York: Knopf, 1945. Discusses radical and protest theatre.

1127. Flanagan, Hallie. **Arena: The History of the Federal Theatre.** New York: Benjamin Bloom, 1965. Head of the New Deal's Federal Theatre Project discusses the Dies Committee charges of Communist influence in the agency.

1128. Frank, Felicia. "The Magazines **Workers Theatre, New Theatre,** and **New Theatre and Films** as Documents of the American Left-Wing Theatre Movement of the 1930s." Ph.D. dissertation. City University of New York, 1976.

1129. Goldman, Harry, and Mel Gordon. "Workers' Theatre in America: A Survey 1913-1978." **Journal of American Culture** 1 (Spring 1978).

1130. Himelstein, Morgan Yale. "Social Drama and the Communist Party in America, 1929-1941." Ph.D. dissertation. Columbia University, 1958. Concludes that the Communist Party played only a small role in the social drama of the 1930s. The organizations under close Communist control [the Prolebuehne, the Workers' Laboratory Theatre, Theatre Collective, Theatre of Action, League of Workers' Theatres (1932-1934), and the New Theatre League (1934-1941)] were short lived or popular failures. Most social drama was produced outside of Communist circles except for Clifford Odets' "Waiting For Lefty" and Irwin

Shaw's "Bury the Dead." Judges that Communist insistence on conformity to rigid political themes stifled production of good drama.

1131. Himelstein, Morgan. **Drama Was a Weapon: The Left-Wing Theatre in New York 1929-1941.** New Brunswick: Rutgers University Press, 1963.

1132. Levine, Ira Alan. "Theatre in Revolt: Left-wing Dramatic Theory in the United States (1911-1939)." Ph.D. dissertation. University of Toronto (Canada), 1980. Examines attempts to formulate a revolutionary aesthetic for dramatic art. Discusses the attitudes of Van Wyck Brooks, Emma Goldman, John Howard Lawson, Michael Gold, John Dos Passos, John Gassner, and Mordecai Gorelik. Finds that one tendency was the revolutionary dramatic form such as the experiments of the New Playwrights Theatre, agit-prop theatre, and left-wing musical revues, and living newspapers; another tendency was to invest dramatic realism with Marxist precepts.

1133. Mathews, Jane DeHart. **The Federal Theatre, 1935-1939: Plays, Relief, and Politics.** Princeton: Princeton University Press, 1967. Discusses controversy over Communist influence in the Federal Theatre.

1134. Miller, M. Lawrence. "Original Federal Theatre Protest Plays -- 1936-1939: New Deal Contributions to the American Drama of Social Concern." Ph.D. dissertation. University of California, Los Angeles, 1968. Notes that a sample of Federal Theatre plays shows strong Left-radical orientation.

1135. Samuels, Raphael, ed. **Theatres of the Left, 1880-1935.** Boston: Routledge & Kegan Paul, 1985. Analysis of the workers' theatre movement in the U.S. and Britain.

1136. Stewart, Donald Ogden. **By a Stroke of Luck: An Autobiography.** London: Paddington Press, 1975. Stewart was a prominent playwright and secret Communist Party member in the 1930s. See item 1048.

1137. Todras, Arthur. "The Liberal Paradox: Clifford Odets, Elia Kazan, and Arthur Miller." Ph.D. dissertation. Indiana University, 1980. Examines how Communism and anti-Communism shaped artistic vision.

1138. Vacha, J.E. "The Case of the Runaway Opera: The
       Federal Theatre and Marc Blitzstein's **The Cradle
       Will Rock.**" **New York History** 62 (1981).
       Discusses the controversy regarding the Federal
       Theatre Project administration's cancellation of
       the opening of a proletarian musical play and
       the defiance of the order by producer John
       Houseman and director Orson Wells.

BIOGRAPHICAL MATERIAL

Lawson, John Howard

1139. Brown, Richard P. "John Howard Lawson as an
       Activist Playwright: 1923-34." Ph.D.
       dissertation. Tulane University, 1964. Finds
       that Lawson, a Marxist social protest playwright
       connected to the New Playwright's Theatre, made
       his dramatic point indirectly through a
       portrayal of social structures rather that
       through hortatory dialogue.

1140. McCreath, Harrison W. "A Rhetorical Analysis of
       the Plays of John Howard Lawson." Ph.D.
       dissertation. Stanford University, 1965. A
       close analysis of Lawson's proletarian plays.

       See item 1132.

Odets, Clifford

*   Mendelson, Michael J. **Clifford Odets, Humane
       Dramatist.** Deland: Everett/Edwards, 1969. Cited
       as item 2077.

1141. Murray, Edward. **Clifford Odets: The Thirties and
       After.** New York: Ungar, 1968.

1142. Shuman, R. Baird. **Clifford Odets.** New York:
       Twayne Pub., 1962.

1143. Weales, Gerald. **Clifford Odets: Playwright.** New
       York: Pagasus, 1971.

       See items 1130 and 1137.

23

COMMUNISM, FILM, RADIO, AND TELEVISION

RADICAL PHOTOGRAPHY AND DOCUMENTARY FILM

1144. Alexander, William. **Film on the Left: American Documentary Film from 1931 to 1942.** Princeton: Princeton University Press, 1981. Survey and analysis of social protest and left-wing documentary film making in the 1930s. Includes coverage of the Communist-aligned Workers' Film and Photo League, Nykino, and Frontier Films.

1145. Bethune, Beverly Moore. "The New York City Photo League: A Political History." Ph.D. dissertation. University of Minnesota, 1979. Recounts the political and politically linked photographic activities of the Communist-aligned Film and Photo League (1930-36) and the New York City Photo League (1936-51).

1146. Campbell, Russell. "Radical Cinema in the United States, 1930-1942: The Work of the Film and Photo League, Nykino, and Frontier Films." Ph.D. dissertation. Northwestern University, 1978.

1147. Campbell, Russell. **Cinema Strikes Back! Radical Filmmaking in the United States, 1930-1942.** Ann Arbor: UMI Press, 1982. Scholarly study of the Communist-aligned Workers' Film and Photo League, Nykino, and Frontier Films. Judges that the adoption of a Popular Front stance caused Frontier Films to move away from the class struggle, adopt Hollywood devices, and reinforce the status quo.

1148. Culbert, David. "REDS: Propaganda, Docudrama, and Hollywood." **Labor History** 24,1 (1983). Reviews "REDS," a commercial film portrayal of the life of John Reed.

1149. Fishbein, Leslie. "A Lost Legacy of Labor Films." **Film and History** 9,2 (1979). Discusses the work of the Communist-aligned Workers' Film and Photo League in filming Communist organized marches and strikes during the Depression.

1150.   Hurwitz, Leo. "One Man's Voyage: Ideas and Films in the 1930's." **Cinema Journal** 15 (Fall 1975). Memoir by a radical documentary filmmaker close to the Communist Party.

1151.   Klehr, Harvey. "Seeing Red 'Seeing Red.'" **Labor History** 26,1 (Winter 1985). Critical review-essay on the film "Seeing Red: Stories of American Communists."

1152.   Reichert, Julia, and James Klein. "Seeing Red: Stories of American Communists." Heartland Productions, 1984. Sympathetic documentary film on American Communists. See items 1151 and 2010.

1153.   Rosenzweig, Roy. "Working Class Struggles in the Great Depression: The Film Record." **Film Library Quarterly** 13 (1980).

1154.   Rosenzweig, Roy. "United Action Means Victory: Militant Americanism on Film." **Labor History** 24,2 (1983). Discusses the militant Americanism of a UAW documentary film and the patriotic themes of the Popular Front cultural line. Argues that Popular Front Americanism had radical potential.

COMMUNISM AND HOLLYWOOD

1155.   Ceplair, Larry, and Steven Englund. **The Inquisition in Hollywood: Politics in the Film Community, 1930-1960.** Garden City: Anchor Press, 1980. Looks at Communist and other radical political activity in Hollywood in the late 1930s; sees the controversy over the Hollywood Ten as an attack by largely malignant anti-Communists upon largely benign left-wingers.

1156.   Dunne, Philip. **Take Two: A Life in Movies and Politics.** New York: McGraw-Hill, 1980. Argues that the Screen Writers Guild was never under Communist control.

1157.   Grenier, Richard. "The Curious Career of Costa-Gavras." **Commentary** 73,4 (1982). Reviews the anti-American and pro-Communist content of the films of Costa-Gavras.

1158. Jones, Dorothy B. "Communism and the Movies."
       Report on Blacklisting. John Cogley, ed. New
       York: Fund for the Republic, 1956.

1159. Navasky, Victor S. **Naming Names.** New York: Viking
       Press, 1980. Discusses congressional
       investigations of Communist Party influence in
       Hollywood and the subsequent blacklisting of
       those who refused to cooperate. Treats left-
       wing Hollywood figures as heroic victims of
       anti-Communist hysteria. Judges that any
       cooperation with the House Un-American
       Activities Committee, including telling the
       truth, was immoral and that those who cooperated
       had self-interested motivations in most cases.
       See item 1166.

1160. Schwartz, Nancy Lynn. **The Hollywood Writers'
       Wars.** New York: Alfred A. Knopf, 1982. Covers
       the strife within the movie industry in the late
       1930s and 1940s around the efforts of the Screen
       Writers Guild to establish itself. Sympathetic
       to Communist influence in the SWG, hostile to
       anti-Communists.

1161. Sklar, Robert. **Movie-Made America.** New York:
       Random House, 1975. Discusses congressional
       investigations of Communism in Hollywood.

1162. Small, Melvin. "Buffoons and Brave Hearts:
       Hollywood Portrays the Russians, 1939-1944."
       California Historical Quarterly 52 (Winter
       1973).

1163. Small, Melvin. "How We Learned to Love the
       Russians: American Media and the Soviet Union
       During World War II." **Historian** 36 (May 1974).

1164. Small, Melvin. "Hollywood and Teaching About
       Russian American Relations." **Film and History**
       10,1 (1980). Discusses the attitude toward
       Communism and the Soviet Union suggested by a
       selection of films from the late 1930s to the
       1960s.

1165. Suber, Howard. "Politics and Popular Culture:
       Hollywood at Bay, 1933-1953." **American Jewish
       History** 68,4 (June 1979). Sees hysteria and
       repression dominating the United States during
       the early Cold War. That hysteria was used by
       anti-Semites, adventurers and those opposed to
       trade unions to settle longstanding labor and
       political conflicts in the film industry.

See item 1346.

BLACKLISTING OF COMMUNISTS AND COMMUNIST SYMPATHIZERS

1166. Biskind, Peter. "The Past is Prologue: The Blacklist in Hollywood." **Radical America** 15,3 (1981). Sympathetic commentary on Navasky's Naming Names; concludes that liberal anti-Communists adopted anti-Communism in order to avoid political attacks upon themselves.

1167. Cogley, John. **Report on Blacklisting.** New York: Fund for the Republic, 1956. Vol. I, movies; Vol. II, radio and television.

1168. Kanfer, Stefan. **A Journal of the Plague Years.** New York: Atheneum, 1973. Journalistic and sensationalistic account of discrimination against Communists in the movie and broadcasting industries.

1169. Kramer, Hilton. "The Blacklist and the Cold War." **The New York Times Arts and Leisure Section** (Oct. 3, 1976).

1170. Lardner, Ring, Jr. "My Life on the Blacklist." **Saturday Evening Post** (Oct. 14, 1961).

1171. Spector, Bert A. "'Wasn't That a Time?' Pete Seeger and the Anti-Communist Crusade, 1940-1968." Ph.D. dissertation. University of Missouri, 1977. Sees Seeger as the victim of opportunistic professional anti-Communists and self-proclaimed patriots seeking to impose their own political standards on American popular culture.

1172. Spector, Bert A. "The Weavers: A Case History in Show Business Blacklisting." **Journal of American Culture** 5 (Fall 1982).

1173. Suber, Howard. "The Anti-Communist Blacklist in the Hollywood Motion Picture Industry." Ph.D. dissertation. University of California, Los Angeles, 1968. Finds that 214 people were blacklisted, mostly writers, and that the blacklist was effective until 1959 after which it eased and disappeared when studios decided that there was no loss of audience if blacklisted writers were used. Discusses the criteria used in blacklisting a person and the tactics used by blacklisted persons to continue work in the movie industry.

1174. Vaughn, Robert. **Only Victims: A Study of Show Business Blacklisting.** New York: Putnam's, 1972.

THE COLD WAR AND ANTI-COMMUNISM IN FILMS AND TELEVISION

1175. Adler, Les K. "The Politics of Culture: Hollywood and the Cold War." **The Specter.** Robert Griffith and Athan Theoharis, eds. New York: New Viewpoints, 1974.

1176. Dowdy, Andrew. **The Films of the Fifties.** New York: Morrow, 1973. Discusses reflections of the Cold War in movies.

1177. Leab, Daniel J. "How Red is My Valley: Hollywood, the Cold War Movies, and I MARRIED A COMMUNIST." Unpublished paper, 1983 American Historical Association convention.

1178. Leab, Daniel J. "How Red is My Valley: Hollywood, the Cold War Movies, and I MARRIED A COMMUNIST." **Journal of Contemporary History** 19 (Jan. 1984).

1179. Leab, Daniel J. "The Hollywood Feature Film as Cold Warrior." **OAH Newsletter** 13,2 (May 1985).

1180. MacDonald, J. Fred. "The Cold War as Entertainment in 'Fifties Television." **Journal of Popular Film and Television** 7,1 (1978).

* MacDonald, J. Fred. **Television and the Red Menace: The Video Road to Vietnam.** New York: Praeger, 1985. Cited as item 2068. Argues that television, both in its news coverage and its entertainment programs, heavily promoted rigid Cold War anti-Communism, blacklisted "progressives," presented a negative image of the Soviet Union and Communism, exalted American militarism, and helped bring about America's participation in the Vietnam war.

1181. Maland, Charles. "DR. STRANGELOVE (1964): Nightmare Comedy and the Ideology of Liberal Consensus." **American Quarterly** 31,5 (1979). Regards the American cultural consensus that American society was basically sound and that Communism threatened the United States as a major cause of the Cold War and the nuclear arms

race. Kubrick's film, "Dr. Strangelove," used
black comedy to attack such thinking.

1182.   McConnell, Frank D. "Pickup on South Street and
the Metamorphosis of the Thriller." **Film
Heritage,** 8,3 (1973). Discusses the effects of
McCarthyism on Samuel Fuller's films.

1183.   Rogin, Michael. "Kiss Me Deadly: Communism,
Motherhood, and Cold War Movies."
Representations 6 (Spring 1984).

1184.   Sayre, Nora. **Running Time: Films of the Cold War.**
New York: Dial Press, 1982. Argues that
numerous films in the 1950s contained
objectionable anti-Communist propaganda.

1185.   Skinner, James M. "Cliche and Convention in
Hollywood's Cold War Anti-Communist Films."
North Dakota Quarterly 46,3 (1978). Discusses
anti-Communist themes in films of the late 1940s
and early 1950s.

1186.   Wolfe, Gary K. "Dr. Strangelove, Red Alert, and
Patterns of Paranoia in the 1950's." **Journal of
Popular Film** 5,1 (1976). Sees the film Dr.
Strangelove and the novel **Red Alert** as
demonstrating the paranoid fear of Communism
that obsessed America in the 1950s.

See items 1192-1196.

BIOGRAPHICAL MATERIAL

Bessie, Alvah

1187.   Bessie, Alvah. **Inquisition in Eden.** New York:
Macmillan, 1965. One of the Hollywood Ten
(Hollywood figures who refused to testify to the
House Un-American Activities Committee)
discusses controversies over Communists and
their allies in the Hollywood film industry.

1188.   Bush, Lawrence. **Bessie.** New York: Seaview/Putnam,
1983.

1189.   Miller, Gariel. "Two Alvah Bessies: the Innocent
and the Embittered." **Los Angeles Times** (Nov. 27,
1977).

Cole, Lester

1190.   Cole, Lester. **Hollywood Red: The Autobiography of
        Lester Cole.** Palo Alto: Ramparts Press, 1981.

Geer, Will

1191.   Norton, Sally Osborne. "A Historical Study of
        Actor Will Geer, His Life and Work in the
        Context of Twentieth-Century American Social,
        Political, and Theatrical History." Ph.D.
        dissertation. University of Southern California,
        1981. Discusses Geer's association with
        Communism and his experience with the anti-
        Communist blacklist.

Kazan, Elia

1192.   Hey, Kenneth. "Ambivalence as a Theme in **On the
        Waterfront** (1954): An Inter Disciplinary
        Approach to Film Study." **American Quarterly** 31,5
        (Winter 1979). Discusses the influence of past
        Communist adherence and House Un-American
        Activities Committee testimony on Elia Kazan's
        film **On the Waterfront;** highly critical of Kazan
        for speaking (truthfully) to HUAC.

1193.   Maland, Charles. "ON THE WATERFRONT (1954): Film
        and the Dilemmas of American Liberalism in the
        McCarthy Era." **American Studies in Scandinavia
        [Norway]** 14,2 (1982).

1194.   Pennington, Renee. "The Agony of Kazan's
        Informer." **The Thousand Eyes Magazine** 8 (Jan.
        1976). Sees **On the Waterfront** as an expression
        of Kazan's agony over answering (truthfully)
        questions of the House Un-American Activities
        Committee.

1195.   Tailleur, Roger. "Elia Kazan and the House Un-
        American Activities Committee." **Film Comment** 2
        (Fall 1966).

1196.   Vanderwood, Paul J. "An American Cold-Warrior:
        Viva, Zapata! (1952)." **American History/American
        Film: Interpreting the American Image.** New York:
        Ungar, 1979.

        See item 1137.

Trumbo, Dalton

1197. Cook, Bruce. **Dalton Trumbo.** New York: Scribner,
          1977.   Biography of a Hollywood writer close to
          the Communist Party.

Schary, Dore

1198. Schary, Dore. **Heyday: An Autobiography.** Boston:
          Little, Brown, 1979.   Discusses blacklisting in
          Hollywood.

24

COMMUNISM AND MUSIC

1199. Clurman, Harold. **All People Are Famous.** New York: Harcourt Brace Jovanovich, 1974. Contains a biographical essay on Hans Eisler, a well-known composer and close friend of the Communist Party.

1200. Denisoff, Ronald Serge. "The Proletarian Renascence: The Folkness of the Ideological Folk." **Journal of American Folklore** 82 (1969). Stresses the predominance of Left and Communist political themes and goals over authentic folk elements in the folk music movement of the late 1930s and 1940s.

1201. Denisoff, Ronald Serge. "Urban Folk 'Movement' Research: Value Free?" **Western Folklore** 28 (1969).

1202. Denisoff, Ronald Serge. "Folk Consciousness: People's Music and American Communism." Ph.D. dissertation. Simon Fraser University (Canada), 1970. Concludes that the use of folk music as a propaganda medium was based on the Communist Party's theories about the nature of mass man. These theories defined folk music as "people's music" and folk artists as "people's artists" and led to Communist support for the Almanac Singers, People's Songs, and People's Artists. Judges that the theory was mistaken because folk music was not the music of the bulk of urban dwellers of the 1930s and 1940s, most folk material being unfamiliar to urban audiences, and that the use of folk material tended to isolate rather than expand the radical movements which adopted such music.

1203. Denisoff, Ronald Serge. "'Take It Easy, But Take It': The Almanac Singers." **Journal of American Folklore** 83,327 (1970). Discusses the 1930s and 1940s labor and social protest songs of the

Almanac Singers, a group associated with the
Communist Party.

1204.   Denisoff, Ronald Serge, and Richard Reuss.   "The
Protest Songs and Skits of American
Trotskyists." **Journal of Popular Culture** 6
(1972).

1205.   Dunaway, David King.   "Unsung Songs of Protest:
The Composers Collective of New York." **New York
Folklore** 5,1-2 (1979).   Discusses the formation
the radical Composers Collective in New York
City (1931-1936) and its evolution from a firm
antifolk song position to later support of folk
song materials.

1206.   Dunaway, David King.   "Pete Seeger and Modern
American Topical Song Movements." Ph.D.
dissertation. University of California,
Berkeley, 1981.   Sympathetic discussion of
Seeger, the Composers Collective, the Almanac
Singers, and People's Songs.   Treats song as a
democratic art form and mode of expression of
the poor in America's repressive and heavily
censored society.

1207.   Klein, Joe.   **Woody Guthrie: A Life.** New York:
Knopf, 1980.   Discusses Guthrie's relationship
with Popular Front culture.

1208.   Lieberman, Robbie.   "American Communism and the
Politics of Culture: the Case of People's Songs,
1946-1949." Unpublished paper, 1983 American
Studies Association convention.

1209.   Lieberman, Robbie.   "'My Song Is My Weapon:'
People's Songs and the Politics of Culture,
1946-1949." Ph.D. dissertation. University of
Michigan, 1984.   Treats People's Songs as a link
between the Popular Front of the 1930s and the
civil rights movement and New Left of the 1950s
and 1960s.   Finds that People's Songs sought a
people's culture based on folk and folk-style
songs, group singing, and a vision of a peaceful
and just world.   The group was sustained despite
attacks on it by the 'wholeness' and 'quality'
of the Communist movement culture.

1210.   Peterson, Frank Ross.   "Protest Songs for Peace
and Freedom: People's Songs and the 1948
Progressives." **Rocky Mountain Social Science
Journal** 9 (Jan. 1972).

1211.   Reuss, Richard A.   "The Roots of American Left-
        Wing Interest in Folksong." **Labor History** 12,2
        (Spring 1971).   Notes that prior to Communist
        interest in the 1930s, no political group
        stressed folk materials.   Discusses the
        unsuccessful effort in the late 1920s and early
        1930s of the Composers Collective and other
        groups associated with the Communist Party to
        develop a viable proletarian music and the turn
        to folk materials in the mid-1930s as the
        substitute.

1212.   Reuss, Richard A.   "American Folksongs and Left-
        Wing Politics: 1935-56." **Journal of the Folklore
        Institute** 12,2-3 (1975).   Discusses Communist
        and Leftist influences on American folk songs.

1213.   Seeger, Pete, and David King Dunaway.   **How Can I
        Keep From Singing: Pete Seeger.** New York:
        McGraw-Hill, 1981.

1214.   Warren-Findley, Jannelle.   "Musicians and
        Mountaineers: The Resettlement Administration's
        Music Program in Appalachia, 1935-37."
        Appalachian Journal 7,1-2 (1979-80).   Discusses
        the attempt of Charles Seeger of the Leftist
        Composers' Collective of New York City to use
        the music program of the New Deal's Resettlement
        Administration to mobilize impoverished
        Appalachian families by integrating music, art,
        and political propaganda.

        See items 1171 and 1172.

GENERAL

1215. Alsop, Stewart, and Thomas Braden. **Sub Rosa, the OSS and American Espionage.** New York: Reynal and Hitchcock, 1948. Notes the use of American Communists in the OSS. See item 1225.

1216. Boveri, Margret. **Treason in the Twentieth Century.** New York: Putnam, 1963.

1217. Burnham, James. **The Web of Subversion: Underground Networks in the U.S. Government.** New York: John Day, 1954.

1218. Dallin, David. **Soviet Espionage.** New Haven: Yale University Press, 1955. Discusses the Communist Party's links to Soviet espionage.

1219. de Toledano, Ralph. **Spies, Dupes, and Diplomats.** New York: Duell, Sloane and Pearce, 1952. Journalistic expose.

1220. de Toledano, Ralph. **The Greatest Plot in History.** New York: Duell, Sloan and Pearce, 1963. Journalistic examination of postwar atomic spy cases.

1221. Gramont, Sanche de. **The Secret War.** New York: Putnam, 1962. Discusses the Coplon case and Soviet espionage.

1222. Lamphere, Robert, and Tom Shachtman. **The FBI - KGB War: A Special Agent's Story.** New York: Random House, 1986. Memoir by a veteran FBI agent; discusses links between the Communist Party and Soviet espionage.

1223. Levine, Isaac Don. "The Mystery of Mrs. Earl Browder." **Plain Talk** (Dec. 1948). Charges that Earl Browder's wife entered the U.S. using the

passport of Edith Berkman, a Communist Party
textile union organizer who had dropped out of
sight. See item 1226.

1224. Moorehead, Alan. **The Traitors.** New York: Harper
and Row, 1952. Discusses the atomic spy cases
of the postwar period.

1225. Smith, R. Harris. **OSS.** New York: Delta, 1973.
Notes the recruitment of American Communists by
the OSS. See item 1215.

1226. Solow, Herbert. "Stalin's American Passport
Mill." **American Mercury** (July 1939). Discusses
the Communist Party's cooperation with Soviet
authorities to obtain American passports. See
item 1223.

1227. Valtin, Jan. **Out of the Night.** New York: Alliance
Book Corp., 1941. Memoir by an agent of the
Comintern seamen's organization sent to the US.

1228. Wagner, J. Richard. "Congress and Canadian-
American Relations: The Norman Case." **Rocky
Mountain Social Science Journal** 10,3 (1973).
Recounts the Congressional role in a Communist
espionage case involving a Canadian diplomat.

1229. West, Rebecca. **The New Meaning of Treason.** New
York: Viking, 1964.

1230. Weyl, Nathaniel. **Treason.** Washington, D.C.:
Public Affairs Press, 1950. Weyl was a
Communist Party member and member of the
Ware group in the Department of Agriculture.

1231. Weyl, Nathaniel. **The Battle Against Disloyalty.**
New York: Crowell, 1951.

1232. Wittenberg, Philip, ed. **The Lamont Case.** New
York: Horizon Press, 1957.

ESPIONAGE CASES

Bentley, Elizabeth

1233. Bentley, Elizabeth. **Out of Bondage, The Story of
Elizabeth Bentley.** New York: Devin-Adair Co.,
1951. Autobiography of an ex-Communist who had
taken part in Soviet espionage.

1234. Schneir, Walter, and Miriam Schneir. "The Story
       the 'Red Spy Queen' Didn't Tell." **The Nation**
       (June 15, 1983). Attacks the credibility of
       Elizabeth Bentley, a former Soviet spy.

       See item 1751.

Field, Noel

1235. Field, Noel. "Hitching Our Wagon to a Star."
       Mainstream (Jan. 1961).

1236. Lewis, Flora. **Red Dawn, The Story of Noel Field.**
       New York: Doubleday, 1965. An account of Field,
       who was involved in Soviet espionage in the US
       and who was a victim of Stalin's anti-Semitic
       purges.

The Hiss-Chambers Case

1237. Altman, George T. "The Added Witness." **The Nation**
       (Oct. 1, 1960). A defense of Hiss.

1238. Aptheker, Herbert. "Behind the Hiss Frameup."
       Masses & Mainstream (Oct. 1953). Communist view
       of the Hiss case.

1239. Barros, James. "Alger Hiss and Harry Dexter
       White: The Canadian Connection." **Orbis** 21,3
       (Fall 1977).

1240. Buckholder, Roger Glen. "Whittaker Chambers: The
       Need to Believe." Thesis. Harvard University,
       1965.

1241. Buckley, William F., Jr. "The End of Whittaker
       Chambers." **Esquire** (Sept. 1962).

1242. Buckley, William F., Jr., ed. **Odyssey of a
       Friend: Whittaker Chambers' Letters to William
       F. Buckley, Jr., 1954-1961.** New York: Putnam,
       1969.

1243. Bullitt, William Marshall. **A Factual Review of
       the Whittaker Chambers--Alger Hiss Controversy.**
       New York: privately printed, 1949.

1244. Canby, Vincent. "A Documentary: 'Trials of Alger
       Hiss.'" **New York Times** (March 9, 1980). Reviews
       a documentary film on Hiss.

1245. Chambers, Whittaker. **Witness.** New York: Random
       House, 1952. Powerful autobiography by an ex-
       Communist who took part in Soviet espionage and
       was the chief witness against Alger Hiss.

1246. Chollet, Laurence B. "The Hiss-Chambers Affair:
       An Evaluation of the Case and Its Effect on
       American Intellectuals." Senior thesis.
       Princeton University, 1973.

1247. Clubb, O. Edmund. **The Witness and I.** New York:
       Columbia University Press, 1974.

1248. Cook, Fred J. "New Perspectives on the Strangest
       Case of Our Time." **The Nation** (Sept. 21, 1957).
       Defends Hiss.

1249. Cook, Fred J. **The Unfinished Story of Alger Hiss.**
       New York: Morrow, 1958. Defends Hiss and
       advances the forgery by typewriter theory.

1250. Cook, Fred J. "Nixon Kicks a Hole in the Hiss
       Case." **The Nation** (April 7, 1962). Advances the
       theory that Nixon had some role in carrying out
       forgery by typewriter in order to frame Hiss.

1251. Cook, Fred J. "The Ghost of a Typewriter." **The
       Nation** (May 12, 1962).

1252. Cook, Fred J. "Alger Hiss and the Smoking
       Typewriter." **New Times** (Oct. 14, 1977).

1253. Cooke, Alistair. **Generation on Trial.** New York:
       Knopf, 1950. Excellent journalistic examination
       of the Hiss-Chambers case.

1254. Dawson, Nelson L. "Unequal Justice: McCarthy and
       Hiss." **Midstream** 27,4 (1981). Compares the
       treatment of Alger Hiss and Joseph McCarthy in
       textbooks. Finds bias in favor of Hiss and a
       tendency to treat Communism as a political
       movement without dangers to a democratic
       society.

*   de Toledano, Ralph, and Victor Lasky. **Seeds of
       Treason: The True Story of the Hiss-Chambers
       Tragedy.** New York: Funk and Wagnalls, 1950.
       Cited as item 2078. Journalistic expose which
       treats the Communist Party as a conspiracy
       linked to Soviet espionage.

1255. Elniff, Terrill I. "Re-writing History: Thomas A.
      Bailey Takes on a Co-author." **The Conservative
      Historians' Forum** 4, (Dec. 1980). Notes the
      changing treatment of the Hiss case in different
      editions of a long-used textbook.

1256. Fox, John D. "The Hiss Hassle Revisited."
      Princeton Alumni Weekly (May 3, 1976).
      Discusses the controversy regarding Hiss's
      appearance at the Whig-Clio lecture, his first
      public appearance after leaving prison in 1956.

1257. Glotzer, Albert. "The Glotzer-Reedy-Farrell
      File." **The Warbler** [The Pumpkin Papers
      Irregulars] 2,1 (July 1980). Correspondence
      regarding the Hiss-Chambers case between
      Glotzer, active in the Communist Party, the
      Trotskyist movement, and the Socialist Party at
      various times, with George Reedy, a reporter who
      covered the case, and James T. Farrell.

1258. Goulden, Joseph. "The Hiss Case: An Ideal
      Tarnished." **The Best Years, 1945-1950.** New York:
      Atheneum, 1976.

1259. Green, Gil. "Forgery by Typewriter." **The Nation**
      (Nov. 10, 1984). Veteran Communist Party leader
      maintains that there is proof that the FBI has
      used forgery by typewriter to frame innocent
      people, a claim made in regards to the Hiss
      case.

1260. Gwynn, Beatrice V. **The Discrepancy in the
      Evidence.** privately printed, 1972. Pamphlet
      defending Hiss.

1261. Hiss, Alger. **In the Court of Public Opinion.** New
      York: Knopf, 1957. A brief for the defense.

1262. Hollinger, David A. "The Confidence Man." **Reviews
      in American History** 7,1 (1979). Review-essay
      discussing Weinstein's **Perjury.**

1263. Hook, Sidney. "The Faiths of Whittaker Chambers."
      The New York Times Book Review (May 25, 1952).

1264. Hook, Sidney. "An Autobiographical Fragment: The
      Strange Case of Whittaker Chambers." **Encounter
      [Great Britain]** 46,1 (1976). Comments on
      Chambers' life and his role in the Hiss case.

1265.   Hook, Sidney. "The Case of Alger Hiss." **Encounter [Great. Britain]** (Aug. 1978). Review of the Hiss case.

1266.   Hook, Sidney. "Arguments (New & Old) About the Hiss Case." **Encounter [Great Britain]** (March 1979). Reviews recent writings about the Hiss case.

1267.   Howe, Irving. "Madness, Vision, Stupidity." **Steady Work: Essays in the Politics of Democratic Radicalism, 1953-1966.** New York: Harcourt, Brace & World, 1966. Critical examination of the views of Whittaker Chambers.

1268.   Irons, Peter H. **Commentary** Dec. 1975 letters column. Argues that the journalist Isaac Don Levine was part of a conspiracy to frame Hiss.

1269.   Irons, Peter H. **Law Library Journal** (Nov. 1976). Argues that the China Lobby was behind the prosecution of Hiss.

1270.   Josephson, Matthew. "Scenes of the Nineteen Thirties: A Soiree with Whittaker Chambers." **Southern Review** 3 (1967).

1271.   Jowitt, William Allen, 1st Earl. **The Strange Case of Alger Hiss.** Garden City: Doubleday, 1953. Suggests that the evidence against Hiss was perjured or faked.

1272.   Kaiser, Robert Blair. "Film About Hiss Trials Revives Controversy." **New York Times** (Feb. 26, 1980).

1273.   Kinsley, Michael and Arthur Lubow. "Alger Hiss and the Smoking Gun Fallacy." **Washington Monthly** (Oct. 1975).

1274.   Lasky, Melvin J. "John Reed & Alger Hiss: Two Cases in Ideology." **Encounter [Great Britain]** 59,2 (1982). Compares the careers of and the films about Reed and Hiss.

1275.   Ledeen, Michael. "Hiss, Oswald, the KGB and Us." **Commentary** 65,5 (1978). Based on Allen Weinstein's **Perjury: The Hiss-Chambers Case** and Edward J. Epstein's **Legend: The Secret World of Lee Harvey Oswald,** this article discusses the reluctance to accept evidence of KGB activities.

1276. Levin, David. "In the Court of Historical
       Criticism: Alger Hiss's Narrative." **The Virginia
       Quarterly Review** (Winter 1976).

1277. Levitt, Morton, and Michael Levitt. **A Tissue of
       Lies: Nixon vs. Hiss.** New York: McGraw-Hill,
       1979. A defense of Hiss.

1278. Lowenthal, John. "Woodstock N230099: What the FBI
       Knew But Hid from Hiss and the Court." **The
       Nation** (June 26, 1976). Argues that the FBI
       framed Hiss.

1279. Matthews, T.S. **Name and Address.** New York: Simon
       and Schuster, 1960. A leading **Time** editor
       remembers his association with Whittaker
       Chambers.

1280. McWilliams, Carey. "Will Nixon Exonerate Hiss?"
       The Nation (Sept. 20, 1975). Argues that some
       words on the Watergate tapes exonerate Hiss.

1281. Morris, Richard B. "The Case of Alger Hiss." **Fair
       Trial.** New York: Knopf, 1953.

1282. Navasky, Victor S. "The Case Not Proved Against
       Alger Hiss." **The Nation** (April 8, 1978).
       Attacks Weinstein's **Perjury.**

1283. Navasky, Victor S. "New Republic, New Mistakes."
       The Nation (May 6, 1978). Attacks Weinstein's
       defense of **Perjury.**

1284. Navasky, Victor S. "The Hiss-Weinstein File." **The
       Nation** (June 17, 1978).

1285. Navasky, Victor S. "Weinstein, Hiss, and the
       Transformation of Historical Ambiguity into Cold
       War Verity." **Beyond the Hiss Case.** Athan
       Theoharis, ed. Philadelphia: Temple University
       Press, 1982.

1286. Nixon, Richard M. **Six Crises.** New York:
       Doubleday, 1962. The Hiss-Chambers case is one
       of the six.

1287. Nobile, Philip. "The State of the Art of Alger
       Hiss." **Harper's** (April 1976).

1288. Packer, Herbert L. "A Tale of Two Typewriters."
       10 **Stanford Law Review** No. 3 (May 1958).
       Examines arguments regarding typewriter evidence
       in the Hiss-Chambers case.

1289.   Popkin, Richard H.   "Hiss Story Repeats Itself."
        University Review (April 1974).   Argues that the
        Watergate scandal indicates that Hiss was the
        American Dreyfus.

1290.   Reuben, William.   **The Honorable Mr. Nixon and the
        Alger Hiss Case.** New York: Action Books, 1956.
        Asserts that Nixon manufactured a case against
        Hiss.

1291.   Reuben, William.   **Footnote On An Historic Case: In
        Re Alger Hiss.** New York: The Nation Institute,
        1984.   Defense of Hiss.

1292.   Reuben, William.   "New Development." **The Nation**
        (Nov. 10, 1984).   Discusses new evidence said to
        show Hiss's innocence.

1293.   Schlesinger, Arthur, Jr.   "Whittaker Chambers and
        His 'Witness.'" **Saturday Review** (May 24, 1952).

1294.   Seth, Ronald.   **The Sleeping Truth.** New York: Hart,
        1968.   Argues that Hiss was framed by the KGB
        and that Chambers was a KGB agent.

1295.   Shapiro, Edward S.   "The Trials of Alger Hiss."
        The Conservative Historians' Forum 4 (Dec.
        1980).

1296.   Shapiro, Edward S.   "The Perjury of Alger Hiss:
        Icon of the Cold War." **Intercollegiate Review**
        (Fall-Winter 1980).

1297.   Sherrill, Robert.   **The New York Times Book Review**
        (April 25, 1976).   Argues that there was an FBI
        conspiracy to frame Hiss.

1298.   Smith, John Chabot.   **Alger Hiss: The True Story.**
        New York: Holt, Rinehart & Winston, 1976.
        Maintains that Hiss was innocent; advances a
        number of possible conspiracies to account for
        the evidence against Hiss.

1299.   Smith, John Chabot.   "The Debate of the Century
        (cont'd)." **Harper's** (June 1978).   A defense of
        Hiss.

1300.   Theoharis, Athan G.   "Unanswered Question:
        Chambers, Nixon, the FBI, and the Hiss Case."
        Beyond the Hiss Case. Athan Theoharis, ed.
        Philadelphia: Temple University Press, 1982.

1301. Tiger, Edith, ed. **In Re Alger Hiss.** New York:
       Hill & Wang, 1979. Contains Hiss' petition to
       have his case reviewed.

1302. Trilling, Diana, and Sidney Hook. "Remembering
       Whittaker Chambers." **Encounter [Great Britain]**
       (June, 1975). An exchange of letters between
       Hook and Trilling regarding contacts with
       Chambers in the 1930s.

1303. Trilling, Lionel. "Whittaker Chambers and 'The
       Middle of the Journey.'" **The New York Review of
       Books** (April 17, 1975).

1304. Van Dusen, George. "The Continuing Hiss:
       Whittaker Chambers, Alger Hiss, and **National
       Review** Conservatism." **Cithara** (Nov. 1971).

1305. Weinstein, Allen. The Hiss Case Revisited." **The
       American Scholar** (Winter 1971-1972).

1306. Weinstein, Allen. "The Symbolism of Subversion:
       Notes on Some Cold War Icons." **Journal of
       American Studies** 6 (1972).

1307. Weinstein, Allen. "Nixon vs. Hiss." **Esquire** (Nov.
       1975).

1308. Weinstein, Allen. "Was Hiss Framed? The New
       Evidence." **The New York Review of Books** (April
       1, 1976). Argues that Hiss was not framed;
       exchanges with critics in the May 27th and Sept.
       16th issues.

1309. Weinstein, Allen. "The Hiss and Rosenberg Files."
       The New Republic (Feb. 14, 1976).

1310. Weinstein, Allen. "F.B.I.'s Hiss Files Show
       Bumbling, Not Malice." **The New York Times Week
       in Review** (Feb. 1, 1976).

1311. Weinstein, Allen. **Perjury: The Hiss-Chambers
       Case.** New York: Alfred A. Knopf, 1978. This
       scholarly and highly detailed history of the
       Hiss-Chambers case is essential reading for
       those interested in the affair; strongly
       suggests that Hiss was guilty. See items 1262,
       1275, 1282-1285, 1312, and 2012.

1312. Weinstein, Allen. "'Perjury,' Take Three." **The
       New Republic** (April 29, 1978). Discusses the
       Communist Party's underground work. Critical

letter by Victor Navasky and response, May 13, 1978 issue.

1313.   Werchen, Raymond A., and Fred J. Cook.   "New Light on the Hiss Case." **The Nation** (May 28, 1973).

1314.   Wills, Garry.   "The Hiss Connection Through Nixon's Life." **The New York Times Magazine** (Aug. 25, 1974).

1315.   Younger, Irving.   "Was Alger Hiss Guilty?" **Commentary** 60,2 (1975).   Reviews the Hiss case.

1316.   Zeligs, Meyer A.   **Friendship and Fratricide.** New York: Viking, 1967.   Psychobiography of the Hiss-Chambers case which argues that Chambers framed Hiss out of a pathological desire for revenge for having been rejected by Hiss.

See item 1351.

Krivitsky, Walter

1317.   Giffin, Frederick C.   "The Death of Walter Krivitsky." **Social Science** 54,3 (1979). Discusses the 1941 death by suicide or assassination of Walter Krivitsky, a official of Soviet military intelligence who defected in 1937.   He wrote a book and several articles critical of the Soviet Union and his testimony to the Dies Committee linked the CPUSA closely to the Soviet Union.

1318.   Krivitsky, Walter.   **I Was Stalin's Agent.** Bristol, England: Right Book Club, 1940.

Oppenheimer, J. Robert

1319.   Alsop, Joseph, and Stewart Alsop.   "We Accuse!" **Harper's Magazine** (Oct. 1954).

1320.   Alsop, Joseph, and Stewart Alsop.   **We Accuse: The Story of the Miscarriage of Justice in the Case of J. Robert Oppenheimer.** New York: Simon & Schuster, 1954.

1321.   Bernstein, Barton J.   "In the Matter of J. Robert Oppenheimer." **Historical Studies in the Physical Sciences** 35,1 (1983).

1322.   Curtis, Charles P.   **The Oppenheimer Case.** New York: Simon and Schuster, 1955.   Includes most of the relevant testimony on the case.

1323.   Newman, Steven L.   "The Oppenheimer Case: A
        Reconsideration of the Role of the Defense
        Department and National Security." Ph.D.
        dissertation. New York University, 1977.   Sees
        the removal of Oppenheimer's security clearance
        as having been manufactured by factions in the
        Air Force and the defense scientific community
        who thought that Oppenheimer's views on nuclear
        strategy would damage their budgets.

1324.   Schlesinger, Arthur, Jr.   "The Oppenheimer Case."
        The Atlantic Monthly (Oct. 1954).

1325.   Stern, Philip M.   **The Oppenheimer Case: Security
        on Trial.** New York: Harper & Row, 1969.

1326.   Strout, Cushing.   "The Oppenheimer Case:
        Melodrama, Tragedy, and Irony." **Virginia
        Quarterly Review** 40 (1964).

Rosenbergs, The

1327.   Anders, Roger M.   "The Rosenberg Case Revisited:
        The Greenglass Testimony and the Protection of
        Atomic Secrets." **American Historical Review** 83,2
        (April 1978).   Examines Atomic Energy Commission
        records regarding the Rosenberg case. Concludes
        that David Greenglass's testimony on atomic bomb
        technology was generally accurate and that the
        Commission was gravely worried that his
        testimony might further compromise secret
        technology.

1328.   Buitrago, Ann Marie.   "The Fraud of the Century."
        Our Right to Know. Fund for Open Information and
        Accountability, Inc. (Fall 1983).   Discusses the
        Rosenberg case as an act of government
        misconduct.

1329.   **Columbia Law Review** 54 (1954). "The Rosenberg
        Case: Some Reflections on Federal Criminal Law."

1330.   Diamond, Arlyn.   "A Legacy." **Massachusetts Review**
        16,3 (1975).   Essay review of Michael and Robert
        Meeropol's **We Are Your Sons.**

1331.   Edelman, Irwin.   "The Rosenberg Case: Some
        Observations." **Contemporary Issues [Great
        Britain]** 5 (Oct.-Nov. 1954).   Suggests some kind
        of conspiracy between the FBI, the Communist
        Party, and the Rosenberg's lawyers to execute
        the Rosenbergs.

1332. Fineberg, S. Andhil. **The Rosenberg Case: Fact and Fiction**. New York: Oceana, 1953.

1333. Gordon, Max. "The Rosenbergs and the Communist Party." **In These Times** 8,2 (Nov. 1983). Critical comment on Radosh and Milton's **The Rosenberg File.**

1334. Markowitz, Gerald E. "Secrecy, Duplicity, and Dirty Tricks: The Incomplete Record of the Rosenberg Case." **Our Right To Know**. Fund for Open Information and Accountability, Inc. (Fall 1983).

1335. Markowitz, Gerald E. "How Not to Write History: A Critique of Radosh & Milton's **The Rosenberg File." Science & Society** 48,1 (Spring 1984). See item 1330.

1336. Meeropol, Robert, and Michael Meeropol. **We Are your Sons: The Legacy of Ethel and Julius Rosenberg**. Boston: Houghton, Mifflin, 1975. A defense of the Rosenbergs' by their sons.

1337. Nizer, Louis. **The Implosion Conspiracy**. Garden City: Doubleday, 1973. Finds the evidence against the Rosenberg's to be overwhelming and the trial and review fair; deplores use of the death penalty.

1338. **Northwestern University Law Review** 48 (1954). "The Rosenberg Case: A Problem of Statutory Construction." Reviews legal issues in the Rosenberg case.

1339. Parrish, Michael. "Cold War Justice: The Supreme Court and the Rosenbergs." **American Historical Review** 82,4 (1977). Discusses Supreme Court consideration of the Rosenberg case. Concludes that a majority of the court was guilty of "capitulation to the Red Scare."

1340. Pessen, Edward. "The Rosenberg Case Revisited: A Critical Essay on a Recent Scholarly Examination." **New York History** 65 (Jan. 1984). Critical of Radosh and Milton's **The Rosenberg File.**

1341. Pilat, Oliver. **The Atom Spies**. New York: G. P. Putnam's Sons, 1952. Journalistic account of the Rosenberg case and other atomic spy cases.

1342.   Radosh, Ronald and Joyce Milton. **The Rosenberg
        File: A Search for the Truth.** New York: Holt,
        Rinehart and Winston, 1983. Detailed and
        extremely well researched scholarly examination
        of the Rosenberg case; finds that Julius
        Rosenberg was guilty of spying and that Ethel
        may not have been; however, the government
        included Ethel in the indictment in an
        unsuccessful attempt to pressure Julius into a
        confession. See items 1333, 1335, and 1340.

1343.   Reuben, William. **The Atom Spy Hoax.** New York:
        Action Books, 1960. Argues that the Rosenbergs
        were innocent and that their trial was unfair.

1344.   Schneir, Walter, and Miriam Schneir. **Invitation
        to an Inquest: A New Look at the Rosenberg-
        Sobell Case.** New York: Dell, 1968. Argues that
        the Rosenbergs were innocent and that their
        trial was unfair.

1345.   Shapiro, Edward S. "The Rosenbergs and the Claims
        of History." **The Intercollegiate Review** 20,2
        (Winter 1984).

1346.   Strout, Cushing. "Reconsidering the Rosenbergs:
        History, Novel, Film." **Reviews in American
        History** 12,3 (Sept. 1984). Review-essay on
        recent coverage of the Rosenberg case.

1347.   Wexley, John. **The Judgement of Julius and Ethel
        Rosenberg.** New York: Cameron and Kahn, 1955. A
        defense of the Rosenbergs.

1348.   Yergin, Daniel. "Were the Rosenbergs Framed?"
        New Times (May 16, 1975).

Straight, Michael

1349.   Haynes, John Earl. "Speak No Evil: Michael
        Straight and **After Long Silence.**" **Chronicles of
        Culture** 7,11 (1983). Discusses the
        contradictions between Straight's version of his
        editorial policy in his autobiography and his
        actual editorial policy as publisher of **The New
        Republic** in the 1940s and early 1950s.

1350.   Hook, Sidney. "The Incredible Story of Michael
        Straight." **Encounter [Great Britain]** (Dec.
        1983). Examines the contradictions in
        Straight's autobiography **After Long Silence**
        regarding Straight's association with Soviet
        espionage.

1351. Straight, Michael. **After Long Silence.** New York:
       Norton, 1983. The one-time editor and publisher
       of **The New Republic** discusses his recruitment as
       a Soviet spy in the 1930s.

White, Harry Dexter

1352. Hudson, G.F. "The Dexter White Case." **The
       Twentieth Century** (Jan. 1954). Examines
       President Truman's actions regarding White's
       governmental positions and charges that White
       passed documents to Soviet agents.

1353. Rees, David. **Harry Dexter White: A Study in
       Paradox.** New York: Coward, McCann & Geoghegan,
       1973.

1354. White, Nathan I. **Harry Dexter White, Loyal
       American.** Waban: Bessie White Bloom, 1956.
       Defends Harry Dexter White.

       See items 1239 and 2041.

26

SUBSIDIARY TREATMENTS OF COMMUNIST HISTORY

1355. Alexander, Robert J. "Splinter Groups in American Radical Politics." **Social Research** 20 (1953).

1356. Alexander, Robert J. "Schisms and Unifications in the American Old Left, 1923-1940." **Labor History** 14,4 (Fall 1973). Surveys the organizational history of Leftist organizations.

1357. Bimba, Anthony. **History of the American Working Class.** New York: International Publishers, 1927. Written by a Communist official who sees all of prior American history demonstrating the need for and leading to the formation of the Communist Party.

1358. Buhle, Paul. "Marxism in the United States, 1900-40." Ph.D. dissertation. University of Wisconsin, 1975. Discusses and analyses the dilemmas that faced Marxist strategies for political and cultural revolution under the Socialist Party, the IWW, and the Communist Party.

1359. Cantor, Milton. **The Divided Left: American Radicalism, 1900-1975.** New York: Hill and Wang, 1978. Critical of the Communist Party's Popular Front tactics of the 1930s and 1940s.

*   Davis, Mike. **Prisoners of the American Dream: Politics and Economics in the History of the US Working Class.** New York: Shochen (Verso Books), 1986. Cited as item 2042.

1360. Dennis, Peggy. "On Learning from History." **Socialist Revolution** (July/Sept. 1976). Critique of Weinstein's **Ambiguous Legacy.**

1361. Diggins, John P. **The American Left in the Twentieth Century.** New York: Harcourt Brace Jovanovich, 1973. Interpretive essay examining

the intellectual outlook, social origins and
historical setting of three generations of the
Left: the Lyrical Left of World War I and after,
the Old Left of the 1930s, and the New Left of
the 1960s.

1362. Egbert, Donald Drew, and Stow Persons. **Socialism
and American Life.** Princeton: Princeton
University Press, 1952.

1363. Fine, Nathan. **Labor and Farmer Parties in the
United States, 1828-1928.** New York: Rand School,
1928. Treats the Communist Party as a utopian
and sectarian organization.

1364. Issacs, William. **Contemporary Marxian Political
Movements in the United States, 1917-1939.** New
York: New York University Press, 1942.

1365. Johnpoll, Bernard K., and Lillian Johnpoll. **The
Impossible Dream: The Rise and Demise of the
American Left.** Westport: Greenwood, 1981.

1366. Kolko, Gabriel. "The Decline of American
Radicalism in the Twentieth Century." **Studies on
the Left** 6 (Sept.-Oct. 1966).

1367. Lader, Lawrence. **Power on the Left: American
Radical Movements Since 1946.** New York: W. W.
Norton, 1979.

1368. Lasch, Christopher. **The Agony of the American
Left.** New York: Knopf, 1969.

1369. Laslett, John H.M. "Why Is There Not More of a
Socialist Movement in the United States?"
Reviews in American History 5,2 (1977). Review-
essay discussing Stave's **Socialism and the
Cities** and Weinstein's **Ambiguous Legacy.**

1370. Laslett, John H.M., and Seymour M. Lipset, eds.
**Failure of a Dream? Essays in the History of
American Socialism.** Garden City: Anchor Press,
1974.

1371. Lowy, M. "Marxism and Revolutionary Romanticism."
Telos 14 (Fall 1981).

1372. Mairowitz, David Zane. **The Radical Soap Opera: An
Impression of the American Left from 1917 to the
Present.** London: Wildwood House, 1974.

1373. Deleted

1374. Miller, Douglas T., and Marion Nowak. **The Fifties: The Way We Really Were.** Garden City: Doubleday, 1977.

1375. O'Brien, Jim. "The Ambiguous Legacy." **Radical America** 10 (July-August 1976).

1376. Simon, Rita J. **As We Saw the Thirties.** Urbana: University of Illinois Press, 1967. Vignettes by Hal Draper, Earl Browder, Granville Hicks, and Max Shachtman.

1377. Starr, Jerold M., ed. **Cultural Politics: Radical Movements in Modern History.** New York: Praeger, 1985. Contains items 246, 1054, and 1124.

1378. Taylor, Telford. **Grand Inquest.** New York: Simon and Schuster, 1955.

1379. Verba, Sidney, and Kay Lehman Schlozman. "Unemployment, Class Consciousness, and Radical Politics: What Didn't Happen in the Thirties." **Journal of Politics** 39 (May 1977).

1380. Weinstein, James. "The Premature Crusade." **Studies on the Left** 2 (1961).

1381. Weinstein, James. "Radicalism in the Midst of Normalcy." **Journal of American History** 52,4 (March 1966).

1382. Weinstein, James. "The Left, Old and New." **Socialist Revolution** 2 (July-Aug. 1972).

1383. Weinstein, James. **Ambiguous Legacy: The Left in American Politics.** New York: New Viewpoints, 1975. Maintains that the Communist Party's Popular Front strategy of the 1930s, adopted due to concern with Soviet interests, led to the co-option of militant energies into New Deal liberalism. See items 1360 and 1369.

1384. Young, Alfred, ed. **Dissent: Explorations on the History of American Radicalism.** DeKalb: Northern Illinois University Press, 1968.

27

BIOGRAPHICAL MATERIAL

Bedacht, Max

1385. Bedacht, Max. "The Memoirs of Your Father: On the
       Path of My Life." Unpublished autobiography,
       Tamiment Library, New York University.

Bittelman, Alexander

1386. Bittelman, Alexander. Unpublished autobiography,
       Tamiment Library, New York University.

Bloor, Ella Reeve

1387. Bloor, Ella Reeve. **We Are Many.** New York:
       International Publishers, 1940.

Browder, Earl

1388. Bittelman, Alexander. **A Communist Views America's
       Future.** Privately published, 1960. Bittelman, a
       longtime ally of William Foster, offers a
       sometimes positive evaluation of Browder's
       leadership. The Party expelled Bittelman in
       1959 for these views.

1389. Browder, Earl. Unpublished autobiography, Earl
       Browder Papers, Syracuse University.

1390. Cleath, Robert Leroy. "Earl Russell Browder,
       American Spokesman for Communism, 1930-1945: An
       Analysis of Adaption of Communist Ideas and
       Goals to a Capitalist Society." Ph.D.
       dissertation. University of Washington, 1963.

1391. Rosenberg, Roger E. "Guardian of the Fortress: A
       Biography of Earl Russell Browder, U.S.
       Communist Party General-Secretary from 1930-
       1944." Ph.D. dissertation. University of
       California, Santa Barbara, 1982. Sympathetic
       political biography interpreting Browder's
       revisionism as a necessary modification of
       Marxism to fit American conditions.

1392.   Ryan, James G. "The Making of a Native Marxist:
        The Early Career of Earl Browder." **Review of
        Politics** 39,3 (1977). Recounts the evolution of
        Browder from orthodox Stalinist to independent
        Marxist.

1393.   Ryan, James G. "Earl Browder and American
        Communism at High Tide: 1934-1945." Ph.D.
        dissertation. University of Notre Dame, 1981.
        History of Browder and the Communist Party
        during Browder's reign.

1394.   Stein, Harry. "Before the Colors Fade: Marx's
        Disenchanted Salesman." **American Heritage** 23,1
        (1971). Discusses Earl Browder's reminiscences
        regarding the Communist Party in the 1930s in an
        interview shortly after Browder's 80th birthday.

        See items 57 and 58.

Bryan, Louise

1395.   Gardner, Virginia. **Friend and Lover, the Life of
        Louise Bryan.** New York: Horizon Press, 1982.
        Biography of the companion of John Reed.

Burnham, James

1396.   Gilbert, James B. "James Burnham: Exemplary
        Radical of the 1930s." **A New History of
        Leviathan: Essays on the Rise of the American
        Corporate State.** Ronald Radosh and Murray N.
        Rothbard, eds. New York: Dutton, 1972.

1397.   Hoffman, Benjamin G. "The Political Thought of
        James Burnham." Ph.D. dissertation. University
        of Michigan, 1969.

        See item 1033.

Chamberlain, John

1398.   Annunziata, Frank. "The Political Thought of John
        Chamberlain: Continuity and Conversion." **South
        Atlantic Quarterly** 74 (1975). Discusses
        Chamberlain's shift from Communist intellectual
        to conservatism.

Charney, George

1399.   Charney, George. **A Long Journey.** Chicago:
        Quadrangle, 1968. Memoir of a former Communist

leader who left the Communist Party in 1958.
See item 2009.

1400. Charney, George. "Out of the Communist Past."
       Dissent, 15,5 (1968). Memoir.

Chernin, Rose

1401. Chernin, Kim. **In My Mother's House, A Daughter's
       Story.** New Haven: Ticknor & Fields, 1983.

Corey, Lewis

1402. Apter, David. "Lewis Corey." **Antioch Alumni
       Bulletin** (Nov. 1953).

1403. Apter, David E. "Lewis Corey: A Portrait of an
       American Radical." **Columbia Library Columns** 8,2
       (Feb. 1959). Biographical essay on the early
       Communist Party leader Louis Fraina who left the
       party and later became a noted scholar under the
       name of Lewis Corey.

1404. Bixler, Paul. "A Memorial Tribute." **Antioch
       Review** Winter 1953/54. Biographical essay on
       Lewis Corey.

1405. Corey, Esther. "Lewis Corey (Louis C. Fraina),
       1892-1953: A Bibliography with Autobiographical
       Notes." **Labor History** 4,2 (Spring 1963).

1406. Corey, Esther. "Passage to Russia, II." **Survey: A
       Journal of Soviet and East European Studies** 55
       (1965).

1407. Gruliow, Leo. "Lenin and Lewis Corey (Louis
       Fraina)." **Columbia Library Columns** (Feb. 1959).

       See item 757.

Davis, Angela

1408. Davis, Angela. **An Autobiography.** New York: Random
       House, 1974.

1409. Huntley, Richard Thomas. "Events and Issues of
       the Angela Davis Dismissal." Ph.D. dissertation.
       University of Southern California, 1976.
       Discusses the dismissal of Davis, a Communist,
       from a university faculty post.

1410. Williams, Irene. "Women in the Dark Times: Three
       Views of the Angela Davis Trial." **San Jose
       Studies** 4,1 (1978). Review-essay on Davis' **An
       Autobiography,** Bettina Aptheker's **The Morning
       Breaks,** and Mary Timothy's **Jury Woman.**

Darcy, Samuel Adams

1411. Darcy, Samuel Adams. Unpublished autobiography in
       the possession of Samuel Darcy. Darcy, a
       prominent Communist official in the 1930s, was
       expelled in 1944 for opposition to Browder's
       policies.

Dennis, Peggy

1412. Dennis, Peggy. **The Autobiography of An American
       Communist: A Personal View of a Political Life,
       1925-1975.** Westport: Lawrence Hill, 1977. See
       items 612, 827, and 835. Dennis, an active
       Communist organizer, discusses her own
       experiences and those of her husband, Gene, who
       was second highest official in the Party in the
       late 1940s and 1950s.

Dodd, Bella

1413. Dodd, Bella. **School of Darkness.** New York:
       Kenedy, 1954. Memoir by a ex-Communist who had
       been active in New York City politics and in the
       teachers' union.

Dolson, James

1414. Dolson, James. **Bucking the Ruling Class: Jim
       Dolson's Story.** Privately printed, 1984. Memoir
       of a Communist militant.

Equi, Marie

1415. Krieger, Nancy. "Queen of the Bolsheviks: The
       Hidden History of Dr. Marie Equi." **Radical
       America** 17 (Sept./Oct. 1983). Notes that
       Elizabeth Gurley Flynn lived with Equi from 1926
       until 1936. Equi, not herself a Communist, had
       been a well known and active radical and IWW
       supporter in the Pacific Northwest

Field, Frederick

1416. Field, Frederick. **From Right to Left: An
       Autobiography.** Westport: Lawrence Hill, 1983.

Scion of a wealthy family discusses his life as a Communist.

Flynn, Elizabeth Gurley

1417.   Baxandall, Rosalynn. "Dreams and Dilemmas: An introduction to Elizabeth Gurley Flynn's Writing on Women." Unpublished paper, 1984 Berkshire Conference on the History of Women.

1418.   Baxandall, Rosalynn. "Elizabeth Gurley Flynn: The Early Years." **Radical America** 9,1 (1975). Biographical essay.

1419.   Camp, Helen Collier. "'Gurley': A Biography of Elizabeth Gurley Flynn, 1890-1964." Ph.D. dissertation. Columbia University, 1980.

1420.   Flynn, Elizabeth Gurley. **I Speak My Own Piece: Autobiography of "The Rebel Girl."** New York: Masses and Mainstream, 1955.

1421.   Flynn, Elizabeth Gurley. **The Alderson Story: My Life as a Political Prisoner.** New York: International Publishers, 1963.

1422.   Flynn, Elizabeth Gurley. **The Rebel Girl: An Autobiography, My First Life: 1906-1926.** New York: International Publishers, 1973.

1423.   Kizer, Benjamin H. "Elizabeth Gurley Flynn." **Pacific Northwest Quarterly** 57 (1966).

Foster, William Z.

1424.   Flynn, Elizabeth Gurley. **Labor's Own: William Z. Foster.** New York: New Century, 1949.

1425.   Foster, William Z. **From Bryan to Stalin.** New York: International Publishers, 1937. Autobiographical.

1426.   Foster, William Z. **Pages From a Worker's Life.** New York: International Publishers, 1939. Autobiographical.

1427.   North, Joseph. **William Z. Foster: An Appreciation.** New York: International Publishers, 1955.

1428.   Zipser, Arthur. **Working Class Giant: The Life of William Z. Foster.** New York: International Publishers, 1981.

1429.   Zipser, Arthur. "The Life of William Z. Foster --
        the Steel Strike Chapter." **Political Affairs** 60
        (Feb. 1981).

Freeman, Joseph

1430.   Beck, Kent M. "The Odyssey of Joseph Freeman."
        Historian 37,1 (1974). Examines the writings
        and life of a Jewish Communist intellectual.

1431.   Freeman, Joseph. **An American Testament; a
        Narrative of Rebels and Romantics.** New York:
        Farrar & Rinehart, 1936. Autobiography.

1432.   Lowenfish, Lee. "The American Testament of a
        Revolutionary." **Columbia Library Columns**
        (February 1978). Discusses Joseph Freeman's
        break with the Communist Party.

Gates, John

1433.   Gates, John. **The Story of an American Communist.**
        New York: Thomas Nelson and Sons, 1958. Gates,
        a prominent Party leader and editor of the **Daily
        Worker,** led the failed drive to democratize and
        Americanize the Party after Khrushchev's
        speech regarding Stalin's crimes and the
        Hungarian Revolution. He subsequently left the
        Party.

Gitlow, Benjamin

1434.   Gitlow, Benjamin. **I Confess, The Truth About
        American Communism.** New York: E.P. Dutton and
        Co., 1940. Autobiography by a disillusioned
        early Communist Party leader.

1435.   Gitlow, Benjamin. **The Whole of Their Lives:
        Communism in America -- A Personal History and
        Intimate Portrayal of Its Leaders.** New York:
        Scribner's, 1948.

Gold, Ben

1436.   Gold, Ben. **Memoirs.** New York: International
        Publishers, 1985.

Green, Gil

1437.   Green, Gil. **Cold War Fugitive.** New York:
        International Publishers, 1985.
        Autobiographical.

Katz, Otto

1438. Draper, Theodore. "The Man Who Wanted to Hang."
       Reporter (Jan. 6, 1953). Sketch of Otto Katz
       (Andre Simone), a Czech-born Communist who used
       anti-Nazi themes to raise money for
       international Communist causes from wealthy
       Americans.

Kinoy, Arthur

1439. Kinoy, Arthur. "The Making of a People's Lawyer."
       Science and Society 45 (Fall 1981). See item
       2037.

Kling, Jack

*   Kling, Jack. **Where The Action Is: Memoirs of a
       U.S. Communist.** New York: New Outlook, 1986.
       Cited as item 2035.

Lawrenson, Helen

1440. Lawrenson, Helen. **Whistling Girl.** Garden City:
       Doubleday, 1978. Memoir by the managing editor
       of **Vanity Fair** in the 1930s recounts anecdotes
       about Communists.

Malkin, Maurice

1441. Malkin, Maurice. **Return to My Father's House.** New
       Rochelle: Arlington House, 1972. Memoir by an
       ex-Communist. Malkin maintained that the
       Communist Party had instructions from the Soviet
       Union to infiltrate charitable foundations.

Massing, Hede

1442. Massing, Hede. **This Deception.** New York: Duell,
       Sloan and Pearce, 1951. Memoir by a
       disillusioned ex-Communist and former wife of
       Gerhardt Eisler, a Communist who fled the United
       States to become a propagandist for East
       Germany.

Mitford, Jessica

1443. Mitford, Jessica. **A Fine Old Conflict.** New York:
       Knopf, 1977.

Nelson, Ella Chase

1444. Tunis, Mildred. "Ella Chase Nelson." **Dartmouth College Library Bulletin** 1968. Biographical essay on a New Hampshire Communist Party activist who later became a Maoist.

Nelson, Steve

1445. Nelson, Steve. **The Volunteers.** New York: Masses and Mainstream, 1953.

1446. Nelson, Steve, James R. Barrett, and Rob Ruck. **Steve Nelson, American Radical.** Pittsburgh: University of Pittsburgh Press, 1981. Autobiography of a Communist Party leader who left the Party after the invasion of Czechoslovakia. See items 2009, 2011, and 2031.

Pollack, Sandy

1447. U.S. Peace Council. "Sandy Pollack: Her Life, 1985." U.S. Peace Council, 1985. Eulogy to a Communist official of the Council who died in a plane crash in Cuba.

Putnam, Samuel

1448. Wolfe, Bertram D. **Strange Communists I Have Known.** New York: Bantam, 1967. Contains essays on Samuel Putnam, a Communist and gifted translator, and on John Reed.

Rapoport, Joe

1449. Kann, Kenneth. **Joe Rapoport: The Life of a Jewish Radical.** Philadelphia: Temple University Press, 1981. An edited oral history biography.

Richmond, Al

1450. Richmond, Al. **A Long View From the Left, Memoirs of an American Revolutionary.** New York: Delta, 1972. See items 2009 and 2011.

Rovere, Richard

*   Rovere, Richard. **Final Reports.** Garden City: Doubleday, 1984. Cited as item 2043. Rovere, later a prominent journalist, discusses his early experiences in the Communist Party.

Ruthenberg, Charles

1451. Johnson, Oakley C. **The Day is Coming, Life and Work of Charles E. Ruthenberg.** New York: International Publishers, 1957.

1452. Millett, Stephen M. "Charles E. Ruthenberg: The Development of an American Communist, 1909-1927." **Ohio History** 81,3 (1972). Recounts Ruthenberg's evolution from supporter of progressive Mayor Tom Johnson of Cleveland in 1901, to the Socialist Party in 1909, to a leading left-wing Socialist Party activist who was jailed for anti-war activity, to a conciliator of the factions of the early Communist movement, and finally to the leadership of the united Communist Party as a faithful follower of Moscow.

1453. Millett, Stephen M. "The Midwest Origins of the American Communist Party: The Leadership of Charles E. Ruthenberg, 1919-1927." **Old Northwest** 1,3 (1975).

Stokes, Rose Pastor

1454. Renshaw, Patrick. "Rose of the World: The Pastor-Stokes Marriage and the American Left, 1905-1925." **New York History** 62 (1981).

1455. Sharp, Kathleen A. "Rose Pastor Stokes: Radical Champion of the American Working Class, 1878-1933." Ph.D. dissertation. Duke University, 1979.

1456. Tamarkin, Stanley R. "Rose Pastor Stokes: The portrait of a Radical Woman, 1905-1919." Ph.D. dissertation. Yale University, 1983. Biography of an immigrant who married into a wealthy family, became a Socialist Party and labor movement militant, was convicted under the wartime Espionage Act in 1918 and helped to launch the Communist Party.

Sugar, Maurice

1457. Johnson, Christopher. "Maurice Sugar: The Law, Labor, and the Left in Detroit, 1912-1950." Manuscript, 1984.

Schneiderman, William

1458. Schneiderman, William. **Dissent on Trial: The Story of a Political Life.** Minneapolis: Marxist Education Press, 1983.

Sennett, William

*   Sennett, William. **Communist Functionary and Corporate Executive.** Berkeley: University of California, Bancroft Library, 1984. Cited as item 2040. Edited oral history interview.

Voros, Sandor

1459. Voros, Sandor. **American Commissar.** Philadelphia: Chilton Company, 1961. Memoir.

Weinstone, William

1460. Weinstone, William. "Labor Radical: An Insider's Story of the CIO." **Political Affairs** (May 1971).

Weisbord, Vera Buch

1461. Weisbord, Vera Buch. **A Radical Life.** Bloomington: Indiana University Press, 1977. This autobiography discusses her role in the Passaic textile workers strike of 1926, the National Textile Workers Union organizing drive in Gastonia, as well as her role in the early Communist Party and the Communist League of Struggle, a Communist Party splinter led by her husband Albert.

Whitney, Anita

1462. Richmond, Al. **Native Daughter: The Story of Anita Whitney.** San Francisco: Anita Whitney 75th Anniversary Committee, 1942.

Williamson, John

1463. Williamson, John. **Dangerous Scot, The Life and Work of an American "Undesirable."** New York: International Publishers, 1969.

Wolfe, Bertram D.

1464. Feuer, Lewis S. "Bertram David Wolfe 1896-1977." **Survey [Great Britain]** 23,3 (1977-78). Obituary

noting Wolfe's career as a founder of the CPUSA,
Comintern advisor to the Mexican Communist
Party, and leading supporter of Jay Lovestone.
Later disenchanted with Communism, Wolfe turned
to scholarship and research.

1465. Treadgold, Donald W. "Bertram D. Wolfe: A Life in
       Two Centuries." **Studies in Soviet Thought
       [Netherlands]** 20,4 (1979). Tribute to the
       scholar whose early career included important
       posts in the American Communist Party and the
       Comintern. See 2036.

*   Wolfe, Bertram D. **A Life in Two Centuries.** New
       York: Stein & Day, 1979. Cited as item 2036.
       Autobiographical.

See item 2039.

28

PUBLIC PERCEPTION OF COMMUNISM AND THE SOVIET UNION

1466. Adler, Leslie K., and Thomas G. Paterson. "Red Fascism: The Merger of Nazi Germany and Soviet Russia in the American Image of Totalitarianism, 1930's-1950's." **American Historical Review** 75,4 (April 1970). Finds that the notion of structural similarity between Nazism and Communism developed after the Hitler-Stalin Pact; judges the idea to be intellectually flawed.

1467. Adler, Leslie. "The Red Image: American Attitudes Toward Communism in the Cold War." Ph.D. dissertation. University of California, Berkeley, 1970. Finds that America's hostile image of Communism was based largely on fantasies and irrational fears.

1468. Al-Naqeeb, Khaldoun H. "Socio-cultural Factors in the Perception of Internal Communist Threat: A Sociological Approach to the Problem of Perceptual Distortion." Master's thesis. University of Louisville, 1969.

1469. Bronfenbrenner, Urie. "The Mirror Image in Soviet-American Relations: A Social Psychologist's Report." **Journal of Social Issues** 17 (1961).

1470. Bulsys, Joseph Algirdas. "An Analysis of Dwight D. Eisenhower's Public Imagery of the Soviet Union and Communist China as presented in Selected Speeches and News Conferences: 1953-1961." Ph.D. dissertation. Pennsylvania State University, 1984.

1471. Cantril, Hadley. **Gauging Public Opinion.** Princeton: Princeton University Press, 1947. Discusses public attitudes toward Communism.

1472. Davis, James A. "Communism, Conformity, Cohorts,
       and Categories: American Tolerance in 1954 and
       1972-73." **American Journal of Sociology** 81 (Nov.
       1975). Compares a 1972-73 survey of attitudes
       toward Communists and atheists with Samuel
       Stouffer's 1954 study. Finds an increase in
       tolerance.

1473. Filene, Peter. **Americans and the Soviet
       Experiment, 1917-1933.** Cambridge: Harvard
       University Press, 1967.

1474. Jefferson, Bonnie Sharp. "The Rhetorical
       Restrictions of a Devil Theory: The Anti-
       Communist Press's View of Communism, 1945-1947."
       Ph.D. dissertation. University of Pittsburgh,
       1984. Finds that the major media had a devil
       theory of Communism and the Soviet Union.

1475. Josephson, Harold. "Ex-Communists in Crossfire: A
       Cold War Debate." **Historian** 44,1 (1981).
       Discusses how the testimony of ex-Communists
       influenced the public perception of Communism as
       a conspiracy and how such testimony was
       manipulated by various political factions;
       highly critical of ex-Communists and hostile to
       anti-Communists.

1476. Josephson, Harold. "Ex-Communist Witnesses and
       the Cold War." Unpublished paper, 1984
       Organization of American Historians convention.

1477. Kacewicz, Laura Ann. "Anti-Communism and the
       Foreign Policy Consensus: A Study of Public
       Opinion." Master's thesis. California State
       University, Long Beach, 1973.

1478. Keefe, Robert. "Of Cowboys and Collectives: The
       Kennedy-Nixon Generation." **Massachusetts Review**
       21,3 (1980). Psychological analysis of
       Kennedy's **Profiles in Courage** and Nixon's **Six
       Crises.** Finds that both reflected a fantasy
       world; Nixon saw Communists as a threat to the
       group whereas Kennedy's book shows fear of
       regional hatred.

1479. Koger, Daniel Allan. "The Liberal Opinion Press
       and the Kennedy Years in Vietnam: A Study of
       Four Journals." Ph.D. dissertation. Michigan
       State University, 1983. Discusses the breakdown
       of the liberal anti-Communist consensus in the
       course of looking at the **New Leader, Reporter,
       The New Republic,** and **The Nation.**

1480.   Koppes, Clayton R., and Gregory D. Black. "What
        to Show the World: The Office of War Information
        and Hollywood, 1942-1945." **Journal of American
        History** 64,1 (June 1977). Briefly discusses OWI
        encouragement of a favorable image of the Soviet
        Union in films.

*   Lasch, Christopher. **The American Liberals and the
        Russian Revolution.** New York: Columbia
        University Press, 1962. Cited as item 2054.

1481.   Levering, Ralph B. **American Opinion and the
        Russian Alliance, 1939-1945.** Chapel Hill:
        University of North Carolina Press, 1976.
        Analysis of the attitude of opinion makers and
        the public toward the Soviet Union. Holds
        Roosevelt at fault for not preparing public
        opinion for the necessity to accommodate Soviet
        foreign policy goals after World War II.

1482.   Lovenstein, Meno. **American Opinion of Soviet
        Russia.** Washington, D.C.: American Council on
        Public Affairs, 1941.

1483.   MacLean, Elizabeth Kimball. "Joseph E. Davies and
        Soviet-American Relations, 1941-1943."
        Diplomatic History 4 (Winter 1980). Discusses
        Davies's influence on American domestic opinion
        toward the Soviet Union.

1484.   Maddux, Thomas R. "Red Fascism, Brown Bolshevism:
        The American Image of Totalitarianism in the
        1930s." **The Historian** 40,1 (November 1977).
        Maintains that the public identification of
        Fascism and Communism as similar
        totalitarianisms developed before 1939.

1485.   Maddux, Thomas R. "American News Media and Soviet
        Diplomacy, 1934-41." **Journalism Quarterly** 58,1
        (1981). Prior to World War II, conservative US
        newspapers presented the Soviet Union as
        ideologically expansionist. Moderate papers saw
        Soviet policy as chiefly one of national self-
        interest. After the invasion of Finland,
        moderates linked Soviet policy to Czarist
        imperialism. Notes that press coverage
        influenced Roosevelt's foreign policy.

1486.   Margolis, Barbara. "The Cold War, the Mass Media
        and American Culture, 1945-60." Unpublished
        paper, 1983 American Historical Association
        annual meeting.

1487. Ruggiero, Josephine A. "Socio-economic Status
       Factors and Attitudes Toward Nonconformists: A
       Secondary Analysis of Samuel A. Stouffer's
       Communism, Conformity, and Civil Liberties."
       Ph.D. dissertation. Fordham University, 1973.
       See item 1490.

1488. Smith, Tom W. "The Polls: American Attitudes
       toward the Soviet Union and Communism." **Public
       Opinion Quarterly** 47,2 (1983). Surveys national
       polls on attitudes toward the Soviet Union and
       Communism. Finds that attitudes moved from
       hostility in the 1950s to near neutrality in the
       early 1970s and back toward hostility in the
       middle and late 1970s.

1489. Sorenson, Dale. "The Language of a Cold Warrior:
       A Content Analysis of Harry Truman's Public
       Statements." **Social Science History** 3,2 (1979).
       Finds Truman's rhetoric regarding Communism and
       the USSR was consistent whereas public opinion
       changed independently of Truman's statements.
       Rejects the theory that Truman' rhetoric laid
       the groundwork for McCarthyism.

1490. Stouffer, Samuel. **Communism, Conformity, and
       Civil Liberties: A Cross-Section of the Nation
       Speaks Its Mind.** Garden City: Doubleday, 1955.
       Analyzes popular American attitudes toward
       dissent and the Communist Party. See items 1472
       and 1487.

1491. Sylvester, Harold James. "American Public
       Reaction to Communist Expansion: From Yalta to
       NATO." Ph.D. dissertation. University of Kansas,
       1970.

1492. Tyler, Gerry Ruth Sack. "A Contextual Analysis of
       Public Opinion Polls: The Question of the
       Admission of Communist China to the United
       Nations." Ph.D. dissertation. Yale University,
       1972.

1493. Willen, Paul. "Who 'Collaborated' with Russia."
       Antioch Review (Sept. 1954). Surveys enthusiasm
       for Russia in the popular press during the World
       War II alliance.

See items 8, 841, 872, 1162-1164, 1175, and 1186.

29

THE COLD WAR AND THE DOMESTIC COMMUNIST ISSUE

GENERAL

1494. Alberts, Florence G. "Domestic Aspects of the Marshall Plan." Master's thesis. University of Missouri-Kansas City, 1968.

1495. Aronson, James. **The Press and the Cold War.** Indianapolis: Bobbs, Merrill, 1970. Critical of the press for deference to capitalism, accommodation of anti-Communism, and hostility to the Soviet Union. Aronson was an editor of the hard Left **National Guardian.**

1496. Blanchard, Margaret A. "Americans First, Newspapermen Second? The Conflict between Patriotism and Freedom of the Press during the Cold War, 1946-1952." Ph.D. dissertation. University of North Carolina, 1981.

1497. Dobriansky, Lev E. "Reflections on the '20th.'" **Ukrainian Quarterly** 35,4 (1979). Recounts the history of Captive Nations Week.

1498. Freeland, Richard M. "The Cold War and Domestic Communism." Ph.D. dissertation. University of Pennsylvania, 1969.

1499. Freeland, Richard M. **The Truman Doctrine and the Origins of McCarthyism; Foreign Policy, Domestic Politics, and Internal Security, 1946-1948.** New York: Knopf, 1972. Argues that Truman was responsible for McCarthyism because his Cold War policies and his loyalty-security program legitimated anti-Communism.

1500. Hofmann, George F. "Major General Robert W. Grow, the News Media and the American Military Justice System: An Episode in Cold War Politics." Ph.D. dissertation. University of Cincinnati, 1983. Discusses the history of a confusing incident

involving the use of General Grow's private
diary for propaganda purposes by Communists and
the Army's reaction to that use.

1501. Kolko, Gabriel. **The Politics of War: The World
and United States Foreign Policy, 1943-1945.** New
York: Random House, 1978. Denies that the
Duclos article indicated a more aggressive
Soviet foreign policy.

1502. Schlesinger, Arthur, Jr. "Origins of the Cold
War." **Foreign Affairs** 46 (Oct. 1967). Treats
the Duclos article regarding the American
Communist Party as evidence of a change in
Soviet foreign policy.

1503. Theoharis, Athan G. "The Yalta Myths: An Issue in
American Politics, 1945-1955." Ph.D.
dissertation. University of Chicago, 1965.

1504. Theoharis, Athan G. "James F. Byrnes: Unwitting
Yalta Myth-maker." **Political Science Quarterly**
81 (Dec. 1966).

1505. Theoharis, Athan G. **The Yalta Myths: An Issue in
U.S. Politics, 1945-1955.** Columbia: University
of Missouri Press, 1970. Discusses the growth
and manipulation of the idea of betrayal of
American interests at Yalta in domestic
politics.

1506. Tucker, Robert W. **The Radical Left and American
Foreign Policy.** Baltimore: Johns Hopkins, 1971.

1507. Walker, Samuel. "Communists and Isolationism."
Maryland Historian 4,1 (1973).

1508. Welch, Richard E., Jr. "Herbert L. Matthews and
the Cuban Revolution." **The Historian** 47,1 (Nov.
1984). Describes the controversy around the **New
York Times** journalist whose stories in the
period before Fedel Castro took power indicated
that Castro was not a Communist.

POLAND

1509. Karcz, Valerian. "The Polish American Congress,
1944-1959." **Polish American Studies** 16,3-4
(1959). A history of the Polish American
Congress and its hostility to Communism in
Poland and in the US.

1510. Pienkos, Donald E. "The Polish American Congress:
       An Appraisal." **Polish American Studies** 36,2
       (1979). Notes the Polish American Congress was
       formed in 1944 to pressure President Roosevelt
       to save Poland from Communist control.

1511. Sadler, Charles. "Pro-Soviet Polish-Americans:
       Oskar Lange and Russia's Friends in the Polonia,
       1941-1945." **Polish Review** 22,4 (1977). Recounts
       the activities of Oscar Lange in promoting U.S.
       acceptance of Soviet annexation of eastern
       Poland and political domination of Poland.

1512. Theoharis, Athan G. "The Republican Party and
       Yalta: Partisan Exploitation of Polish American
       Concern Over the Conference, 1945-1960." **Polish
       American Studies** (Spring 1971).

CHINA

1513. Bachrack, Stanley D. **The Committee of One
       Million: "China Lobby" Politics, 1953-1971.** New
       York: Columbia University Press, 1976.
       Describes a major anti-Communist, pro-
       Nationalist China lobby organization.

1514. Briggs, Philip J. "Congress and the Cold War:
       U.S.-China Policy, 1955." **China Quarterly (Great
       Britain)** 85 (1981). Discusses the role of
       domestic anti-Communism in passage of the
       Formosa Resolution.

1515. Deleted.

1516. Hedley, John H. "The Truman Administration and
       the 'Loss' of China: A Study of Public Attitudes
       and the President's Policies from the Marshall
       Mission to the Attack on Korea." Ph.D.
       dissertation. University of Missouri, 1964.

1517. Kahn, E.J., Jr. **The China Hands: America's
       Foreign Service Officers and What Befell Them.**
       New York: Viking, 1975. Discusses attacks on
       some foreign service officers for partiality to
       Communist forces in the Chinese civil war.

1518. Keeley, Joseph. **The China Lobby Man.** New
       Rochelle: Arlington House, 1969.

1519. Klehr, Harvey, and Ronald Radosh. "Anatomy of a
       Fix." **The New Republic** (April 21, 1986).
       Discusses how the cross purposes of John Stewart

Service, the FBI, and Tommy Corcoran (a powerful lobbyist associated with the Nationalist Chinese) combined to frustrate a thorough investigation of the **Amerasia** case.

1520. Koen, Ross Y. **The China Lobby in American Politics.** New York: Macmillan, 1960. Studies pro-Kuomintang and anti-Maoist activity.

1521. Kubek, Anthony. **How the Far East Was Lost: American Policy and the Creation of Communist China, 1941-1949.** Chicago: Regnery, 1963.

1522. May, Gary. **China Scapegoat: The Diplomatic Ordeal of John Carter Vincent.** Washington, D.C.: New Republic Books, 1979.

1523. Newman, Robert P. "The Self-Inflicted Wound: The China White Paper of 1949." **Prologue** (Fall 1982).

1524. Service, John S. **Lost Chance in China: The World War II Despatches of John S. Service.** J. Estherick, ed. New York: Random House, 1974. Reprints diplomatic despatches which led to attacks on Service by some anti-Communists.

1525. Shewmaker, Kenneth E. "The American Liberal Dream: Evans F. Carlson and the Chinese Communists, 1937-1947." **Pacific Historical Review** 38,2 (1969). Discusses the history of Evans Carlson, a Marine officer (Carlson's Raiders) who visited China as an intelligence officer and admired the Chinese Communists. Finds that although Joseph McCarthy tried to link Carlson to a Communist conspiracy, Carlson was only one of a number of persons who innocently believed that the Chinese Communists were liberal democrats.

1526. Shewmaker, Kenneth E. **Americans and Chinese Communists, 1927-1945: a Persuading Encounter.** Ithaca: Cornell University Press, 1971. A study of the early encounters between Americans and the Chinese Communists and the image of Chinese Communism these observers tried to convey to other Americans.

1527. Thomas, John N. **Institute of Pacific Relations: Asian Scholars and American Politics.** Seattle: University of Washington Press, 1974. Describes the controversy regarding the IPR's attitude toward Communism. See item 1519.

See items 1981-1983 and 2004.

Strong, Anna Louise

1528. Alley, Rewi. "Some Memories of Anna Louise
       Strong." **Eastern Horizon [Hong Kong]** 9,2 (1970).
       Admiring biographical article regarding Strong's
       political journalism in China, the Soviet Union,
       and the United States.

1529. Duke, David C. "Anna Louise Strong and the Search
       for a Good Cause." **Pacific Northwest Quarterly**
       66,3 (1975). Biographical essay on Strong's
       involvement with Soviet and Chinese Communism.

1530. Duke, David C. "Spy Scares, Scapegoats, and the
       Cold War." **South Atlantic Quarterly** 79,3 (Summer
       1980). Recounts the involvement of Agnes
       Smedley and Anna Louise Strong with Soviet and
       Chinese Communism.

1531. Ogle, Stephanie F. "Anna Louise Strong:
       Progressive and Propagandist." Ph.D.
       dissertation. University of Washington, 1981.

1532. Ostrander, Lucy. "Witness to Revolution: The
       Story of Anna Louise Strong." Seattle: Ostrander
       Production. A documentary film.

1533. Pringle, Robert William, Jr. "Anna Louise Strong:
       Propagandist of Communism." Ph.D. dissertation.
       University of Virginia, 1970. Critical
       biography.

1534. Strong, Tracy B., and Helene Keyssar. **Right in
       Her Soul: The Life of Anna Louise Strong.** New
       York: Random House, 1983. Tracy Strong is Anna
       Strong's great nephew.

1535. **Survey [Great Britain].** "The Strange Case of Anna
       Louise Strong." **Survey [Great Britain]** 53
       (1964). Biographical essay on Strong's
       political journalism on behalf of Soviet and
       Chinese Communism. Judges that her sympathy for
       Communism was based on an emotional and romantic
       socialism rather than ideological Marxism-
       Leninism.

1536. Deleted

Smedley, Agnes

1537. Jaffe, Philip J. "Agnes Smedley: A Reminiscence."
       Survey [Great Britain] 20,4 (1974).

1538. MacKinnon, Jan, and Steve MacKinnon. "Agnes
       Smedley." **Eastern Horizon [Hong Kong]** 19,8
       (1980). Surveys the association of American
       writer Agnes Smedley with Chinese Communists and
       Indian nationalists.

1539. Smedley, Agnes. **Daughter of Earth.** New York:
       Coward-McCann, 1973.

30

ANTI—COMMUNIST LIBERALS AND RADICALS

GENERAL

1540. Bernstein, Barton J. "America in War and Peace:
The Test of Liberalism." **Towards a New Past:
Dissenting Essays in American History.** Barton J.
Bernstein, ed. New York: Pantheon Books, 1967.

1541. Bernstein, Barton J., ed. **Politics and Policies
of the Truman Administration.** Chicago:
Quandrangle Books, Inc., 1970.

1542. Boudna, Martin K. **Concerned About the Planet: The
Reporter Magazine and American Liberalism, 1949-
1968.** Westport: Greenwood, 1977. History of an
influential anti-Communist liberal journal.

1543. Bristol, James E., et al. **Anatomy of Anti-
Communism, A Report Prepared for the Peace
Division of the American Friends Service
Committee.** New York: Hill & Wang, 1969. Judges
anti-Communism to be inherently evil.

1544. **Commentary.** "Liberal Anti-Communism Revisited: A
Symposium." **Commentary** 44,3 (1967). Survey of
twenty-one anti-Communist liberals and Leftists
of the 1940s and 1950s regarding their current
attitude toward anti-Communism, the Vietnam war,
and the consequences of postwar anti-Communism.
Those surveyed were Lionel Abel, Daniel Bazelon,
Daniel Bell, Lewis Coser, Paul Goodman, Michael
Harrington, Sidney Hook, Irving Howe, Murray
Kempton, Robert Lowell, Dwight Macdonald,
William Phillips, Robert Pickus, Philip Rahv,
Harold Rosenberg, Richard Rovere, Arthur
Schlesinger, Jr., Stephen Spender, Diana
Trilling, Lionel Trilling, and Dennis H. Wrong.

1545. Diamond, Sigmund. "On the Road to Camelot." **Labor
History** 21,2 (1980). Notes that Representative
John F. Kennedy linked the 1946 Allis-Chalmers

strike in Milwaukee to the Communist Party at a 1947 Congressional hearing.

1546.   Epstein, Jason. "The CIA and the Intellectuals." **New York Review of Books** (April 20, 1967). Suggests that anti-Communist liberal intellectuals prepared the way for American intervention in Vietnam.

1547.   Erickson, Gerald M., and Judith Joel, eds. **Anti-Communism: The Politics of Manipulation.** Minneapolis: Marxist Education Press, 1986. Various essays which share the themes that anti-Communism is always hostile to working people and "progressives" and that anti-Communism results from deliberate campaigns promoting narrow class interests.

1548.   Fiedler, Leslie. **An End To Innocence: Essays on Culture and Politics.** Boston: Beacon Press, 1955. Discusses the shift of view of intellectuals from the 1930s to the 1950s; vindicates the conviction of the Rosenbergs and examines why liberals tended to regard them as innocent victims. Suggests that McCarthyism is a product of Populism gone sour.

1549.   Fowler, Robert Booth. **Believing Skeptics: American Political Intellectuals, 1945-1964.** Westport: Greenwood Press, 1978. Highly critical examination of the anti-Communist liberalism of postwar intellectuals. Discusses the views of Richard Hofstadter, Daniel Bell, Arthur Schlesinger, Jr., Seymour Martin Lipset, and others.

1550.   Hamby, Alonzo. "The Liberals, Truman, and FDR as Symbol and Myth." **Journal of American History** 56 (March 1970).

1551.   Hamby, Alonzo. "The Vital Center, the Fair Deal, and the Quest for a Liberal Political Economy." **American Historical Review** 77 (June 1972).

1552.   Hamby, Alonzo. **Beyond the New Deal: Harry S. Truman and American Liberalism.** New York: Columbia University Press, 1973. Well researched, scholarly history of postwar liberal politics which discusses the development of anti-Communist liberalism and its conflict with Popular Front liberalism within the context of mainstream postwar politics.

1553. Harper, Alan D. **The Politics of Loyalty; The White House and the Communist Issue, 1946-1952.** Westport: Greenwood, 1969.

1554. Lasch, Christopher. "The Cultural Cold War: A Short History of the Congress for Cultural Freedom." **Towards a New Past: Dissenting Essays in American History.** Barton J. Bernstein, ed. New York: 1968. Argues that anti-Communism is inherently evil and that intellectuals cannot honestly support the West in the Cold War.

1555. Lazarowitz, Arlene. "Years in Exile: The Liberal Democrats, 1950-1959." Ph.D. dissertation. University of California, Los Angeles, 1982. Sees anti-Communism as a force which shaped and distorted liberal Democrats in the 1950s.

1556. Matusow, Allen. "John F. Kennedy and the Intellectuals." **Wilson Quarterly** 7,4 (1983). Discusses the influence of anti-Communist liberal intellectuals on Kennedy. See item 1545.

1557. McAuliffe, Mary Sperling. "The Red Scare and the Crisis in American Liberalism, 1947-1954." Ph.D. dissertation. University of Maryland, 1972.

1558. McAuliffe, Mary Sperling. "Liberals and the Communist Control Act of 1954." **Journal of American History** 63,2 (Sept. 1976). Asserts that Senate liberals, motivated chiefly by concern for their political careers, compromised their principles and endangered civil liberties by supporting the Communist Control Act of 1954.

1559. McAuliffe, Mary Sperling. **Crisis on the Left: Cold War Politics and American Liberals, 1947-1954.** Amherst: The University of Massachusetts Press, 1978. This critical history of anti-Communism liberalism at the national level examines in detail the anti-Communist legislation backed by anti-Communist liberals. Treats the concerns of anti-Communist liberals with the role of the Communist Party in American politics as largely without a basis in fact. See items 2012 and 2014.

1560. O'Neill, William L. **A Better World, The Great Schism: Stalinism and the American Intellectuals.** New York: Simon and Schuster, 1982. Well researched study of the ideological

conflict between Left anti-Communist
intellectuals and those who cooperated with the
Communist Party or supported the Soviet Union.

1561. O'Reilly, Kenneth. "Liberal Values, the Cold War,
and American Intellectuals." **Beyond the Hiss
Case.** Athan Theoharis, ed. Philadelphia: Temple
University Press, 1982.

1562. Parenti, Michael. **The Anti-Communist Impulse.** New
York: Random House, 1969. Finds anti-Communism
to be without any redeeming value.

1563. Steinke, John, and James Weinstein. "McCarthy and
the Liberals." **For a New America: Essays in
History and Politics from "Studies on the Left,"
1959-1967.** James Weinstein and David W. Eakins,
eds. New York: Vintage Books, 1970. Discusses
Wisconsin politics in the late 1940s, holds
anti-Communist liberals responsible in part for
the moral degeneration of the Cold War because
of their own red baiting and their attempt to
respond to McCarthy's by holding him to be
indirectly aiding the Communist cause by his
irresponsible tactics.

1564. Theoharis, Athan G. **Seeds of Repression: Harry S.
Truman and the Origins of McCarthyism.** Chicago:
Quadrangle Books, 1971. Maintains that Truman
and his aides betrayed FDR's policy of
accommodation with the USSR, ignited the Cold
War, and created a climate of fear and suspicion
regarding Communism.

1565. Theoharis, Athan G. "Ignoring History: HST,
Revisionism, and the Press." **Chicago Journalism
Review** (March 1973).

1566. Theoharis, Athan G. "The Politics of Scholarship:
Liberals, Anti-Communism, and McCarthyism." **The
Specter.** Robert Griffith and Athan Theoharis,
eds. New York: New Viewpoints, 1974.

1567. Tyler, Robert L. "The American Veterans
Committee: Out of a Hot War and into the Cold."
American Quarterly 18,3 (1966). Recounts the
history of the AVC as a liberal,
internationalist veterans organization and its
split between Popular Front and anti-Communist
liberal factions.

1568.   Wright, Palmer W. "The 'New Liberalism' of the
        Fifties: Reinhold Niebuhr, David Riesman, Lionel
        Trilling, and the American Intellectual." Ph.D.
        dissertation. University of Michigan, 1966.

        See items 1498 and 1499.

THE AMERICANS FOR DEMOCRATIC ACTION

1569.   Ayer, Douglas R. "American Liberalism and British
        Socialism in a Cold War World, 1945-1951." Ph.D.
        dissertation. Stanford University, 1983.
        Discusses the relationship between the ADA's
        liberalism and Bevanite socialism.

1570.   Brock, Clifton. **Americans for Democratic Action:**
        Its Role in National Politics. Washington, D.C.:
        Public Affairs Press, 1962. Sympathetic survey.

*   Gillon, Steven M. "Liberal Dilemmas: The ADA and
        American Liberalism, 1947-1968." Ph.D.
        dissertation, Brown University, 1985. Cited as
        item 2086.

1571.   Epstein, Marc Joel. "The Third Force: Liberal
        Ideology in a Revolutionary Age, 1945-1950."
        Ph.D. dissertation. University of North
        Carolina, 1971. Finds that the Americans for
        Democratic Action and the Progressive Party
        supported a finding a third way of a mixed
        economy welfare state between unregulated
        capitalism and collectivism. The ADA's anti-
        Communism, however, was not compatible with the
        Progressive Party's rejection of confrontation
        with the Soviet Union.

1572.   Pierce, Robert C. "Liberals and the Cold War:
        Union for Democratic Action and Americans for
        Democratic Action 1940-1949." Ph.D.
        dissertation. University of Wisconsin, 1979.
        Highly critical history of the ADA; treats anti-
        Communism as a betrayal of liberalism and holds
        postwar anti-Communists liberals responsible in
        part for the Vietnam war.

1573.   Wilderson, Frank. "The Roots of the ADA: An
        Interview with Jim Loeb." **ADA World** 37,2
        (Spring, 1982). Discusses the ADA's founding.

1574.   Yarnell, Allen. "Liberals in Action: The
        Americans for Democratic Action and the 1948
        Presidential Election." Unpublished paper, 1971
        American Historical Association meeting.

THE SOCIALIST PARTY

1575.   Gens, Stephen Mark. "Paranoia Bordering on
        Resignation: Norman Thomas and the American
        Socialist Party, 1939-48." Ph.D. dissertation.
        University of Oklahoma, 1982. Notes that the
        Socialist Party became steadily more anti-
        Communist over the period.

1576.   Gershman, Carl. "Totalitarian Menace." **Society**
        18,1 (1980). Recounts from a Social Democratic
        perspective the clashing attitude toward
        Communism which led to the 1972 split between
        the Social Democrats-USA (successor to the
        Socialist Party) and Michael Harrington of the
        Democratic Socialist Organizing Committee.

1577.   Johnpoll, Bernard K. **Pacifist's Progress: Norman
        Thomas and the Decline of American Socialism.**
        Chicago: Quandrangle Books, 1970.

1578.   McGreen, John D. "Norman Thomas and the Search
        for the All-Inclusive Socialist Party." Ph.D.
        dissertation. Rutgers University, 1976.
        Discusses Thomas' attempt to open the Socialist
        Party to all types of radicals in the 1930s and
        the subsequent revolt of the Old Guard, loss of
        union support, entry and exit of the
        Trotskyists, and the breakdown of Socialist
        Party internal democracy.

1579.   Salvatore, Nick. **Eugene V. Debs: Citizen and
        Socialist.** Urbana: University of Illinois Press,
        1982. Discusses Debs' attitude toward Communism.

1580.   Shannon, David. **The Socialist Party of America: A
        History.** New York: Macmillan, 1955. Discusses
        the split over Bolshevism.

1581.   Swanberg, W.A. **Norman Thomas: The Last Idealist.**
        New York: Scribner, 1976.

PARTISAN REVIEW

1582.   Barrett, William. **The Truants: Adventures Among
        the Intellectuals.** Garden City: Anchor Press,
        1947. Memoir by an editor of **Partisan Review.**

1583.   Cooney, Terry Arnold. "High Ideals and Political
        Realities: Literary Radicalism at **Partisan
        Review,** 1934-1937." Ph.D. dissertation. State
        University of New York, Stony Brook, 1976.

1584. Cooney, Terry A. "Cosmopolitan Values and the
       Identification of Reaction: **Partisan Review** in
       the 1930s." **Journal of American History** 68,3
       (Dec. 1981). Argues that the shift of **Partisan
       Review** under the editorship of William Phillips
       and Philip Rahv from Communism to Left anti-
       Stalinism flowed from their views on the need
       for cultural cosmopolitanism, literary
       sophistication, and artistic advance.

1585. Crews, Frederick. "The Partisan." **New York Review
       of Books** (Nov. 23, 1978). Review essay prompted
       by Rahv's **Essays on Literature and Politics,
       1932-1972.**

*   Gilbert, James. "The <u>Partisan Review</u>." **The Left-
       Wing Intellectuals Between the Wars, 1919-1939.**
       Walter Laqueur and George L. Mosse, eds. New
       York: Harper & Row, 1966. Cited as item 2080.

*   Gilbert, James. **Writers and Partisans: A History
       of Literary Radicalism in America.** New York:
       Wiley, 1968. Cited as item 2081.

1586. Glaberson, Eric Abraham. "Historical Humanism in
       the Work of Two New York Intellectuals: Irving
       Howe and Alfred Kazin." Ph.D. dissertation. New
       York University, 1982. Discusses the political
       evolution of Howe, Kazin, and **Partisan Review.**

1587. Kirby, Linda Kaye. "Communism, The Discovery of
       Totalitarianism, and the Cold War: **Partisan
       Review**, 1934 to 1948." Ph.D. dissertation.
       University of Colorado, 1974. Examines the
       shift of **Partisan Review** from a pro-Communist to
       an anti-Communist position; finds its support
       for avant-garde literature, distaste for
       bourgeois culture, and support for artistic and
       intellectual freedom remained unchanged in the
       process. The chief change was a shift from
       optimism to realism about the nature of man and
       rejection of the 'artist as revolutionary' for
       the 'artist as critic of society.'

1588. Lasch, Christopher. "Modernism, Politics, and
       Philip Rahv." **Partisan Review** 47,2 (1980).
       Review-essay prompted by Philip Rahv's **Essays on
       Literature and Politics, 1932-1972.**

1589. Longstaff, S.A. "The New York Family." **Queen's
       Quarterly** 83 (Winter 1976). Discusses Left
       anti-Communist intellectuals grouped around
       Partisan Review.

1590. Longstaff, S.A. "**Partisan Review** and the Second
       World War." **Salmagundi** 43 (Winter 1979).
       Examines the reaction of Left anti-Communist
       intellectuals to the war.

1591. Phillips, William. **A Partisan View: Life Among
       the Intellectuals.** New York: Stein & Day, 1983.
       Memoir by a leading figure of **Partisan Review.**

1592. Rahv, Philip. **Essays on Literature and Politics,
       1932-1972.** Arabel J. Porter and Andrew J.
       Dvosin, eds. Boston: Houghton Mifflin, 1978.
       Essays by the leading figure of **Partisan Review.**
       See items 1585 and 1588.

       See item 1034.

V.F. CALVERTON AND **THE MODERN QUARTERLY**

1593. Genizi, Haim. "V.F. Calverton: Independent
       Radical." Ph.D. dissertation. City University of
       New York, 1968. Intellectual biography
       discussing Calverton's evolution from Communist
       sympathizer to independent radical.

1594. Genizi, Haim. "V.F. Calverton, A Radical
       Magazinist for Black Intellectuals, 1920-1940."
       Journal of Negro History 57 (1972).

1595. Genizi, Haim. "Edmund Wilson and **The Modern
       Monthly,** 1934-5: A Phase in Wilson's
       Radicalism." **Journal of American Studies [Great
       Britain]** 7,3 (1973). Discusses Wilson's unhappy
       association with the anti-Stalinist Marxism of
       The Modern Monthly.

1596. Genizi, Haim. "Disillusionment of a Communist:
       the Case of V.F. Calverton." **Canadian History** 9
       (1974).

1597. Genizi, Haim. "The **Modern Quarterly,** 1923-1940:
       An Independent Radical Magazine." **Labor History**
       15,2 (Spring 1974). Discusses the evolution of
       the journal from Communist-aligned to
       independent Marxist, and to anti-Stalinist
       Marxist.

1598. Hook, Sidney. "**Modern Quarterly,** A Chapter in
       American Radical History." **Labor History** 10,2
       (Spring 1969).

1599. Nash, Michael. "Schism on the Left: The Anti-
       Communism of V.F. Calverton and His **Modern
       Quarterly.**" **Science and Society** 45,4 (1981-82).
       Discusses the movement of Calverton, a literary
       critic, from Communist to anti-Communist and his
       influence on other Left intellectuals. Factors
       affecting the split between Calverton and the
       Communist Party included the Communist Party's
       reaction to his admiration for Trotsky, his
       dislike of party discipline, and Communist Party
       criticism of his detachment from the day-to-day
       political struggle.

1600. Wilcox, Leonard I. "Marxism, Death, and Social
       Hypnosis: V.F. Calverton and the Old Left's
       'Crisis of Reason.'" **History of Political
       Thought** 5 (Spring 1984).

BIOGRAPHICAL MATERIAL

Amlie, Thomas R.

1601. Rosenof, Theodore. "The Political Education of an
       American Radical: Thomas R. Amlie in the
       1930's." **Wisconsin Magazine of History** 58
       (Autumn 1974). Discusses an important anti-
       Communist radical political figure of the 1930s.

1602. Weiss, Stuart L. "Thomas Amlie and the New Deal."
       Mid-America 59 (Jan. 1977).

Becker, Carl

1603. Cairns, John C. "Carl Becker: An American
       Liberal." **Journal of Politics,** 16,4 (1964).
       Discusses the attitude of Becker, a leading
       historian, toward Communism.

Bell, Daniel

1604. Liebowitz, Nathan. **Daniel Bell and the Agony of
       Modern Liberalism.** Westport: Greenwood, 1985.
       Intellectual biography of a prominent anti-
       Communist intellectual.

       See item 1549.

Douglas, Paul H.

1605. Douglas, Paul H. **In the Fullness of Time: The
       Memoirs of Paul H. Douglas.** New York: Harcourt
       Brace Javanovich, 1972. Douglas was a leading

anti-Communist liberal and U.S. Senator from Illinois.

Hook, Sidney

1606.   Crimmins, Carolyn Codamo. "In Search of Sidney Hook: An Interpretative Analysis of Hook's Social, Political and Educational Philosophy from 1930 to 1970." Ph.D. dissertation. Georgia State University - College of Education, 1984. Hook was a leading Left anti-Communist intellectual.

Humphrey, Hubert

1607.   Eisele, Albert. **Almost to the Presidency: A Biography of Two American Politicians.** Blue Earth: The Piper Co., 1972. Discusses the careers of Hubert Humphrey and Eugene McCarthy. Both came into national office as anti-Communist liberals and both became U.S. Senators.

1608.   Gorey, Hays. "'I'm A Born Optimist': The Era of Hubert H. Humphrey." **American Heritage** 29,1 (1978). A short survey of the life and times of a key anti-Communist liberal.

1609.   Griffith, Winthrop. **Humphrey: A Candid Biography.** New York: William Morrow, 1965.

1610.   Humphrey, Hubert H. (Norman Sherman, ed.). **The Education of a Public Man: My Life in Politics.** Garden City: Doubleday, 1976. Discusses the fight within the Minnesota Democratic-Farmer-Labor Party with a pro-Communist faction.

1611.   Nordstrand, Marty. **Humphrey.** Washington, D.C.: Robert B. Luce, 1964.

1612.   Solberg, Carl. **Hubert Humphrey: A Biography.** New York: W. W. Norton, 1984.

Kefauver, Estes

1613.   Gorman, Joseph Bruce. **Kefauver: A Political Biography.** New York: Oxford University Press, 1971. Kefauver was a anti-Communist liberal U.S. Senator.

Lehman, Herbert

1614. Lehman, Herbert. **Liberalism: A Personal Journey.**
        New York: 1958. Lehman was an anti-Communist
        liberal Senator from New York.

1615. Nevins, Allan. **Herbert H. Lehman and His Era.** New
        York: Scribner, 1963.

Lewisohn, Ludwig

1616. Singer, David. "Ludwig Lewisohn: The Making of an
        Anti-Communist." **American Quarterly** 23,5 (1971).
        Argues that Lewisohn's stay in Europe in the
        late 1920s gave him a new respect for
        individualism and prompted his intellectual
        evolution from a prominent intellectual critic
        of American society to a critic of Communism and
        collectivism.

Macdonald, Dwight

*   Cummings, Robert. "Dwight Macdonald in the
        1940s." **New Politics** (1986). Cited as item
        2046.

1617. Macdonald, Dwight. **Memoirs of a Revolutionist.**
        New York: Farrar, Straus, & Cudahy, 1957.
        Essays and memoirs of an influential independent
        Leftist journalist and editor of **Politics.**

1618. Whitfield, Stephen J. **A Critical American: The
        Politics of Dwight Macdonald.** Hamden: Archon,
        1984.

        See item 2046.

Morse, Wayne

1619. Smith, A. Robert. **Tiger in the Senate: The
        Biography of Wayne Morse.** Garden City:
        Doubleday, 1962. Morse was a prominent anti-
        Communist liberal Senator.

Muste, A.J.

1620. Robinson, Jo Ann Ooiman. **Abraham Went Out: A
        Biography of A.J. Muste.** Philadelphia: Temple
        University Press, 1981. Muste led an
        independent Marxist movement in the 1930s. See
        item 563.

Niebuhr, Reinhold

1621. Bingham, June. **Courage to Change: An Introduction to the Life and Thought of Reinhold Niebuhr.** New York: Scribner, 1961. Discusses the intellectual background of a leading postwar anti-Communist liberal intellectual associated with the Americans for Democratic Action.

1622. Black, Claude L. "The Agony of Christian Realism: The Historical Relevance of the Pre-World War II Thought of Reinhold Niebuhr." Ph.D. dissertation. Southern Illinois University at Carbondale, 1981.

1623. Harland, Gordon. **The Thought of Reinhold Niebuhr.** New York: Oxford University Press, 1960.

1624. Kegley, Charles W., and Robert W. Bretall, eds. **Reinhold Niebuhr: His Religious, Social and Political Thought.** New York: Macmillan, 1956.

1625. Link, Michael. **The Social Philosophy of Reinhold Niebuhr: An Historical Introduction.** Chicago: Adams, 1975. Survey of the Niebuhr writings on Communism, Fascism, and liberalism from 1920 to 1971.

1626. Merkley, Paul. "Reinhold Niebuhr: the Decisive Years, 1916-1941: A Study of the Interaction of Religious Faith and Political Commitment in an American Intellectual." Ph.D. dissertation. University of Toronto, 1966. Finds that Niebuhr came to regard Marxist socialism as a religious distortion derived from the Christian heresy of the immanent kingdom of God.

1627. Merkley, Paul. **Reinhold Niebuhr: A Political Account.** Montreal: McGill-Queen's University Press, 1975. Analysis of the theological basis of Niebuhr's political stance.

1628. Odegarde, Holton P. **Sin and Science: Reinhold Niebuhr As Political Theologian.** Yellow Springs: Antioch Press, 1956.

1629. Poole, Thomas George. "Contemporary Christian Realism: The Ongoing Relevance of Reinhold Niebuhr." Ph.D. dissertation. Pennsylvania State University, 1984. Argues for a fruitful dialogue between Liberation Theology and Christian Realism.

1630.   Tietje, Louis H. "Was Reinhold Niebuhr Ever a
        Marxist? An Investigation in the Assumptions of
        His Early Interpretation and Critique of
        Marxism." Ph.D. dissertation. Union Theological
        Seminary, 1984. Argues that the anthropology of
        Niebuhr's Christian Realism was fundamentally at
        variance with Marxism and that Niebuhr had
        developed this anthropology before the period
        when he was a self-avowed socialist.

        See item 1568.

Pepper, Claude D.

1631.   Stoesen, Alexander R. "The Senatorial Career of
        Claude D. Pepper." Ph.D. dissertation.
        University of North Carolina, 1965. Discusses
        Pepper's involvement in the factional struggle
        within postwar liberalism.

Schlesinger, Arthur M., Jr.

1632.   Engelhardt, Carroll. "Man in the Middle: Arthur
        M. Schlesinger, Jr., and Postwar American
        Liberalism." **South Atlantic Quarterly** 80,2
        (1981). Analyses the political thought of
        Schlesinger as a representative of the centrist,
        anti-Communist liberal intellectuals of the
        postwar period.

1633.   Nuechterlein, James A. "Arthur M. Schlesinger,
        Jr., and the Discontents of Postwar American
        Liberalism." **Review of Politics** 39 (Jan. 1977).

1634.   Wreszin, Michael. "Arthur Schlesinger Jr.,
        Scholar-Activist in Cold War America: 1946-
        1956." **Salmagundi** 1984.

        See item 1549.

Voorhis, Jerry

1635.   Bullock, Paul. **Jerry Voorhis: The Idealist as
        Politician.** New York: Vantage Press, 1978.

1636.   Voorhis, Jerry. **Confessions of a Congressman.**
        Garden City: Doubleday, 1947.

31

ANTI-COMMUNIST LAWS AND DEMOCRATIC LIBERTIES

1637. Alexander, Milnor. "Political Repression in the
        USA." **Canadian Dimension** 11,6 (1976). Judges
        that radicals, Communists, and ordinary citizens
        were repressed by the House Un-American
        Activities Committee, loyalty oaths, the
        International Security Act of 1950, and the
        McCarran-Walter Immigration Act.

1638. Auerbach, Jerold S. "Patrician as Libertarian:
        Zechariah Chafee, Jr. and Freedom of Speech."
        New England Quarterly 42 (Dec. 1969). Notes
        Chafee's role in defending free speech rights of
        Communists and other radicals. See item 1693.

1639. Baker, Liva. **Felix Frankfurter**. New York: Coward-
        McCann, 1969. Discusses Frankfurter's
        involvement and views on the legality of various
        internal security prosecutions.

1640. Barber, Kathleen L. "The Legal Status of the
        American Communist Party: 1965." **Journal of
        Public Law** 15 (1966).

1641. Barth, Alan. **The Loyalty of Free Men**. New York:
        Viking, 1951. Discusses democratic liberties
        and the Communist Party.

1642. Belknap, Michael R. "The Smith Act and the
        Communist Party: A Study in Political Justice."
        Ph.D. dissertation. University of Wisconsin,
        1973. A history of legal attacks on the
        Communist Party culminating in the Smith Act
        trials.

1643. Belknap, Michael R. **Cold War Political Justice:
        The Smith Act, The Communist Party, and American
        Civil Liberties**. Westport: Greenwood Press,
        1977. Study of the Smith Act trials of the
        leaders of the Communist Party and the reaction
        of the Communist Party to the prosecution.

Attributes the decline of the Communist Party
chiefly to the Smith Act prosecutions.
Discusses the effect on the party of the
decision to go underground. Generally treats
the Communist Party as a harmless organization
devoid of importance except as a victim of
oppression. See item 2014.

1644. Belknap, Michael R., ed. **American Political
Trials.** Westport: Greenwood Press, 1981.
Collection of essays on trials with political
connotations. Included are essays by Harold
Josephson on the New York 1920 trial of Benjamin
Gitlow, a early Communist leader; Charles Martin
on the 1933 Georgia trial of Angelo Herndon, a
black Communist organizer, on incitement to
insurrection charges; and a Belknap article on
the Smith Act trials of Communist leaders in the
1940s and 1950s.

1645. Berman, William C. "Civil Rights and Civil
Liberties." **The Truman Period as a Research
Field.** Richard S. Kirkendall, ed. Columbia:
University of Missouri Press, 1967.

1646. Berns, Walter. **Freedom, Virtue and the First
Amendment.** Baton Rouge: Louisiana State
University Press, 1957. Discusses democratic
liberties and the Communist Party.

1647. Bigel, Alan Ira. "The Supreme Court on
Presidential and Congressional Powers Relating
to Foreign Affairs, War Powers, and Internal
Security 1935-1980." Ph.D. dissertation. New
School for Social Research, 1984.

1648. Blum, Richard H. **Surveillance and Espionage in a
Free Society.** New York: Praeger, 1972.

1649. Bolner, James. "Mr. Chief Justice Vincent and the
Communist Controversy: a Reassessment." **Kentucky
Historical Society Register** 66 (1968).

1650. Brooks, Alexander. **Civil Rights and Liberties in
the U.S., an Annotated Bibliography.** New York:
Civil Liberties Educational Foundation, 1962.

1651. Chafee, Zechariah, Jr. **Free Speech in the United
States.** Cambridge: Harvard University Press,
1941. Discusses abridgements of free speech
rights in cases involving Communists and others.

1652.   Chafee, Zechariah, Jr. **The Blessings of Liberty.**
        Philadelphia: Lippincott, 1956.

1653.   Chase, Harold. "Controlling Subversive
        Activities: An Analysis of the Efforts of
        National Government to Control the Indigenous
        Communists, 1933-1952." Ph.D. dissertation.
        Princeton University, 1954.

1654.   Chase, Harold. **Security and Liberty: The Problem
        of Native Communists, 1947-1955.** Garden City:
        Doubleday, 1955.

1655.   Clardy, J.V. "Communist Publications in the U.S.
        Mail." **Western Humanities Review** 20 (1966).

1656.   Connolly, Peter M. "The Early Fifties: Another
        Look." **Dissent** 24,4 (1977). Maintains that
        Communists have an absolute right to their
        beliefs and that many were made martyrs in the
        1950s.

1657.   Cook, Thomas I. **Democratic Rights versus
        Communist Activity.** Garden City: Doubleday,
        1954. A discussion (and defense) of the legal
        issues involved in outlawing the Communist
        party.

1658.   Ehrmann, H.W. "Zeitgeist and the Supreme Court."
        Antioch Review 11 (Dec. 1951). Discusses
        democratic liberties and treatment of the
        Communist Party.

1659.   Goldstein, Robert Justin. **Political Repression in
        Modern America: From 1870 to the Present.**
        Boston: G.K. Hall, 1978.

1660.   Grodzins, Morton. **The Loyal and the Disloyal.**
        Chicago: University of Chicago Press, 1956.

1661.   Group, David J. "The Legal Repression of the
        American Communist Party, 1946-1960: a Study in
        the Legitimation of Coercion." Ph.D.
        dissertation. University of Massachusetts,
        1979. A Marxist-Weberian analysis that finds
        legal attacks on the Communist Party to be a
        symptom of the deepening crisis of late
        capitalism and of increasing erosion of legal
        formalism.

1662.   Hull, Elizabeth A. "Sherman Minton and the Cold
        War Court." Ph.D. dissertation. New School for

Social Research, 1977. Regards Minton's record
as undistinguished because of his belief in
judicial restraint and judicial deference to the
policy choices of elected officials in regards
to internal security and foreign policy issues.

1663.   Kinoy, Arthur. **Rights On Trial: The Odyssey of a
People's Lawyer.** Cambridge: Harvard University
Press, 1983.

1664.   Konvitz, Milton R. **Fundamental Liberties of a
Free People.** Ithaca: Cornell University Press,
1957. Discusses democratic liberties and
treatment of the Communist Party.

1665.   Kutler, Stanley I. **The American Inquisition:
Justice and Injustice in the Cold War.** New York:
Hill & Wang, 1982. Case studies of several
internal security prosecutions; included are
Harry Bridges, Owen Lattimore, John William
Powell, and Beatrice Braude. Sees massive
oppression and pervasive political distortion of
the legal system in the persecution of those who
challenged authority.

1666.   Levin, Murray B. **Political Hysteria in America:
The Democratic Capacity for Repression.** New
York: Basic Books, 1971.

1667.   Longaker, Richard P. **The President and Individual
Liberties.** Ithaca: Cornell University Press,
1961.

1668.   Mendelson, Wallace. "Clear & Present Danger --
From Schenck to Dennis." **Columbia Law Review** 52
(March 1952). Discusses the evolution of
Supreme court decisions on free speech and
Communist political activity.

1669.   McAuliffe, Mary S. "The Politics of Civil
Liberties: The American Civil Liberties Union
During the McCarthy Years." **The Specter.** Robert
Griffith and Athan Theoharis, eds. New York: New
Viewpoints, 1974.

1670.   Nagy, Alex. "Federal Censorship of Communist
Political Propaganda and the First Amendment:
1941-1961." Ph.D. dissertation. University of
Wisconsin - Madison, 1973.

1671.   Nathanson, Nathaniel. "The Communist Trial and
the Clear-and-Present Danger Test." **Harvard Law
Review** 63 (1950).

1672. O'Brien, John Lord. "New Encroachments on
       Individual Freedom." **Harvard Law Review** 66 (Nov.
       1952).

1673. O'Brien, Kevin J. "Dennis v. U.S.: The Cold War,
       the Communist Conspiracy and the F.B.I." Ph.D.
       dissertation. Cornell University, 1979. Argues
       that the Smith Act prosecutions were undertaken
       largely to justify and serve the FBI's internal
       security apparatus.

1674. Pahl, Thomas L. "The Dilemma of a Civil
       Libertarian: Francis Biddle and the Smith Act."
       Minnesota Academy of Science Journal 34 (1967).

1675. Pritchett, C.H. **Civil Liberties and the Vinson
       Court.** Chicago: University of Chicago Press,
       1954.

1676. Schaar, John H. **Loyalty in America.** Berkeley:
       University of California Press, 1957.

1677. Sheldon, Charles Harvey. "Constitutionalism and
       Subversion: A Comparative Study of Communist
       Parties and High Courts." Ph.D. dissertation.
       University of Oregon, 1965.

1678. Sheldon, Charles H. "Public Opinion and High
       Courts: Communist Party Cases in Four
       Constitutional Systems." **Western Political
       Quarterly** 20,2 (1967). Examines the
       relationship between public opinion and court
       decisions regarding the Communist Party in
       Australia, Canada, the Federal Republic of
       Germany, and the U.S. in the 1950s.

1679. Somerville, John. **The Communist Trials and the
       American Tradition: Expert Testimony on Force
       and Violence.** New York: Cameron Associates,
       1956. Discusses democratic liberties and
       treatment of the Communist Party.

1680. Somerville, John. "Law, Logic, and Revolution."
       Western Political Quarterly 14 (Dec. 1961).
       Discusses democratic liberties and treatment of
       the Communist Party.

1681. Steinberg, Peter L. "The Great 'Red Menace': U.S.
       Prosecution of American Communists, 1947-1951."
       Ph.D. dissertation. New York University, 1979.

1682. Steinberg, Peter L. **The Great "Red Menace":
       United States Prosecution of American
       Communists, 1947-1952.** Westport: Greenwood
       Press, 1984. Finds that the Communist Party was
       a benign influence on progressive politics and
       that the prosecution of the Communist Party was
       an oppressive act rooted in baseless paranoia.

1683. Sterling, David L. "The 'Naive Liberal,' the
       'Devious Communists' and the Johnson Case." **Ohio
       History** 78,2 (Spring 1969). Recounts the legal
       contest around prosecution of three Communist
       agitators under Ohio's criminal syndicalism law.
       Maintains that the American Civil Liberties
       Union won the case (1930) by taking control from
       International Labor Defense and substituting a
       defense based on freedom of speech for the ILD's
       propagandistic tactics.

1684. Sutherland, Arthur E., Jr. "Freedom & Internal
       Security." **Harvard Law Review** 64 (1951).
       Discusses democratic liberties and treatment of
       the Communist Party.

1685. Tanner, William. "The Passage of the Internal
       Security Act of 1950." Ph.D. dissertation.
       University of Kansas, 1971.

1686. Tanner, William, and Robert Griffith.
       "Legislative Politics and 'McCarthyism': The
       Internal Security Act of 1950." **The Specter.**
       Robert Griffith and Athan Theoharis, eds. New
       York: New Viewpoints, 1974.

       See items 1918-1920.

32

THE "RED SCARE" OF 1919-1920

GENERAL

1687. American Institute for Marxist Studies. "The Soviet Ship **Shilka** in Seattle." New York: American Institute for Marxist Studies, n.d. Memoir by the commissar of the 'Shilka' about the visit to Seattle shortly after the Bolshevik Revolution to explain the revolution to American workers. See item 1690.

1688. Candeloro, Dominic. "Louis F. Post and the Red Scare of 1920." **Prologue** 11 (Spring 1979). Discusses Assistant Secretary of Labor Post's blocking of several hundred deportations of suspected radicals after what Post judged to be irregular procedures.

1689. Coben, Stanley. **A. Mitchell Palmer: Politician.** New York: Columbia University Press, 1963. Biography of the U.S. Attorney General who ordered numerous legal assaults on the early Communist Party and other radical groups in 1919-1920.

1690. Coben, Stanley. "A Study in Nativism: The American Red Scare of 1919-1920." **Political Science Quarterly** 79 (March 1964).

*   Emerson, Hough. **The Web.** Chicago: Reilly and Lee, 1919. Cited as item 2058. Authorized history of the American Protective League, a hyper-patriotic and anti-Bolshevik organization active during World War I and the "Red Scare."

1691. Gengarelly, William Anthony. "Resistance Spokesmen: Opponents of the Red Scare, 1919-1921." Ph.D. dissertation. Boston University, 1972. Discusses criticism and opposition to federal legal attacks on radicals by the American Civil Liberties Union, National Popular

Government League, and others. Finds that the
opposition was in part successful in blunting
and ending the attacks.

1692.   Gengarelly, William Anthony. "Secretary of Labor
William B. Wilson and the Red Scare, 1919-1920."
Pennsylvania History 47,4 (1980). Describes
Wilson's initial acquiescence to Attorney
General Palmer's deportation of suspected
immigrant radicals under arbitrary procedures
and his later decision, initiated by Under
Secretary Louis Post, to end irregular
deportations.

1693.   Irons, Peter H. "'Fighting Fair': Zechariah
Chafee, Jr., the Department of Justice, and the
'Trial at the Harvard Club.'" **Harvard Law Review**
94 (April 1981). Discusses the attempt to
dismiss Chafee from his Harvard post because of
his criticism of Justice Department deportation
of Communist and radical aliens.

1694.   LeWarne, Charles P. "The Bolsheviks Land in
Seattle: The **Shilka** Incident of 1917." **Arizona
and the West** 20 (Spring 1978). See item 1687.

1695.   Murphy, Paul L. "Normalcy, Intolerance, and
American Character." **Virginia Quarterly Review**
40 (1964).

1696.   Murphy, Paul L. **World War I and the Origin of
Civil Liberties in the United States.** New York:
Norton, 1980.

1697.   Murray, Robert K. "Communism and the Great Steel
Strike of 1919." **Labor History** 38,3 (Dec. 1951).
Discusses the clamour in the popular press and
from company circles that radicals inspired the
1919 strike; notes that radicals claimed credit
for the strike and that their claims were used
as evidence by the press.

1698.   Murray, Robert K. **Red Scare: A Study in National
Hysteria, 1919-1920.** New York: McGraw-Hill,
1955.

1699.   Panunzio, C.M. **The Deportation Cases of 1919-
1920.** New York: D.A Capo Press, 1970.

1700.   Preston, William, Jr. **Aliens and Dissenters:
Federal Suppression of Radicals, 1903-1933.**
Cambridge: Harvard University Press, 1963.

1701. Ragan, Fred Donald. "The **New Republic:** Red
       Hysteria and Civil Liberties." Ph.D.
       dissertation. University of Georgia, 1965.
       Discusses **The New Republic's** reaction and
       opposition to the excesses of the post-World War
       I Red Scare.

1702. Scheiber, Harry N. **Wilson Administration and
       Civil Liberties, 1917-1921.** Ithaca: Cornell
       University Press, 1960.

       See item 626.

THE "RED SCARE" IN NEW YORK

1703. Colburn, David R. "Governor Alfred E. Smith and
       the Red Scare, 1919-1920." **Political Science
       Quarterly** 88 (1973).

1704. Jaffe, Julian F. "Red Scare and the New York
       Schools 1917-1920." **Montclair Journal of Social
       Sciences and the Humanities** 1 (1972).

1705. Jaffe, Julian F. **Crusade Against Radicalism: New
       York During the Red Scare, 1914-1924.** Port
       Washington: Kennikat Press, 1972. Study of the
       attacks on Socialists, anarchists, and the new
       Communist Party by public authorities in New
       York.

1706. Josephson, Harold. "The Dynamics of Repression:
       New York During the Red Scare." **Mid-America** 59
       (1977).

1707. Pawa, J. M. "The Search for Black Radicals:
       American and British Documents Relative to the
       1919 Red Scare." **Labor History** 16,2 (Spring
       1975). Discusses Lusk Committee (New York)
       reports on radical activity among Blacks.

1708. Urofsky, Melvin I. "Note on the Expulsion of Five
       Socialists." **New York History** 47 (1966).
       Discusses the expulsion of elected Socialist
       legislators from the New York Legislature.

1709. Vadney, Thomas E. "Politics of Repression: Case
       Study of Red Scare in New York." **New York
       History** 49 (1968).

       See item 17.

THE "RED SCARE" IN NEW HAMPSHIRE

1710. Williams, David. "'Sowing the Wind': The
        Deportation Raids of 1920 in New Hampshire."
        Historical New Hampshire 34 (Spring 1979).
        Discusses federal arrests of suspected alien
        Communists and radicals.

THE "RED SCARE" IN DENVER

1711. Cook, Philip L. "Red Scare in Denver." **Colorado
        Magazine,** 43,4 (1966). Discusses a 1920 panic
        in Denver over Bolshevism; finds that
        sensational press coverage contributed to the
        scare. A trolley car strike in which several
        people were killed became associated with the
        issue.

THE SEATTLE GENERAL STRIKE

1712. Friedheim, Robert. **The Seattle General Strike.**
        Seattle: University of Washington Press, 1964.
        Comprehensive history of the Seattle general
        strike of 1919.

1713. O'Connor, Harvey. **Revolution in Seattle.** New
        York: Monthly Review Press, 1964. Discusses the
        Seattle general strike.

33

THE FEDERAL LOYALTY-SECURITY PROGRAM

1714. Abbott, Roger S. "The Federal Loyalty Program: Background and Problems." **American Political Science Review** 42 (June 1948).

1715. Barth, Alan. **Government by Investigation.** New York: Viking, 1955.

1716. Bontecou, Eleanor. **The Federal Loyalty-Security Program.** Ithaca: Cornell University Press, 1953.

1717. Brown, Ralph S., Jr. **Loyalty and Security: Employment Tests in the United States.** New Haven: Yale University Press, 1958.

1718. Cushman, Robert E. "The Purge of Federal Employees Accused of Disloyalty." **Public Administration Review** 3 (Autumn 1943).

1719. Emerson, Thomas I., and D.M. Helfeld. "Loyalty Among Government Employees." **Yale Law Journal** (1948).

1720. Ernst, Max. "Some Affirmative Legislation for a Loyalty Program." **American Scholar** 19 (Oct. 1950).

1721. Gellhorn, Walter. **Security, Loyalty, and Science.** Ithaca: Cornell University Press, 1950. Discusses democratic liberties and government loyalty and security programs.

1722. Henderson, John. **The United States Information Agency.** New York: F.A. Praeger, 1969. Discusses McCarthy's assault on the agency for suspect loyalty.

1723. Lewy, Guenter. **The Federal Loyalty-Security Program: The Need for Reform.** Washington, D.C.: American Enterprise Institute, 1983.

1724. Merson, Martin. **The Private Diary of a Public
       Servant**. New York: Macmillan, 1955.

1725. Morgenthau, Hans J. "Impact of Loyalty-Security
       Measures on the State Department." **Bulletin of
       Atomic Scientists** 11 (1955).

1726. Nikoloric, L.A. "The Government Loyalty Program."
       American Scholar 19 (Summer 1950).

1727. O'Brien, John Lord. "Loyalty Tests and Guilt by
       Association." **Harvard Law Review** 61 (April
       1948).

1728. Schuman, Frederick L. "'Bill of Attainder' in the
       Seventy-Eighth Congress." **American Political
       Science Review** 37 (Oct. 1943). Discusses the
       attempt to withhold appropriations for salaries
       for specific government employees suspected of
       Communist links.

1729. Shattuck, Henry L. "The Loyalty Review Board of
       the U.S. Civil Service Commission, 1947-1953."
       Massachusetts Historical Society Proceedings 78
       (1966). Memoir by a member of the Board.

1730. Stein, Bruno. "Loyalty and Security Cases in
       Arbitration." **Industrial and Labor Relations
       Review** 16 (Oct. 1963).

1731. Theoharis, Athan G. "Attorney General Clark,
       Internal Security and the Truman
       Administration." **New University Thought** 6
       (Spring 1968).

1732. Theoharis, Athan G. "The Rhetoric of Politics:
       Foreign Policy, Internal Security, and Domestic
       Politics in the Truman Era, 1945-1950." **Politics
       and Policies of the Truman Administration.**
       Barton J. Bernstein, ed. Chicago: Quandrangle
       Books, 1970.

1733. Theoharis, Athan G. "The Escalation of the
       Loyalty Program." **Politics and Policies of the
       Truman Administration.** Barton J. Bernstein, ed.
       Chicago: Quandrangle Books, 1970.

1734. Theoharis, Athan G. "The Threat to Civil
       Liberties." **Cold War Critics: Alternatives to
       American Foreign Policy in the Truman Years.**
       Thomas G. Paterson, ed. Chicago: Quandrangle
       Books, 1971.

1735. Thompson, Francis H. "Truman and Congress: The
       Issue of Loyalty, 1946-1952." Ph.D.
       dissertation. Texas Tech University, 1970.

1736. Thompson, Francis H. **The Frustration of Politics:
       Truman, Congress, and the Loyalty Issue, 1945-
       1953.** Rutherford: Fairleigh Dickinson
       University Press, 1979. Argues that Truman's
       loyalty program was chiefly designed to preempt
       more extreme programs proposed by Congress and
       that Truman's personal rhetoric avoided
       inflaming concern about domestic subversion.

1737. Yarmolinsky, Adam. **Case Studies in Personnel
       Security.** Washington, D.C.: Bureau of National
       Affairs, 1955.

1738. Beck, Carl. **Contempt of Congress: Prosecutions Initiated by the Committee on Un-American Activities, 1951-1957.** New Orleans: Hauser Press, 1959.

1739. Belfrage, Cedric. **The American Inquisition, 1945-1960.** Indianapolis: Bobbs-Merrill Co., 1973. Journalistic expose of congressional investigations of Communism. Likens the investigations to inquisitions into heresy by the Catholic Holy Office.

1740. Bentley, Eric, ed. **Thirty Years of Treason: Excerpts from Hearings Before the House Committee on Un-American Activities, 1938-1968.** New York: Viking Press, 1971.

1741. Buckley, William F., Jr., and the editors of the **National Review.** **The Committee and Its Critics: A Calm Review of the House Committee on Un-American Activities.** New York: Putnam's, 1962. Essays describing and defending many aspects of the activities of the House Un-American Activities Committee. Contains an extensive bibliography of the Committee's hearings and reports.

1742. Cantelon, Philip Louis. "In Defense of America: Congressional Investigations of Communism in the United States, 1919-1935." Ph.D. dissertation. Indiana University, 1971. Summarizes the testimony and surveys the goals and recommendations of various series of hearings.

1743. Carlson, Lewis H. "J. Parnell Thomas and the House Committee on Un-American Activities, 1938-1948." Ph.D. dissertation. Michigan State University, 1967.

1744. Carr, Robert K. **The House Committee on Un-
       American Activities, 1945-1959.** Ithaca: Cornell
       University Press, 1952.

1745. Donner, Frank J. **The Un-Americans.** New York:
       Ballantine, 1961.

1746. Goodman, Walter. **The Committee: The Extraordinary
       Career of the House Committee on Un-American
       Activities.** New York: Farrar, Straus and Giroux,
       1968. A hostile examination of the House
       Committee on Un-American Activities from a
       liberal perspective. Particularly thorough on
       the ignorance, viciousness, and corruption of
       some members of the committee.

1747. Hamilton, James. **The Power to Probe.** New York:
       Random House, 1976. Examines the power of
       Congress to investigate.

1748. Kluger, Richard. **Un-American Activities.** Garden
       City: Doubleday, 1982.

1749. Matusow, Harvey. **False Witness.** New York: Cameron
       and Kahn, 1955. Matusow, an ex-Communist who
       testified in a number of investigations of
       Communist activity, here states that often he
       testified falsely.

1750. Ogden, August Raymond. **The Dies Committee: A
       Study of the Special House Committee for the
       Investigation of Un-American Activities, 1938-
       1944.** Washington, D.C.: Catholic University of
       America, 1945.

1751. Packer, Herbert L. **Ex-Communist Witnesses, Four
       Studies in Fact Finding.** Stanford: Stanford
       University Press, 1962. Examines the testimony
       of Chambers, Bentley, Budenz, and Lautner.

1752. Preston, William, Jr. "The 1940's: The Way We
       Really Were." **Civil Liberties Review** 2,1 (1975).
       Discusses public attitudes toward civil
       liberties and examines the anti-Communist
       campaign of the House Committee on Un-American
       Activities.

1753. Rusher, William A. **Special Counsel: An Insider's
       Report on Senate Investigations into Communism.**
       New Rochelle: Arlington House, 1968.

1754.   Schneier, Edward V.   "The Politics of Anti-
        Communism: A Study of the House Committee on Un-
        American Activities and its Role in the
        Political Process." Ph.D. dissertation.
        Claremont Graduate School, 1964. Finds that the
        House Un-American Activities Committee's
        emphasis on advocacy, exposure and education
        rather than the production of legislation was
        not unusual in congressional history; however, the
        HUAC did have unusual internal cohesiveness and
        stable values among its members.

1755.   Schneier, Edward V.   "White-Collar Violence and
        Anticommunism." **Society** 13,3 (1976). Argues
        that the House Un-American Activities Committee
        waged a form of vigilante violence against the
        Communist Party.

1756.   Simmons, Jerold.   "The Origins of the Campaign to
        Abolish HUAC, 1956-1961, The California
        Connection." **Southern California Quarterly** 64,2
        (1982).

1757.   Swerdlow, Amy.   "Ladies' Day at the Capitol: Women
        Strike for Peace versus HUAC." **Feminist Studies**
        8 (Fall 1982).

        See item 647.

35

THE FEDERAL BUREAU OF INVESTIGATION AND COMMUNISM

1758. Belknap, Michael R. "Uncooperative Federalism: The Failure of the Bureau of Investigation's Intergovernmental Attack on Radicalism." **Publius** 12,2 (1982).

1759. Berens, John F. "The FBI and Civil Liberties from Franklin Roosevelt to Jimmy Carter -- An Historical Overview." **Michigan Academician** 13 (Fall 1980).

1760. Cook, Fred J. **The FBI Nobody Knows.** New York: Pyramid, 1965. Hostile and journalistic.

1761. Corson, William R. **The Armies of Ignorance: The Rise of the American Intelligence Empire.** New York: Dial Press, 1977. Discusses the FBI and other intelligence and security agencies.

1762. Donner, Frank J. "Hoover's Legacy: A Nationwide System of Political Surveillance Based on the Spurious Authority of a Press Release." **The Nation** (June 1, 1974). Charges that Hoover created a police state apparatus based on distorting presidential authorizations.

1763. Donner, Frank J. "Let Him Wear A Wolf's Head: What the FBI did to William Albertson." **Civil Liberties Review** 3,1 (1976). Maintains that Albertson's expulsion from the Communist Party in 1964 was based on evidence fabricated by the FBI in order to disrupt the party.

1764. Donner, Frank J. **The Age of Surveillance: The Aims and Methods of American's Political Intelligence System.** New York: Knopf, 1980. Asserts that a "paranoiac" American government, driven by irrational nativism and anti-Communism, has pursued police state policies.

1765. Gibson, Dirk C. "Neither God nor Devil: A
       Rhetorical Perspective on the Political Myths of
       J. Edgar Hoover." Ph.D. dissertation. Indiana
       University, 1983.

1766. Halperin, Morton, et al. **The Lawless State: The
       Crimes of the United States Intelligence
       Agencies.** New York: Penguin Books, 1976.
       Hostile and journalistic.

1767. Hoover, J. Edgar. **Masters of Deceit: The Story of
       Communism in America and How to Fight It.** New
       York: Holt, 1958. Hoover, the longtime head of
       the FBI, treats the Communist Party as chiefly a
       conspiracy under foreign control.

1768. Horowitz, Irving Louis. "Reactionary Immorality:
       The Private Life in Public Testimony of John
       Edgar Hoover." **Catalyst** 5 (1970). Asserts that
       Hoover was a reactionary who abused the
       authority given by Congress and who pursued
       Communists with more enthusiasm than he showed
       in pursuing right-wing extremists.

1769. Lowenthal, Max. **The Federal Bureau of
       Investigation.** New York: Sloane, 1950.
       Discusses FBI involvement in internal security
       operations against the Communist Party.

1770. Marro, Anthony. "FBI Break-in Policy." **Beyond the
       Hiss Case.** Athan Theoharis, ed. Philadelphia:
       Temple University Press, 1982.

1771. Morgan, Richard E. **Domestic Intelligence:
       Monitoring Dissent In America.** Austin:
       University of Texas Press, 1980.

1772. O'Reilly, Kenneth. "The Bureau and the Committee:
       A Study of J. Edgar Hoover's FBI, the House
       Committee on Un-American Activities, and the
       Communist Issue." Ph.D. dissertation. Marquette
       University, 1981. Asserts that the FBI was
       engaged in promoting its own particular
       conservative political vision in its
       dissemination of information on internal
       security.

1773. O'Reilly, Kenneth. "A New Deal for the FBI: The
       Roosevelt Administration, Crime Control, and
       National Security." **Journal of American History**
       69,3 (Dec. 1982). Finds that the Roosevelt
       administration expanded FBI jurisdiction,

manpower, and authorization to investigate
subversion and political dissent. Examines
Hoover's campaign to achieve popular support;
surveys FBI investigations of political figures
and organizations.

1774. O'Reilly, Kenneth. "The FBI, the Congress and
McCarthyism." **Beyond the Hiss Case.** Athan
Theoharis, ed. Philadelphia: Temple University
Press, 1982.

1775. O'Reilly, Kenneth. **Hoover and the Un-Americans:
The FBI, HUAC, and The Red Menace.** Philadelphia:
Temple University Press, 1983. Finds
surreptitious FBI cooperation with the House Un-
American Activities Committee. Highly critical
of anti-Communist liberals.

1776. O'Reilly, Kenneth. "The Roosevelt Administration
and Legislative-Executive Conflict: The FBI vs.
the Dies Committee." **Congress & the Presidency**
10,1 (1983).

1777. O'Reilly, Kenneth. "The FBI and the Origins of
McCarthyism." **Historian** 45 (May 1983).

1778. O'Reilly, Kenneth. "Herbert Hoover and the FBI."
Annals of Iowa 47 (Summer 1983).

1779. O'Reilly, Kenneth. "Un-American Activities: The
FBI, Congress, and the Search for Subversives."
Unpublished paper, 1984 Organization of American
Historians convention.

1780. Salisbury, Harrison E. "A Comment on Theoharis'
'Unanswered Question.'" **Government Publication
Review** 10,3 (1983).

1781. Salisbury, Harrison E. "The Strange
Correspondence of Morris Ernst and John Edgar
Hoover, 1934-1964." **The Nation** (Dec. 1, 1984).
Notes Ernst's attempts to cooperate with the
FBI.

1782. Spolansky, Jacob. **The Communist Trail in America.**
New York: Macmillan, 1951. Spolansky, a Russian
immigrant and one-time radical, was one of the
first Federal agents to investigate the
Communist Party.

1783. Theoharis, Athan G., and Elizabeth Meyer. "The
'National Security' Justification for Electronic

Eavesdropping: An Elusive Exception." **Wayne Law Review** (Spring 1968).

1784. Theoharis, Athan G. "Misleading the Presidents: Thirty Years of Wiretapping." **The Nation** (June 14, 1971).

1785. Theoharis, Athan G. "The FBI's Stretching of Presidential Directives, 1936-1953." **Political Science Quarterly** 91 (Winter 1976/1977).

1786. Theoharis, Athan G. "The Truman Administration and the Decline of Civil Liberties: The FBI's Success in Securing Authorization for a Preventive Detention Program." **Journal of American History** 64,4 (March 1978). Describes in a sinister light internal FBI and Justice Department debates and policies regarding preventive detention of Communists and others in the event of war with the Soviet Union.

1787. Theoharis, Athan G. **Spying on Americans: Political Surveillance from Hoover to the Huston Plan.** Philadelphia: Temple University Press, 1978. Asserts that there was massive and unjustified abuse of power by the FBI and other security agencies in their countersubversive activities.

1788. Theoharis, Athan G., ed. **The Truman Presidency: The Origins of the Imperial Presidency and the National Security State.** Stanfordville: Earl M. Coleman Enterprises, 1979. Document collection; some deal with internal security operations directed at the Communist Party.

1789. Theoharis, Athan G. "The CIA and the **New York Times**: An Unanswered Question." **Government Publications Review** 10,3 (1983). See item 1780.

1790. Turner, W. W. **Hoover's FBI.** Los Angeles: Sherbourne Press, 1970.

1791. Ungar, Sanford. **FBI.** Boston: Little, Brown, 1976. Discusses FBI involvement in internal security activity directed against the Communist Party.

1792. Whitehead, Don. **The FBI Story.** New York: Random House, 1956. Sympathetic discussion of the FBI's internal security operations.

1793.   Williams, David.   "'They Never Stopped Watching
        Us': FBI Political Surveillance, 1924-1936."
        UCLA Historical Journal 2 (1981). Asserts that
        the FBI often violated Justice Department policy
        in its investigations of radical activities.

1794.   Williams, David.   "'Without Understanding': The
        FBI and Political Surveillance, 1908-1941."
        Ph.D. dissertation. University of New Hampshire,
        1981. Treats the FBI as an out-of-control
        autonomous government agency that unilaterally
        created a political criminal law and set up a
        vast political crimes bureaucracy.

1795.   Williams, David.   "The Bureau of Investigation and
        Its Critics, 1919-1921: The Origins of Federal
        Political Surveillance." **Journal of American
        History** 68,3 (Dec. 1981). Discusses the BI's
        involvement in arresting several thousand people
        suspected of Communist Party and Communist Labor
        Party membership in 1919. Finds that the BI
        reacted to criticism of the arrests and
        subsequent deportations by collecting political
        intelligence regarding the critics.

1796.   Wise, David.   **The American Police State: The
        Government Against the People.** New York: Random
        House, 1976.

        See item 2041.

36

RIGHT-WING ANTI-COMMUNISM AND McCARTHYISM

GENERAL

1797. Adler, Les K. "McCarthyism: The Advent and the Decline." **Continuum** (Autumn 1968).

1798. Bell, Daniel, ed. **The New American Right.** New York: Criterion Books, 1955. Critical essays examining the hard Right of the early 1950s.

1799. Caughey, John W. "McCarthyism Rampant." **The Pulse of Freedom: American Liberties, 1920-1970s.** Alan Reitman, ed. New York: W.W. Norton, 1975.

1800. Caute, David. **The Great Fear: The Anti-Communist Purge under Truman and Eisenhower.** New York: Simon and Schuster, 1978. Maintains that mass hysteria, repression, and political purges swept America in the late 1940s and 1950s. Asserts that the nation was "sweat drenched in fear" and treats anti-Communism as intellectually indefensible. See items 1808 and 2012.

1801. Crandell, William F. "A Party Divided Against Itself: Anticommunism and the Transformation of the Republican Right, 1945-1956." Ph.D. dissertation. Ohio State University, 1983. Finds that the Republican Party was deeply divided between a moderate and a conservative faction after World War II and that initially anti-Communism appeared to be an issue which could unite the party. However, the idea that anti-Communism was politically popular was misleading, and Eisenhower's victory had little to do with anti-Communism. Eisenhower realized the dangers of anti-Communism, isolated McCarthy, and, while talking a strong anti-Communist line, wisely backed away from confrontation with the Soviet Union when he refused to aid the Hungarian revolt against Russian rule.

1802.   Fried, Richard M. "Electoral Politics and
        McCarthyism." **The Specter.** Robert Griffith and
        Athan Theoharis, eds. New York: New Viewpoints,
        1974.

1803.   Fried, Richard M. "The New Deal, the Arsenal of
        Democracy and the Origins of McCarthyism."
        Unpublished paper, 1985 Organization of American
        Historians convention.

1804.   Griffith, Robert W. "The Political Context of
        McCarthyism." **Review of Politics** 33 (Jan. 1971).

1805.   Griffith, Robert W. "The Politics of Anti-
        Communism: A Review Article." **Wisconsin Magazine
        of History** 54,4 (1971). Review-essay on the
        historical treatment of McCarthyism and anti-
        Communism.

1806.   Griffith, Robert W. American Politics and the
        Origins of 'McCarthyism.'" **The Specter.** Robert
        Griffith and Athan Theoharis, eds. New York: New
        Viewpoints, 1974. Places the major
        responsibility for McCarthyism on conservative
        and Republican interest groups.

1807.   Griffith, Robert W., and Athan Theoharis, eds.
        **The Specter: Original Essays on the Cold War and
        the Origins of McCarthyism.** New York: New
        Viewpoints, 1974. Contains a number of
        consciously 'revisionist' essays on McCarthyism
        and anti-Communism; many of the essays are
        particularly critical of anti-Communist
        liberalism. See items 393, 1175, 1566, 1669,
        1686, 1802, 1806, 1810, 1816, 1832, and 1871.

1808.   Hook, Sidney. "David Caute's Fable of 'Fear &
        Terror': on 'Reverse McCarthyism.'" **Encounter
        [Great Britain]** 52,1 (1979). Critical review-
        essay of Caute's **The Great Fear.**

1809.   Irons, Peter H. "America's Cold War Crusade:
        Domestic Politics and Foreign Policy, 1942-
        1948." Ph.D. dissertation. Boston University,
        1972.

1810.   Irons, Peter H. "American Business and the
        Origins of McCarthyism: The Cold War Crusade of
        the United States Chamber of Commerce." **The
        Specter.** Robert Griffith and Athan Theoharis,
        eds. New York: New Viewpoints, 1974.

1811.   Johnson, Ralph H., and Michael Altman.
        "Communists in the Press: A Senate Witch-Hunt of
        the 1950s Revised." **Journalism Quarterly** 55,3
        (1978). Describes Senate Internal Security
        Subcommittee hearings on Communists in the
        press, court cases over the rights of the
        witnesses, and the tendency of press management
        to fire reporters associated with the Communist
        Party. Criticizes the press as slow to see the
        investigation as a threat to constitutional
        liberties.

1812.   Koeppen, Sheilah R. "The Republican Radical
        Right." **Annals of the American Academy of
        Political and Social Science** 382 (1969).
        Analysis of Radical Right Republicans and their
        anti-Communism.

1813.   Lasch, Christopher. "Un-American Activities." **New
        York Review of Books** 7 (Oct. 6, 1966). Review
        essay prompted by Latham's **The Communist
        Controversy**.

1814.   Latham, Earl. **The Communist Controversy in
        Washington: From the New Deal to McCarthy.**
        Cambridge: Harvard University Press, 1966.
        Thorough survey of the Communist Party's
        involvement with mainstream institutions, the
        loyalty-security program, various espionage
        cases, McCarthyism, and the House Committee on
        Un-American Activities. See item 1813.

1815.   Lipset, Seymour M., and Earl Raab. **The Politics
        of Unreason: Right-Wing Extremism, 1790-1970.**
        New York: Harper & Row, 1970.

1816.   Lora, Ronald. "A View From the Right:
        Conservative Intellectuals, the Cold War, and
        McCarthy." **The Specter.** Robert Griffith and
        Athan Theoharis, eds. New York: New Viewpoints,
        1974.

1817.   Marlowe, Lon D., III. "The Roots of McCarthyism:
        The House of Representatives and Internal
        Security Legislation, 1945-1950." Ph.D.
        dissertation. University of Georgia, 1981.
        Maintains that "McCarthyite" proposals were
        winning support in the House before Senator
        McCarthy took up the issue; examines voting
        patterns.

1818.   McAuliffe, Mary Sperling. "Dwight D. Eisenhower
        and Wolf Ladejinsky: The Politics of the
        Declining Red Scare, 1954-55." **Prologue** 14 (Fall
        1982).

1819.   McWilliams, Carey. **Witch Hunt: The Revival of
        Heresy.** Boston: Little, Brown, 1950.

1820.   Potter, Charles. **Days of Shame.** New York: Coward-
        McCann, 1965.

1821.   Sibley, Milford Q. "Ethics and the Professional
        Patriots." **Annals of the American Academy of
        Political and Social Sciences** 363 (1966).
        Hostile evaluation of "professional patriots"
        and their anti-Communism.

1822.   Synder, Robert E. "Margaret Bourke-White and the
        Communist Witch Hunt." **Journal of American
        Studies [Great Britain]** 19,1 (April 1985).
        Discusses the controversy in the early 1950s
        when the photographer-journalist Burke-White was
        allowed access to secret Air Force installations
        in order to prepare a photo article on the
        Strategic Air Command. Right-wing journalists
        pointed to her association with the American
        Youth Congress, the Film and Photo League, the
        League of Women Shoppers, and her photographic
        contributions to **Art Front** and the **Sunday Worker**
        as evidence of Communist sympathies. Burke-
        White denied sympathy for Communism and claimed
        that she was nonpolitical and that her
        association with the former groups during the
        1930s was nonpolitical.

1823.   Steinke, John. "The Rise of McCarthyism."
        Master's thesis. University of Wisconsin, 1960.

1824.   Theoharis, Athan G. "McCarthyism: a Broader
        Perspective." **Maryland Historian** 12,2 (Fall,
        1981).

1825.   Theoharis, Athan G., ed. **Beyond the Hiss Case:
        The FBI, Congress, and the Cold War.**
        Philadelphia: Temple University Press, 1982.
        Collection of essays by historians and others
        with a Left perspective critical of J. Edgar
        Hoover, the FBI, anti-Communist liberalism, and
        Weinstein's **Perjury.** See items 159, 876, 955,
        1285, 1300, 1561, 1771, and 1774.

1826. Toy, Ekard V., Jr. "Ideology and Conflict in
      American Ultra-Conservatism, 1945-1960." Ph.D.
      dissertation. University of Oregon, 1965.

1827. Wallerstein, Immanual. "McCarthyism and the
      Conservatives." Master's thesis. Columbia
      University, 1954.

1828. Westin, Alan F. "Anti-Communism and the
      Corporations." Commentary 36,6 (1963). Surveys
      corporate education programs and finds that a
      significant number use material prepared by
      irresponsible anti-Communists. Larger
      corporations tend to use more balanced,
      responsible anti-Communist material.

1829. Whitfield, Stephen J. "The 1950's: the Era of No
      Hard Feelings." South Atlantic Quarterly 74,3
      (1975). Argues that the prevailing social and
      political mood of the 1950s was one of repose,
      satisfaction, and a disinclination to get
      excited about politics, and that even anti-
      Communism was without deep emotion behind it.

1830. Wildavsky, Aaron. "Exploring the Content of
      McCarthyism." The Australian Outlook (June
      1955).

      See item 614.

McCARTHYISM AND CATHOLICS

1831. Crosby, Donald F. "The Angry Catholics: Catholic
      Opinion of Senator Joseph R. McCarthy, 1950-57."
      Ph.D. dissertation. Brandeis University, 1973.

1832. Crosby, Donald F. "The Politics of Religion:
      American Catholics and the Anti-Communist
      Impulse." The Specter. Robert Griffith and Athan
      Theoharis, eds. New York: New Viewpoints, 1974.

1833. Crosby, Donald F. "The Jesuits and Joe McCarthy."
      Church History 46,3 (1977). Recounts attempts
      to link the Jesuit order either with McCarthy or
      with his opponents; discusses the attitude of
      Jesuit journal America toward McCarthy.

1834. Crosby, Donald F. God, Church, and Flag: Senator
      Joseph R. McCarthy and the Catholic Church,
      1950-1957. Chapel Hill: University of North
      Carolina Press, 1978. Finds that Catholics were
      divided in their attitude toward McCarthy, that

Catholic support for McCarthy paralleled changes
in Protestant support, although it was slightly
stronger than the latter. See items 1837 and
2012.

1835. deSantis, Vincent P. "American Catholics and
McCarthyism." **Catholic Historical Review** 51
(April 1965).

SENATOR JOSEPH McCARTHY

1836. Bayley, Edwin R. **Joe McCarthy and the Press.**
Madison: University of Wisconsin Press, 1981.
Scholarly study discussing the role of the press
in making Senator Joseph McCarthy and his brand
of anti-Communism into a national phenomenon,
McCarthy's use of the media, and the role of the
television in McCarthy's fall from public favor.

1837. Belknap, Michael R. "Joe Must Go." **Reviews in
American History** 7,2 (1979). Review article
discussing Oshinsky's **Senator Joseph McCarthy**
and Crosby's **God, Church, and Flag.**

1838. Buckley, William F., Jr., and L. Brent Bozell.
**McCarthy and His Enemies: The Record and its
Meaning.** Chicago: Henry Regnery Co., 1954.
Defends McCarthy.

1839. Cohn, Roy. **McCarthy.** New York: New American
Library, 1968. Admiring biography by a McCarthy
ally.

1840. Cook, Fred J. **The Nightmare Decade, The Life and
Times of Senator Joe McCarthy.** New York: Random
House, 1971.

*   Deaver, Jean. "A Study of Senator Joseph R.
McCarthy and 'McCarthyism' as Influences upon
the News Media." Ph.D. dissertation. University
of Texas, 1970. Cited as item 2041.

1841. Decter, Moshe, and James Rorty. **McCarthy and the
Communists.** Boston: Beacon Press, 1954.

1842. Evans, Matthew. **The Assassination of Joe
McCarthy.** Boston, Western Islands, 1970.

1843. Ferguson, Mary Jane. "McCarthy vs. Pearson."
Master's thesis. University of Wisconsin, 1969.
Discusses the McCarthy-Drew Pearson feud. See
item 1989.

1844.   Fried, Richard M.   "Men Against McCarthy:
        Democratic Opposition to Senator Joseph R.
        McCarthy, 1950-1954." Ph.D. dissertation.
        Columbia University, 1972.

1845.   Fried, Richard M.   **Men Against McCarthy.** New York:
        Columbia University Press., 1976. Well
        researched narrative history of the reaction of
        Republican and Democrat politicians to Senator
        Joseph McCarthy's anti-Communist campaign.
        Concludes that "McCarthyism" was not a crucial
        election issue, rejects the theme that Truman
        legitimated irresponsible redbaiting, and
        describes the internal divisions which prevented
        either party from taking a clear position on
        McCarthy's activities. See item 1851.

1846.   Griffith, Robert W.   "Joseph R. McCarthy and the
        United States Senate." Ph.D. dissertation.
        University of Wisconsin, 1967-68.

1847.   Griffith, Robert W.   **The Politics of Fear: Joseph
        McCarthy and the Senate.** Lexington: University
        of Kentucky Press, 1970.

1848.   Griffith, Robert W.   "Ralph Flanders and the
        Censure of Senator Joseph R. McCarthy." **Vermont
        History** 39,1 (1971). Recounts the leading role
        of Vermont Republican Senator Ralph Flanders in
        the Senate censure of McCarthy. Notes that
        Flanders regarded McCarthy as a liability for
        the international image of the United States.
        See item 1975.

1849.   Ingalls, Robert P.   **Point of Order: A Profile of
        Senator Joe McCarthy.** New York: Putnam's, 1981.

1850.   Luthin, Reinhard H.   "The Making of McCarthy." **The
        Meaning of McCarthyism.** Earl Latham, ed.
        Lexington: D.C. Heath, 1973.

1851.   Markowitz, Norman D.   "The McCarthy Phenomenon."
        Reviews in American History 5,1 (1977). Review-
        essay prompted by Fried's **Men Against McCarthy.**

1852.   McCarthy, Joe.   **McCarthyism, the Fight for
        America.** New York: Devin-Adair, 1952.

1853.   Matusow, Allen, ed.   **Joseph R. McCarthy.** Englewood
        Cliffs: Prentice-Hall, 1970. Collection of
        documents and essays.

1854.   May, Ronald W. **McCarthy: The Man, the Senator,
        the "Ism."** Boston: Beacon Press, 1952.

1855.   Oshinsky, David. **Senator Joseph McCarthy and the
        American Labor Movement.** Columbia: University of
        Missouri Press, 1976. Examines the relationship
        of McCarthy to the labor movement, and the labor
        movement's reaction to internal security
        legislation.

1856.   Oshinsky, David. **A Conspiracy So Immense: The
        World of Joe McCarthy.** New York: The Free Press,
        1983. Comprehensive narrative of the rise and
        fall of McCarthy. See item 1837.

1857.   Plog, Stanley. "Flanders vs. McCarthy: A Study in
        Technique and Theory of Analyzing Constituent
        Mail." Ph.D. dissertation. Harvard University,
        1961. Examines the reaction to Senator Flanders'
        attack on McCarthy.

1858.   Polsby, Nelson W. "Down Memory Lane with Joe
        McCarthy." **Commentary** 75,2 (1983).

1859.   Reeves, Thomas C. **Freedom and the Foundation: The
        Fund for the Republic in the Era of McCarthyism.**
        New York: Knopf, 1969. Discusses the
        controversy about Fund for the Republic projects
        which were critical of McCarthyism.

1860.   Reeves, Thomas C. "The Search for Joe McCarthy."
        Wisconsin Magazine of History 60 (Spring 1977).

1861.   Reeves, Thomas C. **The Life and Times of Joe
        McCarthy.** New York: Stein and Day, 1982. Well
        researched, comprehensive history of McCarthy
        and McCarthyism.

1862.   Reeves, Thomas C. "Eisenhower's 'Hidden Hand' and
        the Downfall of Senator Joe McCarthy."
        Unpublished paper, 1985 Organization of American
        Historians convention.

1863.   Rovere, Richard H. **Senator Joe McCarthy.** New
        York: Harcourt, Brace, 1959. Negative
        journalistic evaluation.

1864.   Sniegoski, Stephen. "Joseph R. McCarthy and the
        Historians." **Modern Age** 29,2 (Spring, 1985).
        Historiographic review.

1865. Thomas, Lately (Robert V. Steele). **When Even**
       Angels Wept: The Senator Joseph McCarthy Affair
       -- A Story Without a Hero. New York: Morrow,
       1973.

1866. Weintraub, Rebecca. "Joseph McCarthy as Leader:
       An Image Analysis." Ph.D. dissertation.
       University of Southern California, 1983.
       Discusses the successes and failures of
       McCarthy's rhetoric. Attributes his success
       largely to America's need to find an internal
       enemy to blame for its foreign policy defeats in
       China, Korea, and Europe.

1867. Wiebe, G.D. "The Army-McCarthy Hearings and the
       Public Conscience." **Public Opinion Quarterly** 22
       (Winter 1958-59).

       See item 1254.

McCarthy in Wisconsin

1868. Coady, Sharon. "The Wisconsin Press and Joseph
       McCarthy." Master's thesis. University of
       Wisconsin, 1965.

1869. Griffith, Robert W. "The General and the Senator:
       Republican Politics and the 1952 Campaign in
       Wisconsin." **Wisconsin Magazine of History** 54,1
       (Autumn 1970). Discusses Eisenhower's handling
       of Joseph McCarthy's reelection in 1952. Notes
       that Eisenhower decided to drop a paragraph
       defending George Marshall from a draft speech to
       be delivered in Wisconsin.

1870. Meyer, Karl. "The Politics of Loyalty: From La
       Follette to McCarthy in Wisconsin, 1918-1952."
       Ph.D. dissertation. University of Wisconsin,
       1962. Discusses parallels and differences
       between the appeal of La Follette, Sr. and
       Joseph McCarthy. Finds that both campaigned as
       embattled insurgents and had similar patterns of
       county support. However, McCarthy had elite
       support that La Follette never received.

1871. O'Brien, Michael. "McCarthy and McCarthyism: The
       Cedric Parker Case, November 1949." **The Specter.**
       Robert Griffith and Athan Theoharis, eds. New
       York: New Viewpoints, 1974. Discusses
       McCarthy's attack on a liberal Wisconsin
       newspaper.

1872. O'Brien, Michael. "The Anti-McCarthy Campaign in
      Wisconsin, 1951-1952." **Wisconsin Magazine of
      History** 56,2 (Winter 1972-73). Discusses the
      divisions among liberal Republicans and
      Democrats which contributed to McCarthy's
      victory.

1873. O'Brien, Michael. **McCarthy and McCarthyism in
      Wisconsin.** Columbia: University of Missouri
      Press, 1980. Narrative of McCarthy's political
      career in Wisconsin. Notes that "McCarthyism"
      had little impact on Wisconsin schools,
      government, or other institutions.

1874. Oshinsky, David. "Wisconsin Labor and the
      Campaign of 1952." **Wisconsin Magazine of History**
      56 (Winter 1973-74). Finds that unions worked
      effectively against McCarthy in his 1952
      reelection.

1875. Shannon, David. "Was McCarthy a Political Heir of
      La Follette?" **Wisconsin Magazine of History** 45
      (Autumn 1961).

1876. Thelen, David, and Esther Thelen. "Joe Must Go:
      The Movement to Recall Senator Joe McCarthy."
      Wisconsin Magazine of History (Spring 1976).
      Finds that, despite dislike of McCarthy, many
      established Wisconsin institutions were
      reluctant to oppose him due to the desire to
      avoid controversy and risk to the institution.

      See item 1563.

RIGHT-WING ANTI-COMMUNIST ORGANIZATIONS

1877. Broyles, J. Allen. **The John Birch Society:
      Anatomy of a Protest.** Boston: Beacon Press,
      1964. Revised dissertation.

*   Finch, Phillip. **God, Guts, and Guns: A Close Look
      at the Radical Right.** New York: Seaview/Putnam,
      1983. Cited as item 2059. Journalistic expose
      of several extreme right-wing organizations
      which were often, violent, racist, anti-
      Communist, and sometimes based on apocalyptic
      "identity" theology.

1878. Jones, J. Harry, Jr. **The Minutemen.** Garden City:
      Doubleday, 1968.

*   Layton, Edwin. "The Better America Federation: A
        Case Study of Super Patriotism." **Pacific
        Historical Review** 30 (1961). Cited as item
        2062.

1879.   Minott, Rodney. "The Organized Veteran and the
        Spirit of Americanism, 1898-1959." Ph.D.
        dissertation. Stanford University, 1960.

1880.   Minott, Rodney. **Peerless Patriots: Organized
        Veterans and the Spirit of Americanism.**
        Washington, D.C.: Public Affairs Press, 1962.

1881.   McKinley, Wayne. "A Study of the American Right:
        Senator Joe McCarthy and the American Legion."
        Master's thesis. University of Wisconsin, 1962.

1882.   Oliva, A. T. "The D.A.R. as Pressure Group in the
        United States." Ph.D. dissertation. Teachers
        College, Columbia University, 1952. Discusses
        anti-Communist campaigns of the Daughters of the
        American Revolution.

*   Schomp, Gerald. **Birchism Was My Business.** New
        York: Macmillan, 1970. Cited as item 2060.
        Memoir by a disillusioned John Birch Society
        organizer.

        See items 859, 1896, 1908, and 1914.

THE NATURE OF McCARTHYISM AND FAR RIGHT ANTI-COMMUNISM

1883.   Bell, Daniel. "Status Politics and New Anxieties:
        On the 'Radical Right' and Ideologies of the
        Fifties." **The End of Ideology.** Daniel Bell. New
        York: The Free Press, 1961. Associates
        McCarthyism with the status anxieties of middle-
        class groups.

1884.   Bell, Daniel, ed. **The Radical Right.** New York:
        Doubleday, 1963.

1885.   Bernstein, Barton J. "Hindsight on McCarthyism."
        Progressive 35 (June 1971).

1886.   Beth, Loren P. "McCarthyism." **South Atlantic
        Quarterly** 55,2 (1956).

1887.   Breslow, Paul E. "The Relationship Between
        Ideology and Socio-Economic Background in a
        Group of McCarthyite Leaders." Master's thesis.
        University of Chicago, 1955.

1888.   Buckley, William F., Jr., and L. Brent Bozell.
        "The Question of Conformity." **The Meaning of
        McCarthyism.** Earl Latham, ed. Lexington: D.C.
        Heath, 1973.

1889.   Chapman, Philip. "The New Conservatism: Cultural
        Criticism vs Political Philosophy." **Political
        Science Quarterly** 75 (March 1960).

1890.   Chesler, Mark, and Richard Schmuck. "Participant
        Observation in a Super-Patriot Discussion
        Group." **Journal of Social Issues** 19 (April
        1963). Finds participants largely of low socio-
        economic status, fundamentalist in religious
        orientation, and seeking preservation of old
        fashioned moral values.

1891.   Fiedler, Leslie. "McCarthy as Populist." **The
        Meaning of McCarthyism.** Earl Latham, ed.
        Lexington: D.C. Heath, 1973. See item 1548.

1892.   Hofstadter, Richard. "The Pseudo-Conservative
        Revolt." **American Scholar** (Winter 1954-55).
        Speculates that McCarthyism is the product of
        nonclass authoritarianism.

1893.   Hofstadter, Richard. **Anti-Intellectualism in
        American Life.** New York: Knopf, 1963.

1894.   Hofstadter, Richard. **The Paranoid Style in
        American Politics.** New York: Knopf, 1965.
        Discusses episodic popularity of paranoid and
        conspiratorial interpretations of American
        history and links such views to extreme anti-
        Communism in the 1950s and early 1960s.

1895.   Kendall, Willmoore. "McCarthyism: The **Pons
        Asinorum** of American Conservatism." **The Meaning
        of McCarthyism.** Earl Latham, ed. Lexington: D.C.
        Heath, 1973. Kendall was a prominent
        conservative intellectual.

1896.   Koeppen, Sheilah Rosenhack. "Dissensus and
        Discontent: The Clientele of the Christian Anti-
        Communism Crusade." Ph.D. dissertation. Stanford
        University, 1967. Based on questionnaires
        filled out by 475 people attending Christian
        Anti-Communism Crusade schools in California;
        finds that most were white, well educated,
        native born Protestants of northern European
        heritage, held high status jobs, and had above
        average incomes; finds that most did not show a

generalized authoritarianism but held that
Communism was a special case needing special
restrictions.

1897. Latham, Earl, ed. **The Meaning of McCarthyism.**
       Lexington: Heath, 1973. A collection of essays
       and commentaries by scholars.

1898. Lipset, Seymour Martin. "Social Stratification
       and 'Right-Wing' Extremism." **British Journal of
       Sociology** 10 (Dec. 1959).

1899. Lipset, Seymour Martin. **Political Man.** Garden
       City: Doubleday & Co., 1960. Discusses the
       social and class sources of radical Right and
       Left politics.

1900. Lipset, Seymour Martin. "Three Decades of the
       Radical Right: Coughlinites, McCarthyites, and
       Birchers." **The Radical Right.** Daniel Bell, ed.
       Garden City: Doubleday, 1964.

1901. Deleted.

1902. Parsons, Talcott. "McCarthyism as Social Strain."
       The Meaning of McCarthyism. Earl Latham, ed.
       Lexington: D.C. Heath, 1973.

1903. Polsby, Nelson W. "Towards an Explanation of
       McCarthyism." **Political Studies** 8 (Oct. 1960).

1904. Polsby, Nelson W. "McCarthyism at the Grass
       Roots." **The Meaning of McCarthyism.** Earl Latham,
       ed. Lexington: D.C. Heath, 1973.

1905. Reeves, Thomas C. "McCarthyism: Interpretations
       Since Hofstadter." **Wisconsin Magazine of History**
       60 (Autumn 1976).

1906. Rogin, Michael. **The Intellectuals and McCarthy:
       The Radical Spectre.** Cambridge: MIT Press, 1967.
       Thorough scholarly attack on theories
       attributing McCarthyism to "populist" roots.

1907. Rovere, Richard. "McCarthy: As National
       Demagogue." **The Meaning of McCarthyism.** Earl
       Latham, ed. Lexington: D.C. Heath, 1973.

1908. Sellen, Robert W. "Patriotism or Paranoia? Right-
       Wing Extremism in America." **Dalhousie Review**
       43,3 (1963). Discusses the John Birch Society,
       the Christian Anti-Communist Crusade, the
       Minutemen, and others.

1909. Sokol, Robert. "Status Inconsistency." Ph.D.
       dissertation. Columbia Univ., 1961. Supports
       the "status anxiety" explanation of McCarthyism.

1910. Sokol, Robert. "Power Orientation and
       McCarthyism." **American Journal of Sociology** 73
       (1968).

1911. Trow, Martin. "Right-Wing Radicalism and
       Political Intolerance: A Study of Support for
       McCarthy in a New England Town." Ph.D.
       dissertation. Columbia University, 1957.

1912. Trow, Martin. "Small Business, Political
       Tolerance, and Support for McCarthy." **American
       Journal of Sociology** 44 (Nov. 1958). Finds
       strong support for McCarthy among small
       businessmen.

1913. Varney, Harold Lord. "McCarthy: As the Voice of
       the People." **The Meaning of McCarthyism.** Earl
       Latham, ed. Lexington: D.C. Heath, 1973.

1914. Wolfinger, Raymond E., _et al_. "America's Radical
       Right: Politics and Ideology." **Ideology and
       Discontent.** David E. Apter, ed. Glencoe: Free
       Press, 1964. Finds participants in Christian
       Anti-Communist Crusade schools were divided
       between a "sophisticated" group who emphasized
       economic conservatism and a "fundamentalist"
       group of lower socio-economic status who
       emphasized moral issues.

1915. Woodward, C. Vann. "The Populist Heritage and the
       Intellectuals." **American Scholar** 29 (Winger
       1959-60). Attacks theories linking McCarthyism
       to Populism.

1916. Wrong, Dennis. "Theories of McCarthyism: A
       Survey." **Dissent** 1 (Autumn 1954). Attacks
       status anxiety theories of McCarthyism.

1917. Wrong, Dennis H. "McCarthyism as
       Totalitarianism." **The Meaning of McCarthyism.**
       Earl Latham, ed. Lexington: D.C. Heath, 1973.

ANTI-COMMUNISM AND McCARTHYISM IN THE STATES

1918. Dowell, E.F. **A History of Criminal Syndicalism
       Legislation in the United States.** Baltimore:
       Johns Hopkins Press, 1939.

1919. Gellhorn, Walter. **The States and Subversion.**
       Ithaca: Cornell University Press, 1952.

1920. Jenson, Carol E. **The Network of Control: State
       Supreme Courts and State Security Statutes,
       1920-1970.** Westport: Greenwood, 1982. Notes
       that state courts continued to support and
       enforce state antisubversive statutes although
       similar laws were rejected by federal courts.

1921. Prendergast, William. "State Legislatures and
       Communism: The Current Scene." **American
       Political Science Review** 44 (Sept. 1950).

Anti-Communism in the Midwest

1922. Selcraig, James T. "The Red Scare in the Midwest,
       1945 to 1950: A State and Local Study." Ph.D.
       dissertation. University of Illinois, 1981.

1923. Selcraig, James T. **The Red Scare in the Midwest,
       1945-1955: A State and Local Study.** Ann Arbor:
       UMI Research, 1982. A study of Wisconsin,
       Illinois, Ohio, Indiana and Michigan which
       argues that public concern over Communism had
       local sources and did not originate in
       Washington, that there was minimal public
       controversy in Detroit, Chicago, and Cincinnati,
       that there were few instances of library
       censorship, that few teachers were fired, and
       that images of university campuses having been
       under an intellectual reign of terror are overdrawn.

Anti-Communism in the South

1924. Braden, Anne. "A View From the Fringes." **Southern
       Exposure** 9,1 (1981). Discusses use of anti-
       Communist themes against civil rights activists
       in the 1950s and 1960s.

1925. Clark, Wayne Addison. "An Analysis of the
       Relationship Between Anti-Communism and
       Segregationist Thought in the Deep South, 1948-
       1964." Ph.D. dissertation. University of North
       Carolina at Chapel Hill, 1976. Concludes that
       the Southern elite used anti-Communism to
       maintain the white consensus in favor of
       segregation.

1926. Egerton, John. "The Trial of the Highlander Folk
       School." **Southern Exposure** 6,1 (1978). Recounts
       the 1959 trial of Myles Horton, director of the

Highlander Folk School, for illegal alcohol
dispensing, Communist propaganda, and racial
agitation.

Anti-Communism in Arkansas

*   Cobb, William H. "The State Legislature and the
        'Reds': Arkansas's General Assembly v.
        Commonwealth College, 1935-1937." **Arkansas
        Historical Quarterly** 45 (Spring 1986). Cited as
        item 2037.

Anti-Communism In California

1927.   Barrett, Edward. **The Tenney Committee:
        Legislative Investigation of Subversive
        Activities in California.** Ithaca: Cornell
        University Press, 1951.

*   Heale, M.J. "Red Scare Politics: California's
        Campaign Against Un-American Activities, 1940-
        1970." **Journal of American Studies** 20,1 (April
        1986). Cited as item 2048. A survey.

1928.   Long, Edward R. "Loyalty Oaths in California,
        1947-1952: The Politics of Anti-Communism."
        Ph.D. dissertation. University of California,
        San Diego, 1981. Finds that anti-Communism had
        its greatest success with liberal support.

1929.   Long, Edward R. "Earl Warren and the Politics of
        Anti-Communism." **Pacific Historical Review** 51,1
        (1982). Finds that Warren was an anti-Communist
        when he was attorney general and governor of
        California and supported loyalty oaths and other
        anti-Communist measures.

1930.   Pritchard, Robert L. "California Un-American
        Activities Investigations: Subversion on the
        Right?" **California Historical Society Quarterly**
        49,4 (1970). Surveys the California legislative
        investigations of extreme right-wing groups.

1931.   Scobie, Ingrid W. "Jack B. Tenney: Molder of
        Anti-Communist Legislation in California, 1940-
        49." Ph.D. dissertation. University of
        Wisconsin, 1970. Finds that Tenney's dedication
        allowed him to mobilize support for extremist
        legislation against insubstantial fears.

1932.   Scobie, Ingrid W. "Jack B. Tenney and the
        'Parasitic Menace': Anti-Communist Legislation

in California, 1940-49." **Pacific Historical Review** 43 (1974).

1933. Scobie, Ingrid W. "Helen Gahagan Douglas and her 1950 Senate Race with Richard M. Nixon." **Southern California Quarterly** 58,1 (1976). Recounts the Douglas-Nixon Senate campaign. Notes that the Democratic Party was seriously divided and Douglas had to fight a difficult primary. Discusses Nixon's use of anti-Communism against Douglas.

1934. Tenney, Jack. **Red Fascism.** Los Angeles: Federal Printing Co., 1947.

1935. Tyler, Bruce M. "Black Radicalism in Southern California, 1950-1982." Ph.D. dissertation. University of California, Los Angeles, 1983. Argues that the anti-Communism of Mayor Sam Yorty and his police chief contributed to the Watts riot of 1965.

See item 2048.

Anti-Communism in Hawaii

1936. Holmes, Thomas M. "The Specter of Communism in Hawaii, 1947-53." Ph.D. dissertation. University of Hawaii, 1975. Maintains that concern about the Communist presence in labor and political institutions was exaggerated by the oligarchy in order to justify oppression aimed at postponing an inevitable social revolution.

Anti-Communism in Indiana

1937. Murray, Michael D. "To Hire a Hall: 'An Argument in Indianapolis.'" **Central States Speech Journal** 26 (1975).

1938. Sorenson, Dale. "The Anticommunist Consensus in Indiana, 1945-1958." Ph.D. dissertation. Indiana University, 1980. Finds that anti-Communism permeated all levels of society and was neither elite nor mass initiated; political anti-Communism and anti-Communist activity inside unions was locally initiated and was not initiated at the national level. Discusses factionalism in the Indiana CIO and the UE; notes that concern over Communism peaked during the Korean war.

Anti-Communism In Illinois

1939. Harsha, E. Houston. "Illinois: The Broyles
       Commission." **The States and Subversion.** Walter
       Gellhorn, ed. Ithaca: Cornell University Press,
       1952.

Anti-Communism in Maryland

1940. Prendergast, William. "Maryland: The Ober Anti-
       Communist Law." **The States and Subversion.**
       Walter Gellhorn, ed. Ithaca: Cornell University
       Press, 1952.

Anti-Communism in Michigan

1941. Mowitz, Robert J. "Michigan: State and Local
       Attack on Subversion." **The States and
       Subversion.** Walter Gellhorn, ed. Ithaca: Cornell
       University Press, 1952.

Anti-Communism in Minnesota

1942. Henrickson, Gary P. "Minnesota in the 'McCarthy'
       Period: 1946-1954." Ph.D. dissertation.
       University of Minnesota, 1981. Finds that anti-
       Communism in Minnesota was elite-led, not of
       local origin, and inspired by national political
       leaders. Discusses attacks on University of
       Minnesota faculty and the purge of Left elements
       from the Democratic-Farmer-Labor Party.

Anti-Communism in Missouri

1943. Johnson, Ronald W. "The Communist Issue in
       Missouri: 1946-1956." Ph.D. dissertation.
       University of Missouri, 1973. Critical survey
       of popular anti-Communism; treats it as largely
       paranoid fantasy; notes a significant Communist
       Party presence in the Missouri UE.

Anti-Communism in New York

1944. Chamberlain, Lawrence H. **Loyalty and Legislative
       Action: A Survey of Activity By the New York
       State Legislature, 1919-1949.** Ithaca: Cornell
       University Press, 1951.

Anti-Communism in South Dakota

1945. Miller, John E. "McCarthyism before McCarthy: The
       1938 Election in South Dakota." **Heritage of the
       Great Plains** 15 (Summer 1982).

1946. Miller, John E. "Mundt vs. McGovern: The 1960
       Senate Election." **Heritage of the Great Plains**
       15 (Fall 1982).

Anti-Communism In Texas

1947. Carleton, Don E. "McCarthyism in Houston: The
       George Ebey Affair." **Southwestern Historical
       Quarterly,** 80,2 (1976). Recounts the 1952
       attack on a newly hired deputy school
       superintendent for Communist ties by the Minute
       Women and other militant anti-Communist and
       anti-liberal groups.

1948. Carleton, Don E. "A Crisis of Rapid Change: The
       Red Scare in Houston, 1945-1955." Ph.D.
       dissertation. University of Houston, 1978.
       Blames Houston's "Red Scare," directed largely
       at school and several Methodist Church agencies,
       on the social stress of rapid growth; notes that
       concern about Communism appeared to some people
       to be legitimated by the activities of local
       Communists and a lengthy struggle within a
       National Maritime Union local between Communist
       and anti-Communist factions.

1949. Carleton, Don E. **Red Scare! Right-Wing Hysteria,
       Fifties Fanaticism, and Their Legacy in Texas.**
       Austin: Texas Monthly Press, 1985.

1950. Green, George N. "McCarthyism in Texas: The 1954
       Campaign." **Southern Quarterly** 16 (April 1978).

Anti-Communism In Washington State

1951. Countryman, Vern. **Un-American Activities in the
       State of Washington: Canwell Committee.** Ithaca:
       Cornell University Press, 1951.

*   Dwyer, William. **The Goldmark Case: An American
       Libel Case.** Seattle: University of Washington
       Press, 1984. Cited as item 2044. Recounts a
       controversial libel case involving accusations
       of Communist sympathies.

1952. Rader, Melvin. **False Witness.** Seattle: University
       of Washington Press, 1969. Discusses the
       Canwell Committee.

       See item 2044.

BIOGRAPHICAL MATERIAL

Acheson, Dean

1953.   Acheson, Dean. **Present at the Creation.** New York:
        Holt, Rinehart & Winston, 1959. Discusses his
        reaction to Joseph McCarthy's attacks on him and
        on the State Department.

1954.   McLellan, David. **Dean Acheson.** New York: Dodd,
        Mead, 1976.

Adams, Sherman

1955.   Adams, Sherman. **First Hand Report.** New York:
        Harper & Row, 1961. Adams, Eisenhower's chief
        aide, discusses his and Eisenhower's attitude
        toward McCarthy.

Benson, George S.

1956.   Garner, Donald P. "George S. Benson:
        Conservative, Anti-Communist, Pro-Americanism
        Speaker." Ph.D. dissertation. Wayne State
        University, 1963.

Benton, William

1957.   Hyman, Sidney. **The Lives of William Benton.**
        Chicago: University of Chicago Press, 1969.
        Biography of a prominent Senator who opposed
        McCarthy.

Bohlen, Charles

1958.   Bohlen, Charles E. **Witness to History, 1929-1969.**
        New York: Norton, 1973. Discusses McCarthy's
        attacks on his nomination to be ambassador to
        the USSR.

1959.   Rosenau, James. **The Nomination of Chip Bohlen.**
        New York: McGraw-Hill, 1958.

Budenz, Louis

1960.   Alsop, Joseph. "The Strange Case of Louis
        Budenz." **Atlantic Monthly** (April 1952).
        Discusses the contradictions in Budenz testimony
        regarding the association of various people with
        the Communist Party and Soviet espionage.

1961. Budenz, Louis. **This is My Story.** New York: McGraw-Hill, 1947. Autobiography covering Budenz's journey from **Daily Worker** editor to anti-Communist and active Catholic.

See item 1751.

Butler, Hugh

1962. Paul, Justis. "The Political Career of Senator Hugh Butler." Ph.D. dissertation. University of Nebraska, 1966. Discusses the use of anti-Communism by a prominent post-World War II Republican politician.

Calomiris, Angela

1963. Calomiris, Angela. **Red Masquerade.** New York: Lippincott, 1950. Memoir by a longtime FBI informant in the Communist Party.

Dennis, Peggy

1964. Dennis, Peggy. "Memories of the Witchhunts." **Progressive** 45 (Oct. 1981).

Dies, Martin

1965. Dies, Martin. **Martin Dies' Story.** New York: Bookmailer, 1963.

1966. Gellerman, William. **Martin Dies.** New York: The John Day Co., 1944.

Dirksen, Everett

1967. McNeil, Neil. **Dirksen: Portrait of a Public Man.** New York: World Publishing Co., 1970. Discusses Dirksen's attitude toward McCarthy.

1968. Schapsmeier, Edward L., and Frederick H. Schapsmeier. "Everett M. Dirksen of Pekin: Politician Par Excellence." **Journal of the Illinois State Historical Society** 76,1 (1983). Finds that Dirksen's anti-Communism took on a partisan tone in the 1950s when he cooperated for a time with Senator Joseph McCarthy.

Dulles, John Foster

1969. Guhlin, Michael. **John Foster Dulles.** New York: Columbia University Press, 1972. Discusses Dulles's reaction to McCarthyism.

1970. Hoopes, Townsend. **The Devil and John Foster Dulles.** Boston: Little, Brown, 1973.

Eisenhower, Dwight

1971. Divine, Robert. **Eisenhower and the Cold War.** New York: Oxford University Press, 1981. Discusses Eisenhower and McCarthy.

1972. Hughes, Emmet. **The Ordeal of Power.** New York: Atheneum, 1963. A key Eisenhower speech writer discusses Eisenhower's reaction to McCarthy.

1973. Larson, Arthur. **Eisenhower: The President Nobody Knew.** New York: Scribner's, 1968. Discusses Eisenhower's reaction to McCarthy.

1974. Parmet, Herbert S. **Eisenhower and the American Crusades.** New York: Macmillan, 1972.

See items 1869 and 1955.

Flanders, Ralph E.

1975. Flanders, Ralph E. **Senator from Vermont.** Boston: Little, Brown, 1961. Autobiography by the Senator who was instrumental in censuring McCarthy. See items 1848 and 1857.

Hennings, T.C., Jr.

1976. Kemper, Donald. **Decade of Fear: Senator Hennings and Civil Liberties.** Columbia: University of Missouri Press, 1965.

Hoey, Clyde R.

1977. Hatcher, Susan Arden. "The Senatorial Career of Clyde R. Hoey." Ph.D. dissertation. Duke University, 1983. Notes that Hoey of North Carolina was both a strong anti-Communist and hostile to Senator McCarthy.

Hunt, Lester.

1978. Ewig, Rick. "McCarthy Era Politics: The Ordeal of Senator Lester Hunt." **Annals of Wyoming** 55,1 (1983). Sees Hunt as a firm anti-Communist who regarded McCarthy as an opportunist. Harassed by fanatical MaCarthyists and beset by health and family problems, Hunt killed himself in 1954.

Kendall, Willmoore

1979. Wilson, Francis G. "The Political Science of
       Willmoore Kendall." **Modern Age** 16,1 (1972).
       Notes the contribution of Kendall to
       conservative anti-Communist thought.

Kennedy, Robert

1980. Schlesinger, Arthur, Jr. **Robert Kennedy and His
       Times.** Boston: Houghton Mifflin, 1978.
       Discusses Robert Kennedy's association, with
       McCarthy.

Lattimore, Owen

1981. Flynn, John T. **The Lattimore Story.** New York:
       Devin-Adair, 1953.

1982. Lattimore, Owen. **Ordeal by Slander.** Boston:
       Little, Brown, 1950. Lattimore's account of the
       attacks on him for Communist sympathies by
       McCarthy and others.

1983. Newman, Robert P. "Red Scare in Seattle, 1952:
       The FBI, the CIA, and Owen Lattimore's
       'Escape.'" **Historian** 48,1 (Nov. 1985).
       Discusses a controversy regarding an erroneous
       report by the CIA that Lattimore was planning to
       flee the United States.

       See item 1665.

Levine, Isaac Don.

1984. Levine, Isaac Don. **Eyewitness to History.** New
       York: Hawthorn, 1973. Autobiography by a
       leading conservative anti-Communist journalist
       of the 1940s and 1950s.

Luce, Clare Boothe

1985. Mckee, Mary Julianus. "Congresswoman Clare Boothe
       Luce: Her Rhetoric Against Communism." Ph.D.
       dissertation. University of Illinois at Urbana-
       Champaign, 1962. Finds that Luce emphasized the
       clash of Soviet and American philosophies rather
       than the domestic activities of the American
       Communist Party.

Mundt, Karl

1986. Hoogestraat, Wayne Edward. "Evaluation of Karl E.
      Mundt's Advocated Theories of Persuasive
      Speaking in Relation to his Practices in
      Selected Speeches on Communism." Ed.D.
      dissertation. Pennsylvania State University,
      1963.

1987. Lee, R. Alton. "'New Dealers, Fair Dealers,
      Misdealers, and Hiss Dealers': Karl Mundt and
      the Internal Security Act of 1950." South Dakota
      History 10,4 (1980) Discusses the role of South
      Dakota Senator Karl Mundt in the drafting and
      enactment of the Internal Security Act of 1950.

Nixon, Richard M.

1988. Nixon, Richard M. Memoirs. New York: Grosset &
      Dunlap, 1978. Discusses his role as a leading
      anti-Communist politician in the postwar period.

Pearson, Drew

1989. Pilat, Oliver. Drew Pearson. New York: Harper's
      Magazine Press, 1973. Discusses Pearson's feud
      with McCarthy.

Pegler, Westbrook

1990. Pilat, Oliver. Pegler, Angry Man of the Press.
      Boston: Beacon Press, 1963. Biography of a
      popular right-wing anti-Communist journalist.

Pepper, Claude

1991. Malafronte, Anthony F. "Claude Pepper: Florida
      Maverick, the 1950 Florida Senatorial Primary."
      Master's thesis. University of Miami, 1964.
      Notes the use of anti-Communism against Pepper.

Philbrick, Herbert

1992. Philbrick, Herbert. I Led 3 Lives: Citizen,
      "Communist," Counterspy. New York: McGraw Hill,
      1952. Memoir by a longtime FBI undercover
      informant in the Communist Party.

Smith, Margaret Chase

1993. Smith, Margaret Chase. Declaration of Conscience.
      Garden City: Doubleday, 1972. Memoir by a
      leading Senate opponent of McCarthy.

Stevenson, Adlai

1994.   Martin, John B. **Adlai Stevenson and the World.**
        New York: Doubleday, 1977. Discusses
        Stevenson's reaction to McCarthyism.

Taft, Robert A.

1995.   Patterson, James. **Mr. Republican: A Biography of
        Robert A. Taft.** Boston: Houghton Mifflin, 1972.

1996.   Ricks, John. "'Mr. Integrity' and McCarthyism:
        Robert A. Taft, Sr. and Joseph R. McCarthy."
        Cincinnati Historical Society Bulletin 37,3
        (1979). Discusses Taft's support for McCarthy.

Von Mises, Ludwig

1997.   East, John P. "American Conservative Thought: The
        Impact of Ludwig Von Mises." **Modern Age** 23,4
        (1979). Discusses the influence of Mises's
        free market liberalism, anti-Communism, and
        hostility to political intervention on American
        conservatives.

Watkins, Arthur W.

1998.   Watkins, Arthur W. **Enough Rope.** Englewood Cliffs:
        Prentice-Hall, 1969. Memoir by the Republican
        senator from Utah, a firm anti-Communist, who
        chaired the committee that recommended the
        censure of McCarthy.

Wherry, Kenneth S.

1999.   Dahlstrom, H. A. "Kenneth S. Wherry." Ph.D.
        dissertation. University of Nebraska, 1965.
        Biography of a prominent post-World War II
        Republican anti-Communist spokesman.

2000.   Stromer, Marvin E. **The Making of a Political
        Leader: Kenneth S. Wherry and the United States
        Senate.** Lincoln: University of Nebraska Press,
        1969.

37

HISTORIOGRAPHIC AND BIBLIOGRAPHIC WORKS

*   Bloom, Jon, and Paul Buhle, eds. **Guide to the Oral History of the American Left.** New York: Tamiment Library, 1985. Cited as item 2033.

2001. Buhle, Paul. "Historians and American Communism: An Agenda." **International Labor and Working Class History** 20 (Fall 1981). Essay-review.

2002. Charney, George. "American Communism in Perspective: a Review." **Wisconsin Magazine of History** 56 (1973).

2003. Clark, Joseph. "Dreams and Nightmares." **Dissent** (Summer 1978). Review essay criticizing positive appraisals of Communist Party history.

2004. Conlin, Joseph R., ed. **The American Radical Press, 1880-1960.** Westport: Greenwood Press, 1974. Includes recollections by editors: Joseph Hansen of the Trotskyist **Militant,** Joseph Clark of the Communist Party's **Student Review,** Joseph P. Lash of the Popular Front **Student Advocate,** Philip J. Jaffe of the Communist-aligned **China Today** and **Amerasia,** and Daniel Bell of the independent Marxist **Modern Review.** Includes comment on the **Daily Worker** by Harvey A. Levenstein.

2005. Corker, Charles, ed. **Bibliography of the Communist Problem in the United States.** New York: Fund for the Republic, Inc., 1955. Extensive list of primary material.

2006. Delaney, Robert. **The Literature of Communism In America: A Selected Reference Guide.** Washington, D.C.: Catholic University of America Press, 1962. Cites journalistic studies, scholarly works, and primary material.

2007. Dowd, Douglas F. "Making History from the Left."
       Maryland Historian 12 (Fall, 1981).

2008. Draper, Theodore. "The Romanticizing of American
       Communism." **New Leader** 61 (March 13, 1978).
       Review-essay.

2009. Draper, Theodore. "American Communism Revisited."
       New York Review of Books 32,8 (May 9, 1985).
       Review-essay discussing Isserman's **Which Side
       Were Your On?**, Klehr's **The Heyday of American
       Communism**, Nelson's **Steve Nelson**, Charney's **A
       Long Journey**, Richmond's **A Long View**, Painter's
       The Narrative of Hosea Hudson, and Haywood's
       Black Bolshevik. Highly critical of those who
       romanticize Communist history and avoid a
       political approach to Communist history. See
       items 2018 and 2032.

2010. Draper, Theodore. "The Popular Front Revisited."
       New York Review of Books 32,9 (May 30, 1985).
       Review-essay discussing Howe and Coser's **The
       American Communist Party**, Naison's **Communists in
       Harlem**, Keeran's **The Communist Party and the
       Auto Workers Unions**, Gornick's **The Romance of
       American Communism**, and the film "Seeing Red."
       See items 2018 and 2032.

2011. Draper, Theodore. "Revisiting American Communism:
       An Exchange." **New York Review of Books** 32,13
       (Aug. 15, 1985). Comment on letters by Paul
       Buhle, James R. Prickett, James R. Barrett, Rob
       Ruck, Norman Markowitz, Al Richmond, Mark
       Naison, Roy Rosenzweig, Gary Gerstle, and Murray
       Bookchin; a further exchange with Maurice
       Isserman on Sept. 26, 1985.

2012. Fried, Richard M. "Communism and Anti-Communism:
       A review-essay." **Wisconsin Magazine of History**
       63,4 (Summer 1980). Review-essay of Gornick's
       The Romance of American Communism, Caute's **The
       Great Fear**, McAuliffe's **Crisis on the Left,**
       Crosby's **God, Church, and Flag,** and Weinstein's
       Perjury.

2013. Goldwater, Walter. **Radical Periodicals in
       America, 1890-1950.** New Haven: Yale University
       Library, 1966. Annotated bibliography on
       periodicals and their sponsors.

2014. Harper, Alan D. "The Antired Decade Remembered."
       Reviews in American History 7,1 (1979). Review-

essay discussing Belknap's **Cold War Political Justice,** Gornick's **The Romance of American Communism,** and McAuliffe's **Crisis on the Left.**

2015. Hobsbawm, Eric J. "Problems of Communist History." **New Left Review** 54 (March-April 1969).

2016. Hobsbawm, Eric. J. "Intellectuals and Communism." **Revolutionaries.** New York: 1973.

2017. Isserman, Maurice. "The Old and the New History of American Communism, a Comparison of Approach and Interpretation." Unpublished paper, 1985 Organization of American Historians convention.

2018. Isserman, Maurice. "Three Generations: Historians View American Communism." **Labor History** 26,4 (Fall 1985). Detailed bibliographic essay; defends the nonpolitical, social history approach to Communist history; maintains the latter approach has superseded the "traditionalist" approach of the Fund for the Republic school, Theodore Draper, Irving Howe, Lewis Coser, Harvey Klehr, Lowell Dyson, John Haynes, and others.

2019. Isserman, Maurice, and Staughton Lynd. Exchange on the Communist Party and the concept of a usable past for radicals. **Radical America** 14 (July-Aug. 1980).

2020. Johnpoll, Bernard K. "Manuscript Sources in American Radicalism." **Labor History** 14,1 (Winter 1973).

*   Johnpoll, Bernard K., and Harvey Klehr, eds. **Biographical Dictionary of the American Left.** Westport: Greenwood Press, 1986. Cited as item 2039. Contains short biographical sketches of many Communist and radical figures.

2021. Kirkendall, Richard S. **The Truman Period as a Research Field.** Columbia: University of Missouri Press, 1967. **(The Truman Period as a Research Field: A Reappraisal, 1972.** Columbia: University of Missouri Press, 1974.)

2022. Levinson, Mark. "Reds without Politics." **Dissent** (Fall 1984).

2023. Lichtenstein, Nelson. "Another Time: Another Place; Blacks, Radicals and Rank and File

Militancy in Auto in the 30s & 40s." **Radical America** 16,1&2 (1982). Review-essay on Keeran's **The Communist Party and the Auto Workers Unions,** Martin Glabermann's **The Struggle against the No-Strike Pledge,** and August Meier and Elliot Rudwick's **Black Detroit and the Rise of the UAW.**

2024. Lichtenstein, Nelson. "The American Communist Party in Its Heyday: A Case of Premature Eurocommunism?" **International Labor and Working Class History.** (Spring 1984). Review-essay discussing Isserman's **Which Side Are You On?** and Levenstein's **Communism, Anticommunism, and the CIO.**

*   Markowitz, Norman. "The New Cold-War 'Scholars.'" **Political Affairs** 62,1 (Oct. 1983). Cited as item 2083. Criticizes writings on Communist history which do not support orthodox Communist Party interpretations.

2025. Neufeld, Maurice F., Daniel J. Leab, and Dorothy Swanson. **American Workingclass History: A Representative Bibliography.** New York: Bowker, 1983. Detailed bibliography with a section devoted to labor and radical political movements, including Communism.

2026. Peterson, Brian. "Working Class Communism." **Radical America** 5,1 (1971). Bibliographic essay on works discussing the relationship of workers with Communist parties in the US, Great Britain, Germany, and France.

2027. Rosenzweig, Roy. "Oral History and the Old Left." **International Labor and Working Class History** 24 (1983).

2028. Schwarz, Bill. "'The People' in History: The Communist Party Historians' Group, 1946-1956." **Making Histories: Studies in History Writing and Politics.** Richard Johnson et al, eds. Minneapolis: University of Minnesota Press, 1982.

2029. Seidman, Joel. **Communism in the United States - A Bibliography.** Ithaca, Cornell University Press, 1969. Extensive annotated bibliography of primary and secondary material.

2030. Taft, Philip. "The **Party Organizer:** An Introduction and Appraisal." **Labor History** 11,1 (Winter 1970).

2031. Waltzer, Kenneth. "The New History of American
       Communism." **Reviews in American History** 11,2
       (1983). Review-essay discussing Isserman's
       Which Side Were You On?, Nelson's **Steve Nelson,**
       Dyson's **Red Harvest,** and Alexander's **The Right
       Opposition.**

2032. Wilentz, Sean. "Red Herrings Revisited: Theodore
       Draper Blows His Cool." **Village Voice Literary
       Supplement,** 36 (June 1985). Critical review-
       essay on Draper's "American Communism Revisited"
       and "The Popular Front Revisited."

ADDENDA

All ADDENDA items are also listed under the appropriate subject matter headings.

2033. Bloom, Jon, and Paul Buhle, eds. **Guide to the Oral History of the American Left.** New York: Tamiment Library, 1985.

2034. Redlich, Norman. "McCarthy's Global Hoax." **The Nation** (Dec. 2, 1978).

2035. Kling, Jack. **Where The Action Is: Memoirs of a U.S. Communist.** New York: New Outlook, 1986.

2036. Wolfe, Bertram D. **A Life in Two Centuries.** New York: Stein & Day, 1979.

2037. Cobb, William H. "The State Legislature and the 'Reds': Arkansas's General Assembly v. Commonwealth College, 1935-1937." **Arkansas Historical Quarterly** 45 (Spring 1986).

2038. Knight, Rolf. **Traces of Magma: An Annotated Bibliography of Left Literature.** Vancouver, Canada: Draegerman, 1983.

2039. Johnpoll, Arthur, and Harvey Klehr, eds. **Biographical Dictionary of the American Left.** Westport: Greenwood Press, 1986.

2040. Sennett, William. **Communist Functionary and Corporate Executive.** Berkeley: University of California, Bancroft Library, 1984.

2041. Deaver, Jean. "A Study of Senator Joseph R. McCarthy and 'McCarthyism' as Influences upon the News Media." Ph.D. dissertation. University of Texas, 1970.

2042. Davis, Mike. **Prisoners of the American Dream.** New York: Shochen (Verso Books), 1986.

2043. Rovere, Richard. **Final Reports.** Garden City: Doubleday, 1984.

2044. Dwyer, William. **The Goldmark Case: An American Libel Case.** Seattle: University of Washington Press, 1984.

287

2045. Jacobson, Phyllis. "The 'Americanization' of the Communist Party." **New Politics** (1986).

2046. Cummings, Robert. "Dwight Macdonald in the 1940s." **New Politics** (1986).

2047. Rossiter, Clinton. **Marxism: The View from America.** New York: Harcourt, Brace and Co., 1960.

2048. Heale, M.J. "Red Scare Politics: California's Campaign Against Un-American Activities, 1940-1970." **Journal of American Studies** 20,1 (April 1986).

2049. Carew, Anthony. "The Schism within the World Federation of Trade Unions: Government and Trade-Union Diplomacy." **International Review of Social History** 29,3 (1984).

2050. Valelly, Richard M. "State-Level Radicalism and the Nationalization of American Politics: The Case of the Minnesota Farmer-Labor Party." Ph.D. dissertation, Harvard University, 1984.

2051. Carr, Virginia Spencer. **Dos Passos: A Life.** Garden City: Doubleday, 1984.

2052. Halpern, Martin. "Taft-Hartley and the Defeat of the Progressive Alternative in the United Auto Workers." **Labor History** 27,2 (Spring 1986).

2053. Hook, Sidney. "Communists in the Classroom." **The American Spectator** (Aug. 1986).

2054. Lasch, Christopher. **The American Liberals and the Russian Revolution.** New York: Columbia University Press, 1962.

2055. Dyson, Lowell, ed. **Agrarian Periodicals in the United States, 1920-1960.** Westport: Greenwood, 1984.

2056. Dyson, Lowell. "The Milk Strike of 1939 and the Destruction of the Dairy Farmers Union." **New York History** (Oct. 1970).

2057. Dyson, Lowell. "The Farmer and the Left: The Influence of Radical Farm Organizations." **Farmers, Bureaucrats, and Middlemen.** Trudy H. Peterson, ed. Washington, D.C.: Howard University Press, 1981.

2058. Emerson, Hough. **The Web.** Chicago: Reilly and Lee, 1919.

2059. Finch, Phillip. **God, Guts, and Guns: A Close Look at the Radical Right.** New York: Seaview/Putnam, 1983.

2060. Schomp, Gerald. **Birchism Was My Business.** New York: Macmillan, 1970.

2061. Montgomery, David. "The Farmer-Labor Party." **Working for Democracy.** Paul Buhle and Alan Dawley, eds. Urbana: University of Illinois Press, 1985.

2062. Layton, Edwin. "The Better America Federation: A Case Study of Super Patriotism." **Pacific Historical Review** 30 (1961).

2063. Patterson, William L. **The Man Who Cried Genocide** New York: International Publishers, 1971.

2064. Stephenson, Anders. "The CPUSA Conception of the Rooseveltian State." Thesis. New College, Oxford University, 1977.

2065. Schrecker, Ellen W. **No Ivory Tower: McCarthyism and the Universities.** New York: Oxford University Press, 1986.

2066. Bone, Robert. **The Negro Novel in America.** New Haven: Yale University Press, 1968.

2067. Young, James O. **Black Writers of the Thirties.** Baton Rouge: Louisiana State University Press, 1973.

2068. MacDonald, J. Fred. **Television and the Red Menace: The Video Road to Vietnam.** New York: Praeger, 1985.

2069. Fabre, Michel. **The Unfinished Quest of Richard Wright.** New York: Morrow, 1973.

2070. Gayce, Addison. **Richard Wright: Ordeal of a Native Son.** Garden City: Doubleday, 1980.

2071. Web, Constance. **Richard Wright: A Biography.** New York: Putnam's, 1968.

2072. Wright, Richard. **Native Son.** New York: Harper and Brothers, 1940.

2073.   Greenberg, Ken. "Benjamin Jefferson Davis, Jr.,
        in the City Council: Harlem's Reaction to
        Communism During the 1940's." Master's thesis.
        Columbia University, 1970.

2074.   Citron, Alice. "An Answer to John Hatchett."
        Jewish Currents (Sept. 1968).

2075.   Kramer, Hilton. "The Big Red Paintpot." **The New
        York Times Book Review** April 27, 1986.

2076.   Greeley, Andrew. **The Most Distressful Nation.**
        Chicago: Quadrangle, 1972.

2077.   Mendelson, Michael J. **Clifford Odets, Humane
        Dramatist.** Deland: Everett/Edwards, 1969.

2078.   de Toledano, Ralph, and Victor Lasky. **Seeds of
        Treason: The True Story of the Hiss-Chambers
        Tragedy.** New York: Funk and Wagnalls, 1950.

2079.   Mangione, Jerre. **The Dream and the Deal: The
        Federal Writers' Project, 1935-1943.** Boston:
        Little, Brown, 1972.

2080.   Gilbert, James. "The _Partisan Review_." **The Left-
        Wing Intellectuals Between the Wars, 1919-1939.**
        Walter Laqueur and George L. Mosse, eds. New
        York: Harper & Row, 1966.

2081.   Gilbert, James. **Writers and Partisans: A History
        of Literary Radicalism in America.** New York:
        Wiley, 1968.

2082.   Lamont, Corliss. **Yes to Life: Memoirs of Corliss
        Lamont.** New York: Horizon Press, 1981.

2083.   Markowitz, Norman. "The New Cold-War 'Scholars.'"
        Political Affairs 62,1 (Oct. 1983).

2084.   Baigell, Matthew, and Julia Williams, eds.
        **Artists Against War and Fascism: Papers of the
        First American Artists' Congress.** New
        Brunswick: Rutgers University Press, 1986.

2085.   Rossi, John. "Farewell to Fellow Traveling."
        Continuity 10 (Spring 1985).

2086.   Gillon, Steven M. "Liberal Dilemmas: The ADA and
        American Liberalism, 1947-1968." Ph.D.
        dissertation, Brown University, 1985.

AUTHOR INDEX

Index numbers refer to item numbers.

Aaron, Daniel. 610, 1001, 1002, 1029, 1030, 1049

Abbott, Roger S. 1714

Abel, Lionel. 1064

Abella, Irving. 338, 339

Acena, Albert A. 184

Acheson, Dean. 1953

Adamic, Louis. 1065

Adams, Sherman. 1955

Adler, Les K. 1175, 1466, 1467, 1797

Ahola, David John. 585, 586

Ajay, Alex. 759

Alberts, Florence G. 1494

Alexander, Milnor. 1637

Alexander, Robert J. 234, 1355, 1356

Alexander, William. 1144

Alexandre, Laurie Ann. 1053

Allen, R.B. 951

Alley, Rewi. 1528

Almond, Gabriel A. 188

Al-Naqeeb, Khaldoun H. 1468

Alperin, Robert Jay. 41

Alsop, Joseph. 1319, 1320, 1960

Alsop, Stewart. 1215, 1319, 1320

Altenbaugh, Richard J. 587

Altman, George T. 1237

Altman, Michael. 1811

American Institute for Marxist Studies. 7, 263, 666, 754, 1687

Anders, Roger M. 1327

Anderson, Jervis. 728

Anderson, Paul H. 8

Anderson, Quentin. 1101

Andrew, William D. 400

Annunziata, Frank. 1398

Ansheles, Jill L. 662

Appalachian Movement Press. 521, 522

Apter, David. 1402, 1403

Aptheker, Herbert. 1238

Aronson, James. 903, 1495

Arroyo, Luis L. 449

Ashbaugh, Carolyn. 537

Auerbach, Jerold S. 311, 312, 789, 1638

Ayer, Douglas R. 1569

Babson, S. 251

Bachrack, Stanley. 1513

Baigell, Matthew. 2084

Bailey, Percival R. 875, 876

Baker, Liva. 1639

Baker, Susan. 1088, 1089

Bakunin, Jack. 131

Balabanoff, Angelica. 22

Baldwin, Roger. 910

Bancroft, Caroline. 1097

Barbash, Jack. 252, 313

Barber, Kathleen L. 1640

Barnard, John. 401

Barrett, Edward. 1927

Barrett, James R. 1446

Barrett, William. 1582

Barron, James. 937, 1239

Bart, Philip. 1

Barth, Alan. 1641, 1715

Barto, Harold. 106

Baskin, Alex. 402

Baxandall, Rosalynn. 1417, 1418

Baylen, Joseph O. 1035

Bayley, Edwin R. 1836

Beal, Fred. 566

Beck, Carl. 1738

Beck, Kent M. 1430

Bedacht, Max. 1385

Beesley, David. 482

Belfrage, Cedric. 903, 911, 928, 929, 1739

Belknap, Michael R. 1642-1644, 1758, 1837

Bell, Daniel. 9, 189-192, 1003, 1798, 1883-1884

Bellush, Bernard. 91

Bellush, Jewel. 91

Belton, John. 238

Bendiner, R. 1002

Bentley, Elizabeth. 1233

Bentley, Eric. 1125, 1740

Berens, John F. 1759

Berger, Henry. 340, 341

Berman, Hyman. 160, 435

Berman, Marvin H. 938

Berman, Paul. 1057

Berman, William C. 1645

Bernard, Matthew M. 549

Berns, Walter. 1646

Bernstein, Barton J.
    1321, 1540-1541, 1885

Bernstein, Irving. 253,
    254

Bessie, Alvah. 1187

Beth, Loren P. 1886

Bethune, Beverly M. 1145

Betten, Neil. 368, 369,
    370, 371

Bigel, Alan Ira. 1647

Bilderback, William W. 68

Bimba, Anthony. 1357

Bingham, Arthur. 146

Bingham, June. 1621

Bintner, Stuart. 107

Biskind, Peter. 1166

Bittelman, Alexander. 2,
    1386, 1388

Bixler, Paul. 1404

Black, Claude L. 1622

Black, Gregory D. 1480

Blackwood, George D. 403

Blake, Fay M. 178

Blanchard, Margaret. 1496

Bliven, Bruce. 906

Bloom, Jon. 2033

Bloor, Ella Reeve. 1387

Blum, Jacob. 147

Blum, John Morton. 92

Blum, Richard H. 1648

Blumenstock, Dorothy. 220

Blustain, Jonah. 314

Bohlen, Charles E. 1958

Boller, Paul F., Jr. 69

Bolner, James. 1649

Bone, Hugh A. 132, 145

Bone, Robert. 2066

Bongartz, Roy. 1114

Bontecou, Eleanor. 1716

Bonthius, Andrew. 450

Boryczka, Ray. 404, 405

Boudna, Martin K. 1542

Boveri, Margret. 1216

Boyer, Richard. 255

Bozell, L. Brent. 1838,
    1888

Braden, Anne. 1924

Braden, Thomas. 1215

Brandt, Harvey V. 108

Brandt, Joe. 634

Brax, Ralph S. 984

Brecher, Jeremy. 256

Breslow, Paul E. 1887

Bretall, Robert W. 1624

Brickman, William W. 931

Briendel, Eric. 193, 194, 717

Briggs, Philip J. 1514

Bristol, James E. 1543

Brock, Clifton. 1570

Brody, David. 83, 257, 258

Brogna, John J. 1058

Bronfenbrenner, Urie. 1469

Brook, Alexander D. 1650

Brook, Michael. 633

Brooks, Robert R.R. 531

Brooks, T.R. 259, 729

Brooks, Van Wyck. 1067

Brophy, John. 567

Browder, Earl. 45, 46, 1389

Brown, Anthony Cave. 755

Brown, John Cotton. 109

Brown, Lloyd L. 734

Brown, Ralph S., Jr. 1717

Brown, Richard P. 1139

Broyles, J. Allen. 1877

Buckholder, Roger. 1240

Buckley, William F., Jr. 1241, 1242, 1741, 1838, 1888

Budenz, Louis. 195, 196, 1961

Buhle, Paul. 10, 47, 239, 609, 611, 1358, 2001, 2033

Buitrago, Ann Marie. 1318

Buka, Tony. 523

Bullitt, William. 1243

Bullock, Paul. 1635

Bulsys, Joseph. 1470

Burgchardt, Carl R. 48

Burke, Robert. 179

Burkhardt, Richard. 939

Burnham, James. 197, 1217

Bush, Lawrence. 1188

Cairns, John C. 1603

Calomiris, Angela. 1963

Camp, Helen Collier. 1419

Campbell, Katherine. 932

Campbell, Russell. 1146, 1147

Canby, Vincent. 1244

Candeloro, Dominic. 1688

Cannon, James P. 32, 240

Cantelon, Philip. 1742

Cantor, Milton. 1359

Cantril, Hadley. 1471

Carew, Anthony. 2049

Carleton, Don E. 1947–
1949

Carliner, Lewis. 342

Carlson, G. Bert, Jr.
1066

Carlson, Lewis H. 1743

Carlson, Oliver. 241

Carlson, Peter. 26

Carr, Robert K. 1744

Carr, Virginia S. 2052

Carter, Dan. 685

Carter, Robert. 133

Carwell, Joseph. 343

Cary, Lorin Lee. 524,
573, 574

Caughey, John W. 1799

Caute, David. 867, 1800

Centola, Kathleen. 836

Ceplair, Larry. 1155

Chafee, Zechariah, Jr.
1651, 1652

Chaison, Gary N. 260

Chamberlain, Lawrence H.
1944

Chambers, Steven A. 815

Chambers, Whittaker. 1245

Chapman, Philip. 1399,
1400, 1889, 2002

Chase, Harold. 1653, 1654

Chatfield, Charles. 70

Chernin, Kim. 1401

Chesler, Mark. 1890

Chollet, Laurence B. 1246

Christie, Robert A. 507

Christopulos, Diana. 756

Citron, Alice. 2074

Clardy, J.V. 1655

Clark, Wayne. 1925

Clark, Joseph. 49, 2003

Cleath, Robert. 1390

Clecak, Peter. 902, 1004

Cleland, Hugh. 470, 471

Clubb, O. Edmund. 1247

Clurman, Harold. 1126,
1199

Coady, Sharon. 1868

Cobb, William. 790, 791,
2037

Coben, Stanley. 1689,
1690

Cochran, Bert. 381

Cogley, John. 1167

Cohen, Robby. 952

Cohn, Roy. 1839

Cohn, Werner. 199

Colburn, David R. 1703

Cole, Lester. 1190

Columbia Law Review. 1329

Commentary. 1544

Conlin, Joseph. 27, 2004

Connolly, Peter M. 1656

Conrad, David Eugene. 792

Cook, Bruce. 1197

Cook, Fred J. 1248-52,
   1313, 1760, 1840

Cook, Philip L. 1711

Cook, Sylvia. 532

Cook, Thomas I. 1657

Cooke, Alistair. 1253

Cooney, Terry. 1583, 1584

Cooper, Wayne F. 721

Corey, Esther. 757, 1405,
   1406

Corker, Charles. 2005

Corson, William R. 1761

Coulton, Thomas. 953

Countryman, Vern. 1951

Cowley, Malcolm. 1068,
   1069, 1070, 1071

Crampton, John. 785, 786

Crandell, William F. 1801

Crews, Frederick. 1585

Crimmins, Carolyn. 1606

Critchlow, Donald C. 674

Crosby, Donald F. 855,
   1831-1834

Crossman, Richard. 1031

Crowl, James William. 887

Cruse, Harold. 635

Culbert, David. 1148

Cummings, Robert. 2046

Cunningham, Earl L. 735

Curtis, Charles P. 1322

Cushman, Robert E. 1718

Dahlheimer, Harry. 406

Dahlstrom, H. A. 1999

Dallin, David. 1218

Daniel, Cletus E. 315,
   804, 805, 806

Daniels, Roger. 50

Danish, Max. 570

Dann, Jim. 780

Darcy, Samuel Adams. 1411

Davies, Margaret. 344

Davin, Eric Leif. 316

Davis, Angela. 1408

Davis, Benjamin J. 699

Davis, Earle.

Davis, James A. 1472

Davis, Jane Maria. 747

Davis, Jerome. 954

Davis, Lenwood G. 736

Davis, Mike. 317, 2042

Dawidowicz, Lucy. 444

Dawson, Nelson L. 1254

Daykin, Walter L. 318

De Grazia, Victoria.

de Lazarovics, Fedor. 42

de Toledano, Ralph. 1005,
    1219, 1220, 2078

Deaver, Jean. 2041

DeCaux, Len. 569

Decter, Moshe. 1841

Delaney, Robert. 2006

Denisoff, Ronald Serge.
    1200-04

Denison, Dave A. 588

Dennis, Peggy. 72, 612,
    827, 1360, 1412, 1964

deSantis, Vincent P. 1835

Dewitt, Anthony. 667

Diamond, Arlyn. 1330

Diamond, Sigmund. 955,
    1545

Dickstein, Morris. 1006

Dies, Martin. 200, 1965

Diggins, John P. 907,
    1033, 1077, 1361

Dirscherl, Dennis. 201

Divine, Robert. 110,
    1971

Dixler, Elsa. 202, 829

Dobbs, Farrell. 514, 515,
    516

Dobriansky, Lev E. 1497

Dodd, Bella. 1413

Doenecke, Justus D. 71

Dolson, James. 1414

Donner, Frank J. 762,
    1745, 1763, 1764

Donohue, Charles T. 722

Dos Passos, John. 1074,
    1075

Douglas, Paul H. 1605

Dowd, Douglas F. 2007

Dowdy, Andrew. 1176

Dowell, E.F. 1918

Downing, Lyle A. 956

Drachkovitch, Milorad.
    758

Drake, Willie Avon. 700

Drakeford, John W. 837

Draper, Hal. 51, 985

Draper, Theodore. 11, 33,
    203, 525, 533, 1438,
    2008, 2009, 2010,
    2011

Dubinsky, David. 571

Dubofsky, Melvyn. 12, 28,
    576

DuBois, Shirley. 701

DuBois, W.E.B. 702

Duke, David C. 1529, 1530

Duke, David Nelson. 863

Dunaway, David King.
    1205, 1206, 1213

Dunbar, Anthony P. 877

Dunne, Philip. 1156

Dwyer, William. 2044

Dyson, Lowell K. 781,
    782, 783, 793, 816,
    2055, 2056, 2057

Dzierba, Timothy R. 319

Eagan, Eileen. 986, 987

East, John P. 1997

Eastland, Terry. 235

Eastman, Max. 23, 1078

Eaton, William. 487

Eaton, William J. 407

Eby, Cecil. 765

Edelman, Irwin. 1331

Egbert, Donald Drew. 1362

Egerton, John. 1926

Ehrmann, H.W. 1658

Eisele, Albert. 1607

Eisman, Louis. 34

Elniff, Terrill I. 1255

Emerson, Hough. 2058

Emerson, Thomas I. 686,
    1719

Emspak, Frank. 382

Engelhardt, Carroll. 1632

Engelmann, Larry. 448

Englund, Steven. 1155

Enzensberger, Hans. 888

Epstein, Albert. 261

Epstein, Jason. 1546

Epstein, Marc Joel. 1571

Epstein, Melech. 436, 613

Erickson, Gerald M. 1547

Erickson, Herman. 262

Ernst, Max. 1720

Ernst, Morris L. 204

Esherick, John. 1515

Evans, Matthew. 1842

Evans, William. 205

Eversull, Le Roi. 940

Ewig, Rick. 1978

Fabre, Michel. 1104, 2069

Fairclough, Adam. 718

Falk, Doris V. 913

Falk, Julius. 13

Farsoun, Karen. 759

Farsoun, Samih. 759

Fast, Howard. 1081

Feldblum, Esther. 838

Fennero, Matthew. 864

Ferguson, Mary Jane. 1843

Ferrari, Arthur C. 1054

Feuer, Lewis S. 868, 889, 1464

Fiedler, Leslie. 1548, 1891

Field, Frederick. 1416

Field, Noel. 1235

Fields, A.B. 242

Filene, Peter. 1473

Filippelli, Ronald. 472-74

Finch, Phillip. 2059

Fine, Nathan. 1363

Fine, Sidney. 408, 409

Fineberg, S.A. 1332

Finison, Lorenz. 878-80

Fink, Gary M. 557

Fisch, Dov. 614

Fischel, Jacob. 957

Fishbein, Leslie. 1149

Fitzgerald, Richard. 1115

Flanagan, Hallie. 1127

Flanders, Ralph E. 1975

Flournoy, Houston. 134

Flynn, Elizabeth Gurley. 1420-22, 1424

Flynn, John T. 1981

Folsom, Michael. 1059

Foner, Philip S. 437, 636, 675, 830

Foster, Arnold. 615

Foster, James. 320

Foster, William Z. 3, 1425, 1426

Fothergill, Garland. 908

Fountain, Clayton. 410

Fowler, Robert. 1549

Fox, John D. 1256

Frank, Felicia. 1128

Fraser, Steven C. 438

Freeland, Richard. 1498, 1499

Freeman, Joseph. 1431

Freeman, Joshua B. 298, 502, 503

Fried, Richard M. 1802, 1803, 1844, 1845, 2012

Friedheim, Robert. 1712

Friedlander, Peter. 411

Friedman, John S. 1042

Frost, Richard. 180

Fry, William Welz. 206

Furmanovsky, Michael. 181

Gahn, Joseph A. 1116

Galenson, Walter. 264, 383

Gardner, David. 958, 959

Gardner, Virginia. 1395

Garfinkel, Herbert. 730

Garman, Phillips L. 321

Garner, Donald P. 1956

Garraty, John A. 93

Garrow, David J. 719

Gates, John. 1433

Gayce, Addison. 2070

Gedicks, Albert J. 589

Gellerman, William. 1966

Gellhorn, Walter. 1721, 1919

Gengarelly, William Anthony. 1691, 1692

Genizi, Haim. 1593, 1594, 1595, 1596, 1597

Gens, Stephen Mark. 1575

Gerassi, John. 766

Gershman, Carl. 1576

Gerson, Simon W. 135

Gerstle, Gary L. 52, 265, 266, 267, 372, 534

Geschwender, James A. 637

Gettleman, Marvin. 960, 961, 962

Gibson, Dirk C. 1765

Gieske, Millard. 161

Giffin, Frederick C. 1317

Gilbert, James. 1396, 2080, 2081

Gilder, Peggy Allen. 893

Gillon, Steven. 2086

Gitlow, Ben. 1434, 1435

Glaberman, Martin. 268, 299, 412, 988

Glaberson, Eric. 1586

Glazer, Nathan. 207, 208, 914

Glotzer, Albert. 243, 1257

Gnall, Janet Marita. 1083

Godson, Roy. 345-49

Gold, Ben. 1436

Goldberg, Joseph. 452

Goldblatt, Louis. 451

Goldfield, Michael. 708

Goldfinger, Nathaniel. 261

Goldman, Harry. 1129

Goldsmith, William. 881

Goldstein, Robert. 1659

Goldwater, Walter. 2013

Goodman, Walter. 1746

Gordon, Gerald R. 350

Gordon, Linda. 831

Gordon, Max. 53, 54, 136, 493, 989, 1333

Gordon, Mel. 1129

Gorey, Hays. 1608

Gorman, Joseph. 1613

Gornick, Vivian. 209

Goulden, Joseph. 1258

Gower, Calvin W. 990

Graham, Shirley. 737

Gramont, Sanche de. 1221

Graves, John. 638

Gray, Roland F. 941

Greeley, Andrew. 2076

Green, Dan. 703

Green, George N. 1950

Green, Gil. 1259, 1437

Green, James. 269, 270, 300

Greenberg, Ken. 2073

Grenier, Richard. 1157

Griffith, Robert W. 1686, 1804-1807, 1846-1848, 1869

Griffith, Winthrop. 1609

Grob, Gerald N. 271

Grodzins, Morton. 1660

Group, David J. 1661

Grubbs, Donald H. 790, 794, 795

Gruliow, Leo. 1407

Guhlin, Michael. 1969

Gurowsky, David. 439

Gustafson, Merlin. 839, 840

Guttmann, Allen. 616, 617, 767, 1105

Gwynn, Beatrice V. 1260

Hainsworth, Jerome. 942

Hall, Gus. 494

Hall, Tim. 1106, 1107

Halonen, Arne. 590

Halperin, Morton. 1766

Halpern, Martin. 413, 2052

Hamby, Alonzo. 111, 112, 1550, 1551, 1552

Hamilton, James. 1747

Hamilton, John R. 862

Hamilton, Mary A. 113

Haney, Richard. 171

Harland, Gordon. 1623

Harper, Alan D. 1553, 2014

Harrington, Michael. 373, 869

Harris, Abram L. 683

Harris, Benjamin. 882, 974

Harris, Ed. 453

Harris, Herbert. 384

Harris, Lement. 784

Harris, William H. 731

Harsha, E. Houston. 1939

Haskett, William. 272

Hasting, Anne. 114

Hatcher, Susan. 1977

Haynes, John Earl. 84,
162 163, 445, 552,
817, 1349

Haywood, Harry. 709

Haywood, William D. 29

Hazlett, John D. 1072

Heale, M.J. 2048

Healy, Dorothy. 273

Hedley, John H. 1516

Hein, Carl. 30

Hein, Virginia H. 1035

Held, Abraham. 14

Helfeld, D.M. 1719

Hellman, Lillian. 915,
916

Hemenway, Robert E. 713

Henderson, Jeff. 732

Henderson, John. 1722

Henrickson, Gary P. 1942

Hero, Alfred O. 351

Hertz, Howard Lee. 1060

Herz, Martin F. 943

Herzig, Jill H. 186

Hevener, John W. 526

Hey, Kenneth. 1192

Hicks, Granville. 24,
1007, 1086-87

Higgins, James. 476

Hill, George W. 602

Himelstein, Morgan. 1130,
1131

Hincheyst, Mary. 94

Hiss, Alger. 1261

Hobsbawn, Eric. 2015,
2016

Hoffman, Benjamin. 1397

Hofmann, George F. 1500

Hofstadter, Richard.
1892, 1893, 1894

Hoglund, A. William. 591

Holcomb, Ellen Lois. 807

Hollander, Paul. 870,
871, 890, 891

Hollinger, David A. 1262

Holmes, Thomas M. 1936

Holt, Elvin. 714

Homberger, Eric. 1055

Honey, Michael. 676

Hood, Robin. 535

Hoogestraat, Wayne. 1986

Hook, Sidney. 210, 211,
    894, 895, 917, 1263-
    1266, 1302, 1350,
    1598, 2053

Hooker, James. 668

Hoopes, Townsend. 1970

Hoover, J. Edgar. 1767

Horne, Gerald C. 704, 705

Horowitz, Irving. 1768

Howe, Irving. 4, 274,
    414, 918, 1008-1012

Hoyt, Edward. 738

Hronicek, Francis R. 488

Huberman, Leo. 1094

Hudson, G.F. 1352

Hudson, Harriet D. 527

Hudson, Hosea. 677, 710

Hughes, Cicero A. 663

Hughes, Emmet. 1972

Hughes, H. Stuart. 963

Hull, Elizabeth A. 1662

Hummasti, Paul. 592

Humola, Hulda F. 164

Humphrey, Hubert H. 1610

Hunter, Allen. 831

Huntley, Horace. 483, 484

Huntley, Richard. 1409

Hurst, Catherine. 748

Hurwitz, Leo. 1150

Hyman, Sidney. 1957

Ilkka, Richard. 15

Ingalls, Robert. 495,
    496, 1849

Irons, Peter. 1268, 1269,
    1693, 1809, 1810

Issacs, William. 1364

Isserman, Maurice. 55,
    56, 73, 74, 2017,
    2018, 2019

Iversen, Robert W. 933

Jackson, Peter. 148

Jacobson, Phyllis. 2045

Jaffe, Julian F. 1704,
    1705

Jaffe, Philip J. 57, 58,
    115, 1537

James, Estelle. 517, 518

James, Ralph C., 517, 518

Jamieson, Stuart. 808

Jaszi, Oscar. 40

Jefferson, Bonnie. 1474

Jennings, Ed. 301

Jensen, Vernon. 485, 508

Jenson, Carol E. 1920

Joel, Judith. 1547

Johnpoll, Bernard K.
    1365, 1577, 2020,
    2039

Johnpoll, Lillian. 1365

Johnson, Christopher. 1457

Johnson, Oakley C. 16, 968, 1451

Johnson, Ralph H. 1811

Johnson, Ronald. 475, 1943

Johnston, Verle. 768

Joint Legislative Committee. 17

Jones, Dorothy B. 1158

Jones, J. Harry, Jr. 1878

Josephson, Harold. 1475, 1476, 1706

Josephson, Matthew. 546, 575, 1013, 1270

Jowitt, William. 1271

Kaas, Baron Albert. 41

Kacewicz, Laura Ann. 1477

Kagedan, Allan L. 618

Kagel, John. 454

Kahn, E. J., Jr. 1517

Kahn, Eleanor. 559

Kaiser, Robert. 1272

Kakutani, Michiko. 919

Kamp, Joe. 385

Kampelman, Max. 386, 387

Kaner, Norman J. 149

Kanet, Roger. 669

Kanfer, Stefan. 1168

Kann, Kenneth. 1449

Karcz, Valerian. 1509

Karmarkovic, Alex. 841

Karni, Michael G. 593, 594, 595

Karsh, Bernard. 321

Kazin, Alfred. 920, 1014-1017

Kebker, Vant W. 596

Keefe, Robert. 1478

Keeley, Joseph. 1518

Keeran, Roger. 302, 415-418

Kegley, Charles W. 1624

Keiser, John H. 760

Keitel, Robert S. 486

Kemper, Donald. 1976

Kempton, Murray. 1018

Kendall, Willmoore. 1895

Kercher, Leonard C. 596

Keyssar, Helene. 1534

Kinnamon, Keneth. 749

Kinoy, Arthur. 1439, 1663

Kinsley, Michael. 1273

Kintner, William R. 212

Kirby, Linda Kaye. 1587

Kirkendall, Richard. 2021

Kivisto, Peter. 597, 598, 599

Kizer, Benjamin H. 1423

Klehr, Harvey. 18, 59,
    95, 213, 214, 215,
    216, 217, 419, 583,
    1151, 1519, 2039

Klein, James. 1152

Klein, Joe. 1207

Kling, Jack. 2035

Kling, Joseph M. 60

Kluger, Richard. 1748

Knight, Rolf. 2038

Koch, Lene. 322

Koen, Ross Y. 1520

Koeppen, Sheilah R. 1812,
    1896

Koger, Daniel Allan. 1479

Kolehmainen, John I. 600,
    601, 602

Kolko, Gabriel. 1366,
    1501

Konvitz, Milton R. 1664

Koppes, Clayton R. 1480

Korstad, Robert. 639

Kosa, John. 640

Kostiainen, Auvo. 603,
    604

Kramer, Hilton. 218, 921,
    1169, 2075

Kraus, Henry. 420

Krause, Fayette. 165, 185

Kreuger, Thomas. 883

Krieger, Nancy. 1415

Krivitsky, Walter. 1318

Krugman, Herbert. 219

Kubek, Anthony. 1521

Kuczun, Sam. 547

Kumasi, Kandi Baba. 750

Kunkel, Joseph A. 172

Kutler, Stanley I. 1665

Kyser, John L. 842

La Gumina, Salvatore.
    150-153

Lader, Lawrence. 1367

Lamont, Corliss. 884,
    926, 2082

Lamphere, Robert. 1222

Lampman, Robert J. 455

Landis, Arthur. 769

Langer, Elinor. 1084

Laqueur, Walter. 1019,
    1036

Lardner, Ring, Jr. 1170

Larrowe, Charles. 456,
    457

Larson, Arthur. 1973

Larson, Simeon. 352

Lasch, Christopher. 1368,
    1554, 1588, 1813,
    2054

Lash, Joseph. 991

Lasky, Melvin J. 1274

Lasky, Victor. 1219, 2078

Laslett, John H.M. 275, 276, 421, 1369, 1370

Lasswell, Harold D. 220

Latham, Earl. 1037, 1814, 1897

Lattimore, Owen. 1982

Lawless, Ken. 1117

Lawrenson, Helen. 1440

Layton, Edwin. 2062

Lazarsfeld, Paul. 964

Lazarowitz, Arlene. 1555

Lazitch, Branko. 758

Le Blanc, Paul. 221

Leab, Daniel J. 497, 548, 560, 561, 1177-1179, 2025

Ledeen, Michael. 1275

Lee, Mark Wilcox. 75

Lee, R. Alton. 1987

Lefever, Ernest W. 843

Lehman, Herbert. 1614

Leiter, Robert D. 440

Leland, Wilfred. 596

Lembcke, Jerry. 509, 510

Lenburg, LeRoy. 353

Lens, Sidney. 277

Lester, Julius. 706

Levenstein, Harvey. 278, 354, 355, 387

Levering, Ralph B. 1481

Levin, David. 1276

Levin, Harry. 1092

Levin, Murray B. 1666

Levine, Ira Alan. 1132

Levine, Isaac Don. 1223, 1984

Levinson, Edward. 389

Levinson, Mark. 2022

Levitt, Michael. 1277

Levitt, Morton. 1277

LeWarne, Charles P. 1694

Lewinson, Edwin R. 654

Lewis Coser. 4

Lewis, Flora. 1236

Lewy, Guenter. 1723

Libbey, James K. 896

Licht, Walter. 137

Lichtenstein, Nelson. 279, 303-306, 422, 423, 2023, 2024

Lieberman, Donna. 154

Lieberman, Robbie. 1208, 1209

Liebman, Arthur. 619

Liebowitz, Nathan. 1604

Link, Eugene P. 865, 866

Link, Michael. 1625

Lipset, Seymour Martin.
    96, 873, 1370, 1815,
    1898-1900

Lipsitz, George. 323,
    324, 325

Lomis, Dean. 944

Long, Edward. 1928, 1929

Longaker, Richard P. 1667

Longstaff, S.A. 1589,
    1590

Lopez, Ronald W. 809

Lora, Ronald. 1816

Lorence, James J. 173

Lorin, Lewis. 356

Loth, David. 204

Lovin, Hugh T. 97, 98,
    187, 326-329, 556,
    770

Lowenfish, Lee. 872, 1432

Lowenstein, Meno. 1482

Lowenthal, John. 1278

Lowenthal, Max. 1769

Lowy, M. 1371

Lubow, Arthur. 1273

Ludington, Townsend. 1076

Luthin, Reinhard. 1850

Lydenberg, John. 965

Lynd, Alice. 582

Lynd, Staughton. 61, 316,
    330, 498, 581, 582,
    2019

Lynn, Kenneth. 1073, 1093

Lyons, Eugene. 21

Lyons, Paul. 222, 223

Màlusz, Elemèr. 42

Mabon, David. 458

MacDonald, Charles B. 755

Macdonald, Dwight. 1617

MacDonald, J. Fred. 1180,
    2068

MacDougall, Curtis D. 116

MacKay, Kenneth. 88

MacKenzie, Alan J. 715

MacKinnon, Jan. 1538

MacKinnon, Steve. 1538

MacLean, Elizabeth. 1483

Maddux, Thomas R. 1484,
    1485

Mailer, Norman. 922

Mairowitz, David. 1372

Malafronte, Anthony. 1991

Maland, Charles. 1181,
    1193,

Malkin, Maurice. 1441

Mangione, Jerre. 2079

Marable, Manning. 733

Marden, David L. 934

Margolis, Barbara. 1486

Markowitz, Gerald E.
    1334, 1335

Markowitz, Norman D. 117,
    118, 119, 1851, 2083

Marlowe, Lon D., III.
    1817

Marquart, Frank. 280

Marro, Anthony. 1770

Marshall, Herbert. 739

Marshall, Paul. 844

Martin, Charles H. 687,
    688, 689, 690, 691

Martin, John B. 1994

Mason, Daniel. 5

Massing, Hede. 1442

Mast, Charles. 787

Mathews, Allan. 818, 819

Mathews, Jane DeHart.
    1118, 1133

Matles, James J. 476

Matthews, G. 810

Matthews, J.B. 927

Matthews, T.S. 1279

Matusow, Allen. 1556,
    1853

Matusow, Harvey. 1749

Maurer, Marvin. 845

May, Gary. 1522

May, Ronald W. 1854

Mayer, George H. 519

McAuliffe, Mary. 1557-
    1559, 1669, 1818

McCarthy, Joe. 1852

McConnell, Frank D. 1182

McCoy, Donald. 99, 174

McCoy, Garnett. 1119

McCracken, Samuel. 923

McCrackin, Bobbie. 224

McCreath, Harrison. 1140

McCurry, Dan. 536

McDonald, William F. 1120

McDougall, Daniel J. 966

McElvaine, Robert S. 100

McFarland, C.K. 101

McGinley, James J. 504

McGreen, John D. 1578

McIntyre, Edison. 771

McKay, Claude. 723, 724

McKee, Delber. 357

Mckee, Mary J. 1985

McKinley, Wayne. 1881

McKinzie, Richard D. 1121

McLellan, David. 1954

McNeil, Neil. 1967

McPherson, Michael L. 924

McWilliams, Carey. 811,
    1280, 1819

Meeropol, Michael. 1336

Meeropol, Robert. 1336

Meier, August. 678, 679

Mendelson, Michael. 2077

Mendelson, Wallace. 1668

Merkley, Paul. 1626, 1627

Merson, Martin. 1724

Meyer, Elizabeth. 1783

Meyer, Frank S. 225

Meyer, Gerald. 155

Meyer, Karl. 1870

Meyer, Stephen, III. 424

Meyerowitz, Ruth. 425

Mikhailov, B.Y. 281

Miller, Charles. 489

Miller, Donald L. 102

Miller, Douglas T. 1374

Miller, Gariel. 1189

Miller, John. 1945, 1946

Miller, M. Lawrence. 1134

Miller, Michael H. 992

Millett, Stephen. 1452, 1453

Milton, David. 390, 391

Milton, Joyce. 1342

Minott, Rodney. 1879, 1880

Mirel, Jeffrey. 935

Mitau, G. Theodore. 166

Mitchell, H.L. 796, 797

Mitford, Jessica. 1443

Monfross, John. 812

Monnerot, Jules. 226

Monroe, Gerald. 1122, 1123

Monroy, Douglas. 630, 631, 632

Montgomery, David. 578, 2061

Moon, Henry Lee. 692

Moore, Barrington. 227

Moore, Gilbert W. 426

Moore, John Hammond. 63

Moorehead, Alan. 1224

Moremen, Merril. 182

Morgan, Alda. 967

Morgan, J.W. 441

Morgan, Richard E. 1771

Morgenthau, Hans J. 1725

Morray, J.P. 763

Morris, Herbert. 255

Morris, James O. 392

Morris, Richard B. 1281

Mortimer, Wyndham. 427

Mosse, George. 1019, 1036

Mowitz, Robert J. 1941

Mullay, Camilla. 568

Mulvey, Daniel P. 681

Munk, Michael. 904

Muraskin, L.D. 490

Muravchik, Joshua. 846,
    885

Murdock, Steve. 183

Murphy, Paul. 1695, 1696

Murphy, Richard J. 847

Murray, Edward. 1141

Murray, Hugh T., Jr. 693

Murray, Michael D. 1937

Murray, Robert. 1697,
    1698

Myers, Constance. 244-246

Naficy, Azar. 1061

Naftalin, Arthur A. 167

Nagy, Alex. 1670

Naison, Mark. 64, 641,
    655-661, 751, 798,
    799, 930

Nash, Al. 579

Nash, Michael. 1599

Nass, Deanna R. 969

Nathanson, Nathaniel.
    1671

Navasky, Victor. 1159,
    1282-1285

Nelson, Daniel. 331

Nelson, Joseph. 459, 560

Nelson, Steve. 1445, 1446

Neufeld, Maurice F. 2025

Nevins, Allan. 1615

Newman, H. Morton. 178

Newman, Robert. 1523,
    1983

Newman, Steven L. 1323

Nikoloric, L.A. 1726

Ninkovich, Frank A. 1020

Nixon, Richard. 1286,
    1988

Nizer, Louis. 1337

Nobile, Philip. 1287

Nolan, William. 642, 643

Nordstrand, Marty. 1611

North, Joseph. 1427

Norton, Sally. 1191

Notaro, Carmen A. 103

Novak, Estelle G. 1108

Nowak, Marion. 1374

Nuechterlein, James. 1633

Nunn, Clyde Z. 640

O'Brien, David. 374

O'Brien, F.S. 282

O'Brien, Jim. 236, 1375

O'Brien, John. 1672, 1727

O'Brien, Kevin J. 1673

O'Brien, Michael. 1871-73

O'Connell, Thomas. 168

O'Connor, Harvey. 1713

O'Hearn, Michael. 848

O'Leary, Richard. 945

O'Neill, William L. 1079,
    1560

O'Reilly, Kenneth. 1561,
    1772-1779

Odegarde, Holton P. 1628

Ogden, August. 1750

Ogle, Stephanie F. 1531

Oliva, A.T. 1882

Ollila, D. 595

Ollman, Bertell. 970

Olson, Frederick. 175

Olson, James S. 680

Olster, Stacey. 1038

Oneal, James. 6, 19

Orr, Miriam. 1096

Oshinsky, David. 393,
    1855, 1856, 1874

Ostrander, Lucy. 1532

Ottanelli, Michele Fraser.
    65, 66

Ozanne, Robert. 283, 558

Packer, Herbert L. 1288,
    1751

Padmore, George. 670, 671

Pahl, Thomas. 247, 1674

Painter, Nell. 711, 712

Palermo, Patrick F. 1098

Palladino, Grace. 477

Palmer, Bryan D. 31

Palmer, Edward E. 228

Panunzio, C. M. 1699

Papanikolas, Helen. 528

Parenti, Michael. 1562

Parmet, Herbert S. 1974

Parrish, Michael. 1339

Parsons, Talcott. 1902

Paterson, Thomas G. 1466

Patterson, James. 1995

Patterson, William. 2063

Paul, Justis. 1962

Paulston, Rolland G. 587

Pauluch, Peter. 892

Pawa, J.M. 1707

Peck, David R. 1056

Peeler, David P. 1021

Pells, Richard. 1022,
    1023

Penkower, Monty. 1050

Pennington, Renee. 1194

Perdew, Richard M. 946

Perlman, Selig. 86

Perry, Louis B. 550

Perry, Richard S. 550

Persons, Stow. 1362

Pesotta, Rose. 580

Pessen, Edward. 1340

Peters, Norma Jean. 947

Peterson, Brian. 2026

Peterson, Frank. 120,
    121, 122, 1210

Phelps, Marianne. 993

Philbrick, Herbert. 1992

Phillips, William. 925,
    1591

Pienkos, Donald E. 1510

Pierce, Robert C. 1572

Pilat, Oliver. 1341,
    1989, 1990

Pinola, Rudolph. 553

Plog, Stanley. 1857

Podhoretz, Norman. 1024,
    1025, 1039

Polsby, Nelson W. 1858,
    1903

Poole, Thomas. 1629

Pope, Liston. 538

Popkin, Richard H. 1289

Potter, Charles. 1820

Prago, Albert. 562, 621

Pratt, William C. 332,

Preston, William, Jr.
    1700, 1752

Prickett, James R. 284,
    285, 286, 307, 394,
    428, 429, 461

Pries, Art. 395

Pringle, Robert W., Jr.
    1533

Pritchard, Robert L. 1930

Pritchett, C.H. 1675

Prpic, George. 584

Purcell, Theodore V. 681

Pyle, Gordon Bruce. 971

Pyros, John. 1062

Quill, Shirley. 505

Ra'anan, Gavriel. 761

Raab, Earl. 1815

Rader, Melvin. 1952

Radosh, Ronald. 358,
    1342, 1519

Ragan, Fred Donald. 1701

Rahv, Philip. 1592

Raskin, A.H. 571, 729

Rawick, George. 988, 994

Raymond, Orin R., 2d. 35

Record, Jane. 462

Record, Wilson. 644, 645,
     672

Rededip, John H. 859

Redlich, Norman. 2034

Rees, David. 1353

Rees, John. 898

Reeve, Carl. 538, 539

Reeves, Thomas C. 1859-
     1862, 1905

Reichert, Julia. 1152

Renshaw, Patrick. 1454

Reuben, William. 1290-
     1292, 1343

Reuss, Richard. 1204,
     1211, 1212

Reuther, Victor G. 430

Reutter, E. Edmund. 972

Richardson, R. Dan. 772,
     773

Richmond, Al. 1450, 1462

Ricks, John. 1996

Rideout, Walter B. 1049

Riker, William H. 333

Rintala, Harvin. 605

Robeson, Paul. 740

Robeson, Paul, Jr. 741

Robinson, Cedric J. 646,
     716

Robinson, Donald A. 442

Robinson, Jo Ann. 1620

Rogin, Michael. 1183,
     1906

Rolfe, Edwin. 774

Rorty, James. 1841

Rosen, Dale. 800, 801

Rosen, Jerold A. 123

Rosen, Sumner. 682

Rosenau, James. 1959

Rosenberg, Roger E. 1391

Rosengarten, Theodore.
     801, 802

Rosenof, Theodore. 1601

Rosenstone, Robert A. 25,
     775-777

Rosenzweig, Roy. 563,
     564, 1153, 1154, 2027

Ross, Carl. 606

Rossi, John P. 1041, 2085

Rossiter, Clinton. 2047

Roth, Henry. 1042

Rothweiler, Robert. 1043

Rovere, Richard H. 1863,
     1907, 2043

Rowley, William D. 821

Roy, Ralph L. 849

Rozakis, Laurie E. 905

Rubenstein, Annette T.
     156, 1085

Ruck, Rob. 1446

Rudwick, Elliott. 678, 679

Ruggiero, Josephine. 1487

Ruiz, Vicki Lynn. 813

Rusher, William A. 1753

Ryan, James G. 1392, 1393

Ryan, Leo J. 936

Sadler, Charles. 1511

Salisbury, Harrison E. 1780, 1781

Sallach, David. 359

Salmond, John A. 104

Salomone, Jerome J. 956

Salvatore, Nick. 1579

Samuels, Raphael. 1135

Sanders, David. 1044

Sanders, Jane. 973

Sanford, Delacy W., Jr. 647

Santora, Patricia. 1109

Santos, Michael W. 540

Saposs, David. 87, 287, 288

Sarasohn, Stephen. 138

Sargent, S. Stansfeld. 974

Sasuly, Richard. 157

Sayre, Nora. 1184

Schaar, John H. 1676

Schaffer, Alan. 158

Schappes, Morris U. 622

Schapsmeier, Edward L. 124, 1968

Schapsmeier, Frederick. 124, 1968

Schary, Dore. 1198

Schatz, Ronald. 375, 478-481

Scheiber, Harry N. 1702

Schlatter, Richard. 995

Schlesinger, Arthur, Jr. 1293, 1324, 1502, 1980

Schlozman, Kay. 1379

Schmidt, Henry. 463

Schmidt, Karl M. 125, 126

Schmidt, Lester F. 176

Schmuck, Richard. 1890

Schneider, David. 289, 290

Schneiderman, William. 1458

Schneier, Edward V. 1754, 1755

Schneir, Miriam. 1234, 1344

Schneir, Walter. 1234, 1344

Schnell, Rodolph L. 996

Schomp, Gerald. 2060

Schonberger, Howard. 360

Schrecker, Ellen. 975,
    976, 977, 978, 979,
    980, 2065

Schriver, Joe M. 446

Schuman, Frederick. 1728

Schwartz, Donald A. 431

Schwartz, Harvey. 464,
    465

Schwartz, Lawrence H.
    1045, 1046

Schwartz, Nancy L. 1160

Schwarz, Bill. 2028

Scobie, Ingrid W. 1931,
    1932, 1933

Seabrook, John. 696

Seaman, John. 860

Seaton, Douglas. 376, 377

Seeger, Pete. 1213

Seideman, David. 909

Seidman, Joel. 308, 309,
    443, 2029

Selcraig, James T. 1922,
    1923

Sellen, Robert W. 1908

Selvin, David. 551

Selznick, Philip. 229

Sennett, William. 2040

Service, John S. 1524

Sessions, John. 778

Seth, Ronald. 1294

Seton, Marie. 742

Seymour, Helen. 565

Shachtman, Max. 248

Shachtman, Tom. 1222

Shaffer, Ralph E. 36, 37

Shaffer, Robert. 832

Shair, David I. 334

Shannon, David. 76, 1580,
    1875

Shapiro, Edward S. 623,
    1295, 1296, 1345

Shapiro, Stanley. 38

Sharp, Kathleen A. 1455

Shattuck, Henry L. 1729

Shaw, Peter. 873

Sheldon, Charles. 1677,
    1678

Sherrill, Robert. 1297

Shewmaker, Kenneth E.
    1525, 1526

Shi, David E. 1091

Shideler, James H. 89

Shields, Art. 466, 541

Shields, James M. 169

Shils, Edward. 230

Shover, John L. 822, 823,
    824, 825

Shrake, Richard W., II.
    335

Shuldiner, David P. 624

Shuman, R. Baird. 1142

Sibley, Milford Q. 1821

Siegel, Morton. 542

Simama, Jabari Onaje. 648

Simmons, Jerold. 1756

Simon, Rita J. 1376

Simson, Arthur. 90

Singal, Daniel. 1090

Singer, Alan J. 529

Singer, David. 1616

Sistrunk, Walter. 948

Skeels, Jack. 432, 433

Skinner, James M. 1185

Sklar, Robert. 1161

Small, Melvin. 1162,
   1163, 1164

Smedley, Agnes. 1539

Smiley, Sam. 1051

Smith, A. Robert. 1619

Smith, John Chabot. 1298,
   1299

Smith, Margaret Chase.
   1993

Smith, R. Harris. 1225

Smith, Ronald A. 743

Smith, Tom W. 1488

Smith, William Thomas.
   764

Smyle, Robert F. 850

Sniegoski, Stephen. 1864

Soden, Dale Edward. 861

Sofchalk, Donald G. 499,
   500, 554

Sokol, Robert. 1909-1910

Solberg, Carl. 1612

Solomon, Lesley L. 361

Solomon, Mark. 649

Solow, Herbert. 1226

Somerville, John. 1679,
   1680

Sontag, Susan. 874

Sorenson, Dale. 1489,
   1938

Spano, Richard. 447

Spector, Bert A. 1171,
   1172

Spencer, Thomas T. 336

Spero, Sterling D. 683

Spolansky, Jacob. 1782

Spruill, Larry H. 720

Stachowski, Floyd. 177

Stanley, William, III. 67

Starobin, Joseph R. 77,
   78, 79, 80

Starr, Emil. 351

Starr, Jerold M. 1124,
   1377

Steffens, Lincoln. 1099

Stein, Bruno. 1730

Stein, Harry. 1394

Stein, Judith. 650

Steinberg, Peter L. 1681, 1682

Steinberg, Philip A. 491

Steinbock, Julius. 139

Steinke, John. 1563, 1823

Stephenson, Anders. 105, 2064

Sterling, David L. 1683

Stern, Philip M. 1325

Stern, Sol. 997

Steward, William J. 140

Stewart, Donald O. 1136

Stoesen, Alexander. 1631

Stokes, Melvyn. 762

Stolberg, Benjamin. 396, 572

Stouffer, Samuel. 1490

Straight, Michael. 1351

Streater, John, Jr. 664

Stripling, Robert. 231

Strom, Sharon H. 833

Stromer, Marvin E. 2000

Strong, Tracy B. 1534

Strout, Cushing. 1326, 1346

Stuhler, Barbara. 170

Sturmthal, Adolf. 362

Suber, Howard. 1165, 1173

Sugar, Maurice. 434

Sullivan, William C. 651

Sussman, Warren. 1026

Sutherland, Arthur E., Jr. 1684

Swanberg, W.A. 1578

Swanson, Dorothy. 2025

Swearingen, Rodger. 949

Sweeney, Eugene T. 291

Sweezy, Paul M. 1094

Swerdlow, Amy. 1757

Swift, William S. 684

Sylvester, Harold J. 1491

Synder, Robert E. 1822

Szajkowski, Zosa. 625, 626, 627

Taft, Philip. 86, 292-295, 337, 363, 378, 467, 2030

Tailleur, Roger. 1195

Tamarkin, Stanley R. 1456

Tanner, William. 1685, 1686

Tattam, William. 511

Tax, Meridith. 834

Taylor, Brennen. 652

Taylor, Frederick J. 779

Taylor, Telford. 1378

Tenney, Jack. 1934

Thelen, David. 1876

Thelen, Esther. 1876

Theoharis, Athan G. 1300,
     1503-1505, 1512,
     1564-1566, 1731-1734,
     1783-89, 1807, 1824-
     1825

Thielens, Wagner, Jr. 964

Thomas, John N. 1527

Thomas, Lately. 1865

Thompson, Francis H.
     1735, 1736

Thrasher, Sue. 803

Tietje, Louis H. 1630

Tiger, Edith. 1301

Tillery, Tyrone. 725, 726

Tippett, Tom. 543

Todras, Arthur. 1137

Toth, C. 364, 365

Touchet, Francis H. 851

Toy, Eckard V., Jr. 468,
     1826

Trachtenberg, Alan. 912

Treadgold, Donald W. 1465

Trilling, Diana. 1027,
     1302

Trilling, Lionel. 1102,
     1303

Trimberger, Ellen K. 835

Trow, Martin. 1911, 1912

Tselos, George. 555

Tucker, Robert W. 1506

Tunis, Mildred. 1444

Tuomi, Kaarlo. 607

Turner, H. Haines. 608

Turner, W.W. 1790

Tygiel, Jules. 744

Tyler, Bruce M. 1835

Tyler, Gerry. 1492

Tyler, Robert L. 1567

Tyson, James L. 899

Ungar, Sanford. 1791

Urmann, Michael F. 397

Urofsky, Melvin I. 1708

Vacha, J.E. 1138

Vadney, Thomas E. 1709

Valaik, J. David. 856,
     857, 858

Valelly, Richard M. 2050

Valtin, Jan. 1227

Van Den Haag, Ernest. 981

Van Dusen, George. 1304

Van Tine, Warren. 576

Van West, Carroll. 694

Van Zanter, John W. 673

Vanderwood, Paul J. 1196

Varney, Harold Lord. 1913

Vaughn, Robert. 1174

Verba, Sidney. 1379

Vernoff, Edward. 970

Vindex, Charles. 826

Viorst, Milton. 746

Voorhis, Jerry. 1636

Voros, Sandor. 1459

Vorse, M.H. 544

Wagner, J. Richard. 1228

Wald, Alan M. 249, 250,
    628, 1028, 1063,
    1080, 1082, 1110-1113

Waldman, Louis. 141

Walker, Charles R. 520

Walker, Samuel. 1507

Walker, Thomas J. 886

Wallerstein, Immanual.
    1827

Walter, John C. 662, 697,
    698

Walton, Richard J. 127

Waltzer, Kenneth. 142,
    143, 159, 2031

Wandersee, Winifred. 998

Ward, Estolv E. 469

Ward, Roger J. 379

Warren, Frank A., III.
    900, 901

Warren, Stanley. 727

Warren-Findley, Jannelle.
    1214

Watkins, Arthur W. 1998

Watson, George. 897

Wattell, Harold. 380

Weales, Gerald. 1143

Web, Constance. 2071

Wechsler, James. 577, 999,
    1000

Weiler, P. 366

Weinstein, Allen. 1305-
    1312

Weinstein, James. 20,
    1380, 1381, 1382,
    1383, 1563

Weinstone, William. 1460

Weintraub, Rebecca. 1866

Weir, Stan. 310

Weisbord, Albert. 545

Weisbord, Vera Buch. 1461

Weiss, Stuart L. 1602

Welch, Richard E., Jr.
    1508

Welton, Mike. 844

Werchen, Raymond A. 1313

Werner, G.A. 6

West, Charles C. 852

West, Rebecca. 1229

Westin, Alan F. 1828

Wexley, John. 1347

Weyl, Nathaniel. 1230, 1231

Wheeler, Robert. 232

White, George A. 1095

White, Nathan I. 1354

Whitehead, Don. 1792

Whitfield, Stephen J. 1100, 1618, 1829

Whitney, R.M. 21

Whittemore, L.H. 506

Wickersham, Edward D. 530

Widick, B.J. 274, 414

Wiebe, G.D. 1867

Wiener, Jon. 81

Wigren, James C. 82

Wilcox, Leonard I. 1600

Wildavsky, Aaron. 1830

Wilderson, Frank. 1573

Wilentz, Sean. 2032

Wilhelm, John. 147

Willen, Paul. 1493

William Henry. 653

Williams, Pontheolla. 707

Williams, David. 1710, 1793, 1794, 1795

Williams, Irene. 1410

Williamson, John. 1463

Wills, Garry. 1314

Wilson, Edmund. 1103

Wilson, Francis G. 1979

Wilson, Joseph F. 501

Windmuller, John P. 367

Winegarten, Renee. 1047

Winter, Ella. 1048

Wirsing, Marie E. 950

Wise, David. 1796

Wise, Leah. 803

Wittenberg, Philip. 1232

Wittner, Lawrence. 665

Wolfe, Allan. 144

Wolfe, Bertram D. 39, 1448, 2036

Wolfe, Gary K. 1186

Wolfe, Thomas, Jr. 1052

Wolfinger, Raymond. 1914

Wollenberg, Charles. 814

Woodward, C. Vann. 1915

Wreszin, Michael. 1634

Wriggins, William H. 233

Wright, Charles. 745

Wright, Palmer W. 1568

Wright, Richard. 752,
    753, 2072

Wrong, Dennis. 1916, 1917

Yablonsky, Mary Jude. 853

Yarmolinsky, Adam. 1737

Yarnell, Allen. 128, 129,
    130, 1574

Yergin, Daniel. 1348

Young, Alfred. 1384

Young, James O. 2067

Younger, Irving. 1315

Zeligs, Meyer A. 1316

Zeller, Belle. 145

Zieger, Robert H. 296,
    297, 398, 399, 512,
    513

Zimring, Fred R. 982, 983

Zipser, Arthur. 1428,
    1429

Zitron, Celia. 492

Zuker, Bat-Ami. 629